Islam and Contemporary Society

Islam and Contemporary Society

Published by **Longman** in association with the
Islamic Council of Europe

 Longman London and New York

Longman Group Limited,
Burnt Mill, Harlow, Essex

First published 1982

British Library Cataloguing in Publication Data
Islam and contemporary society.
 1. Civilization, Islamic
 I. Islamic Council of Europe
 909'.0917'671   DS35.6
ISBN 0-582-78323-2
ISBN 0-582-78322-4 Pbk

Library of Congress Cataloging in Publication Data
Main entry under title:

Islam and contemporary society.
 Includes index.
 1. Islam—Addresses, essays, lectures.
 2. Islam—20th century—Addresses, essays, lectures.
I. Islamic Council of Europe.
BP161.2.I843 1982   297'.09'04   82-253
ISBN 0-582-78323-2   AACR2
ISBN 0-582-78322-4 (pbk.)

Printed in Great Britain by Butler & Tanner Ltd
Frome and London

Contents

Introduction

Salem Azzam

Secretary General of the Islamic Council

The world of Islam which straddles a broad and strategic belt stretching from Indonesia in the East to Senegal in the West, is today the focus of unprecedented attention.

Though living in different climes and under different customs and political systems, speaking different languages, Muslims all over the world retain an abiding sense of Islamic affinity – an affinity which is the hallmark of the Muslim *Ummah* or the community of Muslim peoples.

It was fourteen centuries ago that the Prophet Muhammad (peace be upon him) left Mecca for Medina where he established the first Islamic state based on the concepts revealed in Al Qur'an. The success of the system dazzled the world. It gave birth to a civilization which continues to be a source of inspiration to mankind to this day.

Within fifty years of its revelation, Islam established creative links with the then major cultures of Persia, Egypt and Greece, leading to an unprecedented flowering of human genius. The great epoch of creative activity which followed manifested itself in remarkable advances in the arts and sciences and laid the foundations of modern knowledge and learning. It was indeed the Muslim scholars who were instrumental in generating the first intellectual stirrings which prepared the ground for the European Renaissance.

The resurgence of Islam, on the eve of the 15th century of the Islamic era, has created a widespread interest, particularly in the West, in the dynamic and revolutionary principles of Islam. The educated, intelligent and inquiring minds in the West want to know and understand the reasons for the baffling resilience and tenacity of this great religion. Unfortunately, some of the publications produced in the West tend to present a highly distorted and often totally false image of Islam and its teachings. This book is an attempt to present the basic concepts of Islam primarily to the Western reader. It is not a complete

treatise on Islam; rather it contains articles on selected topics by leading Muslim scholars. It is my earnest hope that this book will not only
enlighten the reader on the topics covered in it but will also stimulate
his interest to read further in order to learn about all aspects of Islam
and its teachings. It is only thus that he can gain a balanced and complete understanding of Islam which is not only a religion but also a
complete code of life.

Opening the discussion of Islam as a supreme doctrine, Professor
Mohammad Qutb explains the fundamental beliefs of Islam which, in
essence, require complete submission of the believer to God's will in
every detail of his life. Moving on from this outline of the general
form of Islamic belief, subsequent authors treat more specialized
topics. Dr Seyyed Hossein Nasr discusses the relationship of "Intellect" and "Intuition" from an Islamic standpoint, and explains these
two key faculties upon which "knowledge" is based. The precise
meaning of these words is often obscured by the popular usage of
"intellect" as being synonymous with "reason", and "intuition"
with a "sixth sense" concerned with foretelling future events. In
Islamic philosophy, however, the meaning of these words is quite
clear and needs to be understood by anyone seeking the Truth.

Dr Ebrahim El-Khouly, from the University of Al-Azhar, writes
about the "Five Pillars of Islam": the Unity of God (*Shahada*); prayer
(*as-Salah*), and its functions; community wealth tax (*Zakah*); fasting
during the month of Ramadan (*Siyam*); and the pilgrimage to Mecca
(*al-Hajj*).

Mr A.K. Brohi discusses the political and legal principles embodied
in Islam, and outlines their contribution to the development of the
socio-economic institutions associated with Islam.

Al Seyyed Sadiq Al-Mahdi describes the economic practices of
Islam, which were integral from the earliest times. The Prophet (peace
be upon him) took a very positive view of economic enterprise, and
the Qur'an states: "It is He who hath produced you from the earth and
settled you therein to develop it." However, while commercial enterprise was encouraged, all types of unearned income like usury and
gambling were prohibited. Islam has always recognized the importance
of material well-being for everyone, and for women in particular it has
done much to protect their individual economic status. Al Seyyed
Sadiq Al-Mahdi also touches on the economic questions that face the
world today.

Prince Mohammed Al-Faisal Al-Saud, Chairman of the International Union of Islamic Banks, explains the principles upon which the Islamic Bank is based. Unlike many other banks, the Islamic Bank will not indulge in usurious practices. It organizes its functions in a way that is totally compatible with the principles of Islam. He goes on to describe the objectives, characteristics and the means of the Islamic Bank, and the way in which it operates the *Zakah*, the community wealth tax, or as he calls it, the poor due.

Professor Ismail Al Faruqi discusses Islam and Culture. He defines culture in a general sense and describes the relationship of Islamic culture to Arab culture. Islam's specific contribution to the arts is discussed by Dr Lamya' Al Faruqi, who argues that, in Islam, science and art are closely entwined. She also examines the styles, materials and forms of expression used in painting, architecture, sculpture, music and poetry, and explores the role of art in society and civilization.

Dr Seyyed Hossein Nasr makes his second contribution to this collection of articles. Writing about Islam and modern science, he observes that each language means something quite distinct by its equivalent word for science, and that the same concept cannot easily be translated from one language to another, any more than it can from one culture to another. He therefore explains what the word means in Islam, and how Islamic science differs from and often conflicts with what the West understands by modern science.

In his contribution on "Islam and the Secular Thrust of Western Imperialism", Mr Altaf Gauhar formulates the issues arising from colonial domination which are now facing Muslim nations. The last article in the book sets out the Human Rights and Duties in Islam, explained in detail by Mr A.K. Brohi.

The book concludes with a historic document, the *Universal Islamic Declaration*, prepared by the Islamic Council of Europe in consultation with a number of eminent Muslim thinkers, scholars and leaders of Islamic movements all over the world. It was presented and unanimously approved at the Inaugural Session of the International Conference on "Prophet Muhammad (peace be upon him) and his Message" held in April 1980 in London. The declaration not only seeks to guide Muslims in their struggle for the establishment of an Islamic order but also to dispel from the minds of many people the confusion and misapprehensions caused by the spread of false and misleading notions about Islam.

The Islamic Council of Europe is devoted to developing a better understanding of Islam and Muslim culture in the West. It is in the furtherance of this aim that we are sponsoring the publication of this book. We hope that it will be read by Muslims and non-Muslims alike and will be helpful in projecting the image of Islam in its true perspective.

Salem Azzam
Secretary General

Islam as a Supreme Doctrine

Professor Muhammad Qutb

(translated by Muhammad Abdul Majid Barghout)

Islam, in its general and wide sense, means that man should give himself up to God, surrender his soul completely to Him and leave everything, however small, in His hands. In its specific, religious sense, Islam is the last message revealed by God to all mankind, urging them to submit themselves wholly to God and surrender to His Divine Will in every detail of their everyday life.

This message, in essence, was the message revealed to every prophet throughout the history of mankind to be delivered to his own people. Noah, (peace be upon him) addressed his people saying, "O ye my people: worship God, for ye have no other God but Him". The succeeding prophets: Saleh, Hu'd, Abraham, Moses, Christ and others, reiterated the same statement, each to his own people. Prophet Muhammad, (peace be on him) voiced it to all mankind.

The Islam which Prophet Muhammad came with is, in its genuine aspect, the same Islam other preceding prophets had already preached. Nevertheless, there are some differences which make Islam, the acknowledged final message of God, stand unique among other messages that preceded it. For, as each prophet was sent to guide his own people to the straight path of God, our Prophet was sent to guide all mankind. Furthermore, each message was limited to a definite period of time which God only knew, but this message is valid for all time since its revelation until God will inherit the earth and all in it.

Two distinctive features characterize Islam: a) It comprehends every aspect of the human soul because it is revealed for every single person living on this earth irrespective of his race, colour, language, location, environment, historical or geographical circumstances, intellectual or cultural heritage and his contribution to material civilization; b) It comprehends and fulfils all the requirements of life, past and future, until the end of human existence on the earth whether these requirements are spiritual, material, political, economic, social, moral, intellectual or aesthetic.

There is not sufficient room for more details in these particular fields. We shall have to give mere glimpses which will help us draw the broad lines for a general idea of this religion.

The Qur'an, God's revealed book, does not address the Arabs alone, for whom it was revealed and in whose language it was written. It speaks to man as a human being:

"O Man! what has seduced thee from thy Lord, Most Beneficent? He who has created thee, fashioned thee in due proportion, and given thee a just bias. In whatever form He wills, does He put thee together," (*Sura 82 verses 6–8*); "Nay, man will be evidence against himself though he were to put up his excuses," (*Sura 75, verses 14–15*); "Verily, we created Man from a drop of mingled sperm, in order to try him: So we gave him (the gifts) of hearing and sight," (*Sura, 76, verse 2*); "Oh thou Man! verily thou art even toiling towards thy Lord – painfully toiling, but thou shalt meet Him," (*Sura 84, verse 6*); "By the soul, and the proportions and order given to it; and its enlightenment as to its wrong and its right; truly he succeeds that purifies it and he fails that corrupts it." (*Sura 91, verses 7–10*)

The Qur'an addresses Mankind, all Mankind:

"O Mankind! reverence your Guardian Lord who created you from a single Person, created of like nature, his mate, and from them twain scattered (like seeds) countless men and women," (*Sura 4, verse 1*); "Oh Mankind! if ye have a doubt about the resurrection, consider that we created you out of dust, then out of sperm," (*Sura 22, verse 5*); "Say, O Men! I am sent unto you, as the Apostle of God. . . . . ." (*Sura 7, verse 158*)

Since the Qur'an addresses every human spirit and all mankind, it follows that it must meet all the spiritual and physical needs of man in order to help him base his life on sound principles which suit the human nature and are not in contradiction with the aim of human existence on this earth.

What are, then, the basic needs of man, in both his spiritual and physical aspects, on this earth? Proceeding from a materialistic point of view we may argue that since all that man needs is food, drink, clothing, accommodation, sex, and tools of material production, a sufficiently convincing answer should then be sought for the unavoidable question: is the Qur'an or Islam able to provide for such needs? To begin with, we believe that Islam is, in actual fact, able enough to provide for man's basic needs such as have been previously enumerated. But the Qur'an, which is Islam's revealed book, was not originally and primarily meant to speak about physics, chemistry, the properties of matter and how to transform it into manufactured articles.

The Qur'an, no doubt, organizes all the aspects of human life, both the physical and the emotional, in such a way as to create a favourable atmosphere for the healthy growth of man within the limits of sound human nature and man's humanitarianism.

For this reason, the Qur'an does not content itself with systematizing the emotional and physical aspects of human life as did some systems which man had set up for himself in the absence of God's curriculum, for God alone knows that these man-made systems do not cast man "in the best of moulds", as God had created him and willed him to be: "We have indeed created man in the best of moulds," (*Sura 95, verse 4*).

Neither do these systems honour man the way God honoured him:

"We have honoured the sons of Adam, provided them with transport on land and sea, given them for sustenance things good and pure, and conferred on them special favours, above a great part of our Creation." (*Sura 17, verse 70*)

The Qur'an provides all the needs which God, the All-Wise, the All-Knowing, deems necessary for man in his life's journey from its beginning to its very end. Then the Qur'an attaches to these requirements an importance which only God, the Most High, knows to be the truest and the most genuine, arranges them in a manner most suited to the betterment and righteousness of man's life in all its phases.

In short, we can say that the Qur'an speaks of God, the Universe, Life and Man. In the first place, the Qur'an speaks to man about God. Modern man, deeply influenced by the physical world in which he lives, may imagine that the discussion of the concept of man should be given priority over that of God. He may also imagine that man and the universe, that is the physical universe, are the most appropriate topics for detailed discussion since they are visible and tangible, whereas talking about God or life is a metaphysical kind of talk man may resort to after he has completed his investigations into the visible and the tangible or he may not do so at all.

But man's Creator knows more about man than man knows about himself:

"Should He not know He that created? And He is the One that understands the finest mysteries (and) is well acquainted (with them)." (*Sura 67, verse 14*)

Hence God, the Most High, knows that the most serious, significant and effective question in man's life is that of divinity. Therefore, God speaks about all the aspects of this question in a most elaborate manner.

Man is a worshipper by nature:

"When thy Lord drew forth from the children of Adam – from their loins – their descendants, and made them testify concerning themselves (saying): 'Am I not your Lord (who cherishes and sustains you)?' They said: 'Yea! We do testify!'" (*Sura 7, verse 172*)

When man does not worship God, he will not have rid himself of the whole question of worship and set it aside as he may think or imagine, but he will have actually knowingly or unknowingly, worshipped another god, be it money, power, sensuous pleasures or mere desire:

"Seest thou such a one as taketh for his God his own passion (or impulse)?" (*Sura 25, verse 43*)

The Qur'an confirms that all these forms of worship are devil worship:

"Did I not enjoin on you, O ye Children of Adam, that ye should not worship Satan; for that he was to you an enemy avowed? And that ye should worship Me (for that) this was the straight way?" (*Sura 36, verses 60–61*)

There are two states of man's being; he worships God or Satan, and the two forms of worship cannot be equalized:

"Are those equal, those who know and those who do not know?" (*Sura 39, verse 9*); "Is there one who doth know that that which hath been revealed unto thee from thy Lord is the Truth like one who is blind? It is those who are endowed with understanding that receive admonition." (*Sura 13, verse 19*)

Man's life, in all its minutest details, is considerably influenced by this question, the object of worship: is it God, the Most High, the Creator, the Omnipotent or is it some other feigned god which is, in fact, a Satan?

There is no other question or anything else which affects man's life and shapes its smallest details more effectively than this question. This is the only case which confronts man in every single fleeting moment of his life on this earth, in every deed he performs, in every thought or feeling.

Man, in every moment of his life, consciously or unconsciously, cannot take any step or perform any action except through and in accordance with a constitution, whether written or unwritten, derived from God, or from any other source. In other words, he must always follow a certain God in his practical behaviour, intellect or emotional situations, no matter whether this God is Allah or any other worshipped idol. And even when man's actions are uncontrollable, and his steps misguided, he will devise a certain plan at the very outset and his situations will be governed and directed by his personal desire which will become, in the long run, his worshipped idol.

The question of divinity, of who is to be worshipped, must of necessity occupy its proper place in the life of man. It must be the first and most significant since it controls, in actuality, all his actions, emotional and intellectual situations.

Modern man, influenced by the material and non-religious atmosphere in which he lives, undoubtedly does not understand how prodigiously important is the question of belief or religious doctrine. He has always considered belief to be a private emotional relationship between man and his Lord severed from actual life. He also does not believe that when man forsakes the worship of God, he is still a worshipper, not of God but of some other false and invisible god, which is Satan.

God, the All-Knowing, knows man better than man does himself. Therefore, God presents to us a detailed account of this argument according to which man's life on this earth and his life in the hereafter can be righteous and straight or not. Allah speaks to man about the one and peerless God:

"Say: He is God, the One and Only, God the Eternal, the Absolute; He begetteth not, nor is he begotten, and there is none like unto Him," (*Sura 112*); "Say: Praise be to God, who begets no son, and has no partner in (His) dominion, nor (needs) He any to protect Him from humiliation. Magnify Him for His greatness and glory." (*Sura 17, verse 111*)

About God, the Creator, the Designer, Allah says:

"It is He who created all things and ordered them in due proportions," (*Sura 25, verse 2*); "Verily, all things have We created in proportion and measure," (*Sura 54, verse 49*); "Say! Is it that ye deny Him Who created the earth in two days? And do ye join equals with Him? He is the Lord of (all) the worlds. He set on the (earth) mountains standing firm, high above it, and bestowed blessings on the earth, and measured therein all things to give them nourishment in due proportion, in four days, in accordance with (the deeds of) those who seek (sustenance).

".... Moreover, He comprehended in His design the sky, and it had been (as) smoke: He said to it and to the earth: 'Come ye together, willingly or unwillingly'. They said: 'We do come (together) in willing obedience.' So he completed them as seven firmaments in two days, and He assigned to each heaven its duty and command. And We adorned the lower heaven with lights, and (provided it) with guard. Such is the Decree of (Him) the Exalted in Might, full of knowledge." (*Sura 41, verses 9–12*)

About God the sustenance giver, the Qur'an says:

"For God is He Who gives (all) sustenance, Lord of Power, Steadiest (forever)," (*Sura 51, verse 58*); "Among His signs is this, that He sends the winds, as Heralds of Glad Tidings, giving you a taste of His (Grace and) Mercy, that the ships may sail (Majestically) by His command and that ye may seek of His Bounty, in order that ye may be grateful." (*Sura 30, verse 46*)

About God the Almighty, the Qur'an says:

"So glory be to Him in Whose hands is the dominion of all things." (*Sura 36, verse 83*)

About God who knows the unseen the Qur'an says:

"He knows all that goes into the earth, and all that comes out thereof; all that comes down from the sky and all that ascends thereto. And He is the Most Merciful, the Oft-Forgiving." (*Sura 34 verse 2*); "God does know what every female (womb) doth bear, by how much the wombs fall short (of their time or number) or do exceed. Every single thing is before His sight, in (due) proportion. He knoweth the unseen and that which is open. He is the Great, the Most High. It is the same (to Him) whether any of you conceal his speech or declare it openly; whether he lie hid by night or walk forth freely by day." (*Sura 13, verses 8–10*)

About God who gives life and death, the Qur'an says:

"And verily, it is We who give life and who give death: it is We who remain inheritors (after all else passes away)." (*Sura 15, verse 23*); "It is He Who gives Life and Death; and when He decides upon an affair, He says to it, 'Be', and it is." (*Sura 40, verse 68*)

Many other names of God are enumerated in the Qur'an; He is the Almighty, the Proud, the Oft-Forgiving, the Merciful, the Lord of the Worlds and the Owner of the Day of Judgement.

Speaking of God's names, attributes and deeds in a manner that will fill man's heart with submissive awe and make man sense the greatness of God's glory, the Qur'an proceeds to explain man's duties towards this great and mighty God who owns the heavens and the earth and who created everything in due proportion.

What could that duty be except pure worship for this great God? Can it be true that man, having truly known God, will possibly worship one other than Him? And is there any God worthy of worship other than Allah? This is the first part of the argument. The second part is how man should worship Allah.

The gravest problem that had faced mankind since ancient times was that man, even when he performed and directed his duties of worship towards God simultaneously believed in another partner associated with God. Here is a Quranic verse to this effect: "And most of them believe not in God without associating (others as partners) with Him." *(Sura 12, verse 106)*

Associating other partners with God is often reflected in two pictures which, although they are closely overlapping, can sometimes be separated. False worship is evident in matters related to religious rituals; in other words, prayers, imploration and thanksgiving are directed to some other God or partner associated with God. It is also revealed in not abiding by God-given laws, that is, implementing a set of laws other than those divinely inspired, and adhering to a system of life other than that drawn up by God.

Throughout the entire history of mankind, and except at times of moral and spiritual enlightenment, humanity was not devoid of any form of false worship so predominant in the lives of people that they were led astray, forsaking Islam and falling headlong into the *Jahilliyyats* (Times of Darkness and Ignorance), culminating in the 20th century *Jahilliyya.*

Though the first form of false worship has disappeared, at least apparently, in many parts of the world where idols and pagan gods are no longer worshipped, the second form of false worship, namely, the implementation of man-made laws. Prevails in most parts of the world today. Such are the laws which dragged mankind into all miseries and misguidance.

What dominates man in his contemporary *Jahilliyya* (Darkness and Ignorance) is that he believes he knows himself much better than God knows him. Therefore, man and not God ought to be the legislator. Two serious aberrations in the lives of people emerge out of this, in addition to the grave mistake man makes by rejecting God's *Sharia* (Laws). First, people must, unavoidably, be divided into masters and slaves. The masters will be those who set the laws according to their interests and desires, and the slaves will have to implement them. Second, political, economic and social grievances will, inevitably, occur in any society not governed by God's *Sharia* (Laws).

Dialectical materialism, though incapable of providing a material interpretation of the history of mankind, highly affirms this point and states that he who owns rules, and that the entire history of mankind is one of continued enslavement of one class by another. When feudalism prevailed in a society, the feudal lord was the one who owned and ruled while the remaining part of the society were slaves. In like manner, when capitalism prevailed, the industrial capitalist was the one who owned and ruled, and the workers were the slaves.

If dialectical materialism, in reviewing the history of human enslavement, has stopped at this particular point and proceeded no further, it is our responsibility to carry the argument a little further, stating that when the communist theory was transformed into a system of government, the state, the Communist Party, the Supreme Central Committee or the sacred leader owned and ruled while the rest of the people became slaves.

This applies to every individual society where God's laws are not carried out because a group of individuals rise to the stature of self-made gods while other individuals, lacking the pre-requisites and instruments of godliness, are content or forced to worship those human deities in submissive servitude. Man's genuine freedom will not be attained except when human beings abstain, or are made to abstain, from drawing up their own legislation. True freedom will be enjoyed only when the individuals strictly follow God's revealed laws and all become equal in their servitude to God, the Almighty. They will enjoy equal freedom in their behaviour, one towards the other, because they will have to enforce a law not of any one else's making and no one else will have the power to make decrees.

Justice, political, economic or social, cannot exist in a society of lords and slaves because the lords will always hunger for more privileges at the expense of the slaves. Besides, the human outlook is unable to comprehend, grasp or have a clear objective vision of any legislation even if all parties concerned are presumably supposed to have goodwill. Consequently, human beings, in their self-devised curricula, continue to prescribe remedies for existing problems which seldom eliminate them but always create other problems.

God's *Sharia* alone is without defect and any such shortcomings because it is laid down by Him, the All-Knowing, the All-Wise. God the Almighty has no interest to maintain or desire to fulfil, and He alone knows the innermost secrets of the human soul, those which hold good and which do not. His divine knowledge encompasses all man's past, present and future until the Day of Judgement.

The *Sharia* revealed in this last message was meant to comprehend the entirety of man's life in all its political, economic, social, intellectual and spiritual aspects. It was also meant to absorb the sound and normal growth of human life until history ends.

At the moment we do not have sufficient room for more detailed account of this fact (other chapters in this book, however, deal with some of these aspects); we only give a brief reference to a certain specific fact.

Some aspects of human life are stable and unchangeable or ought to be so because they are basic, and life cannot be righteous without them. On the other hand, there are ever-changing and ever-growing aspects of human life which will have to be allowed sufficient room to grow and move in, otherwise humanity will fail to achieve the progress which is part of its function and existence on the earth. But in the course of growth and mobility, the ever-changing and ever-growing aspects of human life must be controlled, otherwise mankind will suffer from the evil consequences of these changes. Divine *Sharia*, revealed to comprehend and absorb human life till the end of history, was intended to respond to both aspects of human life, the changing and the changeless, in order to meet all the needs of man.

The basic and changeless aspects of human life have been regulated by divinely inspired changeless and detailed rules. The question of divinity, for instance, and all that is associated with it: man's slavery to the Creator, the necessity of worshipping Him without associating any partner or partners with Him in matters related to rituals or the implementation of God's *Sharia*, as well as divine laws which guarantee that man's blood, money or moral integrity and reputation should be safeguarded, family laws and the relationships between the two sexes or the international laws that govern the relationships of Muslims and non-Muslims in all walks of life — all the above mentioned questions have been settled and regulated by divine, changeless rules.

As for the ever-changing aspects of human life, the political, economic and social, God's *Sharia* has provided a permanent, stable and firm frame for each, and has entrusted the committed, believing intellect with fixing the right picture into the right frame. Thus the political, social or economic picture of society constantly changes to suit the age and as a consequence the theoretical and applied sciences that man has acquired. But while changing they do not lead people astray or undermine the fundamental principles on which they base their lives as did the Industrial Revolution in Europe, which based the industrial society upon immoral and non-religious principles in the name of progress. The Industrial Revolution in Europe destroyed family bonds: children went truant and teenagers and young men and women turned into delinquents. Communism, in like manner, destroyed human dignity, humiliated man and strangled his freedom in return for food.

This is a brief glimpse of how the Qur'an or Islam speaks of divinity. It is evident, after this rapid review, that it is a question of the gravest importance. It has nothing to do with man's personal temperament, his whims or desires which may find him a god to worship in whichever way he chooses. It is indeed a question of life in its entirety, all its aspects and minute details. It is not even a question of earthly life alone; it is a question of the life to come as well. Life does not cease with the end of the apparent physical existence on earth; it moves into another phase and assumes another form similar to that of the larva in its silk-spun cocoon, invisible, but full of life.

The greatest event in man's life comes when he is risen from the dead to be informed of the deeds, good and bad, he has done in his earthly life and to receive his reckoning which will lead him into everlasting bliss or into the bottomless pit of eternal hell.

The question of divinity is not a case to be pursued and then forgotten. It exists permanently throughout the life-history of man, both in this life and the next. Man's attitude towards this question is the sole determinant of his future either in Hell or in Heaven. For this reason, the Qur'an iterates and reiterates this question as long as man lives on this earth in order to make him respond soundly and correctly to this question before time elapses. The Qur'an still continues to remind even the believers of the sole divinity of God, the Almighty, in order to make them believe more firmly in Him and act accordingly: "But teach (thy Message) for teaching benefits the believers," (*Sura 51, verse 136*).

The Qur'an, Islam's book, also speaks of the universe in a manner which relates it to God, the divine Creator. The universe is the creation of God; He created and ordered it. Talking about the universe implies, in part, God's miraculous creativity of which everything in the heavens or the earth is a visible sign. It also implies God's boundless and infinite greatness. God did not create the universe just by accident. Nothing occurs accidentally or haphazardly; everything is predestined and predetermined. Everything happens by the will of God. He says to a thing "Be" and it is.

Talking about the universe is, on the other hand, a negation of the divinity or the divine character attributed by some to the universe; it also negates the independence of the universe of the creative will of God.

The Universe, Nature and Matter are not gods as ancient and modern *Jahilliyyats* (Ignorances) allege. The natural laws that govern the universe are not an arbitrary authority inherent in or emanating from nature. They are divine signs deposited in nature by God, for He is the one who, "Gave to each (created) thing its form and nature, and further gave (it) guidance," (*Sura 20, verse 50*). Natural laws are not inevitable in the sense that they are binding or restrictive to the will of God so that He cannot change, stop or discontinue them as He pleases. God, the Most High, has laid down the natural laws as they are out of His own divine will, and He alone has the power to modify, stop or discontinue them as He pleases without any restrictions being imposed on His will or any external power affecting His infinite ability. Hence, the occurrence of supernatural miracles when God wills them. Physical phenomena do not conform to physical laws familiar to man.

The sea rips in two when struck by a prophet's cane, Jesus is born of no father, and a murdered body, when struck with a piece of dead meat, comes back to life and tells about his murderer. Sweeping change takes place in the motion of the whole universe on the Day of Judgement through the will of God:

"The Day that the sky will be like molten brass, and the mountains will be like wool." (*Sura 70, verses 8–9*); "When the sky is cleft asunder, when the stars are scattered, when the oceans are suffered to burst forth, and when the graves are turned upside down; (then) shall each soul know what it hath sent forward, and (what it hath) kept back." (*Sura 82, verses 1–5*)

Hence, God's creative will is the sole effective factor behind all physical phenomena which otherwise will never take place whatever the causes are: "Verily, all things have We created in proportion and measure." (*Sura 54, verse 49*)

Causes act through the God-given, effective power deposited in them; they act differently each time through the will of God, not through the personal continuity of the effectiveness deposited in them. Therefore, a Muslim pursues the causes because he knows that they will lead to the effects, according to the current tradition, but he does not cling to the causes, nor does he imagine that they will definitely lead to the desired effects in the absence of God's will. Everything is always in the hands of God, and if God so willed that the causes would not lead to the effects, they will not. And if God so willed that the effects would be contrary to the causes, they will be as God had willed them. Hence

Moses is brought up in the palace of Pharaoh and all effects come out contrary to the causes.

Thus the Muslim combines the two aspects of reasonable thinking: the causal aspect on which religious belief is built, with no emotional contradiction between the two. Science progresses at the hands of the Muslim without losing his belief in the supernatural and without creating a conflict in his mind and heart between his belief in science and its laws and his belief in God. The real history of the Muslim nation bears witness that that nation introduced to all mankind the experimental method in scientific research and made major discoveries in physics, chemistry, medicine and other sciences without ever losing belief in the supernatural and in God.

The universe worships God in its own way, bows to Him, glorifies Him:

"Seest thou that to God bow down in worship all things that are in the heavens and on earth, the sun, the moon, the stars, the hills, the trees, the animals, and a great number among Mankind." (*Sura 22, verse 18*); "There is not a thing but celebrates His praise; and yet ye understand not how they declare His Glory." (*Sura 17, verse 44*)

If the universe and all its enormous stars worship, glorify and obey the orders of God, ought not man to bring his nature into harmony with the nature of the whole universe and become a true worshipper of God and an executor of all His orders? Has the honour which God conferred on man by not oppressing him with worship but by giving him reason, will and freedom, tempted man into disobedience and contradiction of the distinctive nature of the whole universe? Is not the honour with which God associated man bountiful enough to urge him into more worship and submission to God? The universe is a field for man's thoughtful meditation on the one hand, and exploitation of the potentialities and energies God made accessible to him, on the other:

"Behold! In the creation of the heavens and the earth, and the alternation of Night and Day, they are indeed signs for men of understanding, men who celebrate the praises of God, standing, sitting and lying down on their sides, and contemplate the (wonders of) creation in the heavens and the earth (with the thought): 'Our Lord! not for naught hast Thou created (all) this! Glory to Thee! Give us our salvation from the penalty of the Fire'." (*Sura 3, verses 190–191*); "It is God Who hath created the heavens and the earth and sendeth down rain from the skies, and with it bringeth out fruits wherewith to feed you; it is He Who hath made the ships subject to you, that they may sail through the sea by His command, and the rivers (also) hath He made subject

to you. And He hath made subject to you the sun and the moon, both diligently pursuing their courses; and the Night and the Day hath He (also) made
subject to you, as from Him, all that is in the heavens and on earth." (*Sura
45, verse 13*)

The universe is not the avowed enemy of man to wrestle with and conquer as modern *Jahilliyya* (Ignorance) demonstrates when it speaks of
"the conflict with nature" or "man, the conqueror of nature". On the
contrary, the universe, with all its energies, conditions and circumstances is devoted to man by God. Modern science is aware of the fact
that if one single particle which God has assembled in the whole structure of the universe were dislocated, man would never be able to survive. If the earth came closer to the sun all living creatures would be
burned; if it drew further away, they would die of cold. If the moon
came closer to the earth, tide flow would cover up the whole surface
of the earth and drown all living creatures. If the amount of oxygen
increased, all living creatures would catch fire; if it decreased, men
would die. Which of these reconciliations — they are in hundreds and
thousands — has man made or forced nature to make? By the grace and
bounty of God, these reconciliations were made and devoted to man,
who is both powerless and helpless to do any such thing. The God-
gifted exploitation of some energies requires man to know and study
the properties of the matter and the ways by which God runs the universe.

The ability to learn is in itself an energy which God deposited in
man by His divine grace and bounty:

"He taught (the use of) the Pen; taught man that which he knows not." (*Sura
96, verses 4–5*); "It is He Who brought you forth from the wombs of your
mothers when ye knew nothing; and He gave you hearing and sight and intelligence and affections; that ye may give thanks (to God)." (*Sura 16, verse
78*)

When man utilizes his intellectual or muscular energies to exploit
some of the God-given physical energies he is not actually involved in
a conflict with nature or subduing it to his will. He is, as Islam depicts
him, exploiting in reality what God has created for him. The universe
is man's friend; it co-operates with him by the will and command of
God:

"And the earth, moreover, hath He extended (to a wide expanse); He draweth
out therefrom, its moisture and its pasture; and the mountains hath he firmly
fixed, for use and convenience to you and your cattle." (*Sura 79, verses
30–33*)

Thus, the Qur'an's speech about the universe flows gently and majestically into the human soul and becomes part of the gushing live belief which urges man into theoretical meditation into the realm of the intellect and emotional motion into the world of reality. From our knowledge of history, it is well understood that the Muslim nation had introduced to mankind a voluminous intellectual production which illuminated the dark ages of humanity. Moreover, Muslims had roamed the earth exploring its secrets and setting up buildings and civilization. But for the guidance of Islam, those achievements would not have been accomplished.

The Qur'an speaks also of life in general and human life in particular, either in its emotional or moral aspect. Life did not exist by accident as modern *Jahilliyya* (Ignorance) asserts on a non-scientific basis simply to avoid the mention of God. Life was created through the will of God, the Maker who says to anything "Be" and there it is. Life proceeded the way God willed. Nature did not act at random as Darwin stated; it enforced the will of God, the Creator, which neither Darwin nor any other scientist can comprehend. No wonder they call it "random action". True scientists understand and feel the greatness of the Maker through the articles of his own making. They believe in Him and their hearts cling to Him:

"Seest thou not that God sends down rain from the sky? With it we then bring out produce of various colours. And in the mountains are tracts white and red, of various shades of colour and black intense of hue. And so amongst men and crawling creatures and cattle are they of various colours. These truly fear God, among His servants, who have knowledge: for God is Exalted in Might, Oft Forgiving." *(Sura 35, verses 27–28)*; "And has created every animal from water; of them there are some that creep on their bellies; some that walk on two legs; and some that walk on four. God creates what He wills; for verily, God has power over all things. We have indeed sent down signs that make things manifest; and God guides whom He wills to a way that is straight." *(Sura 24, verses 45–46)*

Talk of life, in the Qur'an, is also connected with the question of divinity. It deals partly with God's miraculous creativity, and partly with His power to resurrect the dead which the *Jahilliyyeen* (people who lived in the ages of Ignorance) rejected:

"And the earth, We have spread it out, and set thereon mountains standing firm, and produced therein every kind of beautiful growth (in pairs) to be observed and commemorated by every devotee turning (to God). And We send down from the sky rain charged with blessing, and We produce there with

gardens and grain for harvest; and tall and stately palm trees, with shoots of
fruit-stalks, piled one over another; as sustenance for (God's) servants; and
We give (new) life therewith to land that is dead: thus will be the Resurrection. Before them was denied (The Hereafter) by the people of Noah, the
companions of the Rass, the Thamud, the Add and Pharaoh, the Brethren of
Lut; the Companions of the Wood, and the people of Tubba; each one (of
them) rejected the Apostles and My warning was duly fulfilled (in them). Were
We then weary with the first Creation, that they should be in confused doubt
about a new Creation?'' (Sura 50, verses 7–15); ''O Mankind! if ye have a
doubt about the Resurrection, consider that We created you out of dust, then
out of sperm, then out of a leech-like clot, then out of a morsel of flesh, partly
formed and partly unformed, in order that We may manifest (Our power) to
you. And We cause whom We will to rest in the wombs for an appointed term,
then We do bring you out as babes, then (foster) you that ye may reach your
age of full strength; and some of you are called to die, and some are sent back
to the feeblest of old age; so that they know nothing after having known
(much). And (further), thou seest the earth barren and lifeless, but when We
pour down rain on it, it is stirred (to life), it swells, and it puts forth every
kind of beautiful growth (in pairs). This is so, because God is the Reality: it is
He who gives life to the dead, and it is He who has power over all things. And
verily, the Hour will come: there can be no doubt about it, or about (the fact)
that God will raise up all who are in the graves.'' (Sura 22, verses 5–7)

In this Quranic discourse there are several scientific references, some
of which were unknown to all mankind when the Qur'an was revealed,
and some were only known during the last or this century which all
bear witness that the Qur'an is God's revealed book and not of man's
own making. Neither Muhammad (peace be to Him) nor anyone else
could possibly create it. There is not room here, to elaborate this point
any further. What concerns us in this review is to make a brief reference to the main topics. The Qur'an indicates that the spreading forth
of life on this earth was not accidental nor an unintended event:

''Behold! In the creation of the heavens and the earth; in the alternation of the
Night and Day; in the sailing of the ships through the ocean for the profit of
mankind; in the rain which God sends down from the skies, and life which He
gives therewith to an earth that is dead; in the beasts of all kinds that He
scatters through the earth; in the change of the winds, and the clouds which
they trail like their slaves between the sky and the earth; (here) indeed are
signs for a people that are wise.'' (Sura 2, verse 164)

There is an obvious equilibrium in creation; this Quranic verse refers
to some of its aspects: ''And the earth We have spread out (like a
carpet); set thereon mountains firm and immovable; and produced

therein all kinds of things in due balance." (*Sura 15, verse 19*) The mountains maintain balance in the earth, and the plants grow in due balance. Life, particularly human life does not expire with the end of the earth's limited duration; it extends into the Hereafter. It is unique and purposeful in God's creation. In both behaviour and design life is subject to a compact order. It is forever suspended by the will of God:

"He set on the (earth) mountains standing firm, high above it, and bestowed blessing on the earth, and measured therein all things to give them nourishment in due proportion, in Four Days, in accordance with (the needs of) those who seek (sustenance). Moreover, He comprehended in His design the sky, and it had been (as) smoke; He said unto it and to the earth: 'Come ye together, willingly or unwillingly.' They said: 'We do come (together) in willing obedience.' " (*Sura 41, verses 10–11*)

This is the emotional aspect of human life as elaborated in the Holy Qur'an.

The Qur'an speaks in detail of the moral aspect of life which is closely related to man and which deals with values and principles governing life:

"Wealth and sons are allurements of the life of this world, but the things that endure good deeds are best in the sight of thy Lord as rewards; and best as (the foundations) for hopes." (*Sura 18, verse 46*); "Fair in the eyes of men is the love of things they covet; women and sons, heaped up hoards of gold and silver, horses branded (for blood and excellence) and (wealth of) cattle and well tilled land. Such are the possessions of this world's life. But in nearness to God is the best of the goals (to return to). Say: Shall I give you glad tidings of things far better than those? For the righteous are gardens in nearness to their Lord, with rivers flowing beneath; therein in their eternal home, with companions pure (and holy) and the good pleasure of God. For in God's sight are (All) His servants, namely, those who say: 'Our Lord! we have indeed believed; forgive us, then, our sins, and save us from the agony of the Fire'. Those who show patience, firmness and self-control; who are true (in word and deed); who worship devoutly; who spend (in the way of God), and who pray for forgiveness in the early hours of the morning." (*Sura 3, verses 14–17*)

There are many possessions and pleasures in this world:

"On earth will be your dwelling place and your means of livelihood for a time." (*Sura 2, verse 36*); "The other worldly life has also many pleasures but they are purer, more sublime, are more everlasting . . . Shed over them a Light of beauty and a (blissful) Joy. And because they were patient and constant, He will reward them with a garden and (garments of) silk. Reclining in the (garden) on raised thrones, they will see there neither the sun's (excessive heat) nor the moon's (excessive cold). And the shades of the (garden) will come low over them, and the branches (of fruit) there, will hang low in humility. And amongst them will be passed round vessels of silver and goblets of crystal, crystal clear, made of silver. They will determine the measure thereof (according to their wishes). And they will be given to drink there of a Cup (of Wine) mixed with Zanjabil, a fountain there called salsabil. And round about them will be (serve) youths of perpetual (freshness). If thou seest them, thou wouldst think them scattered Pearls. And when thou lookest it is there thou wilst see a bliss and a Realm Magnificent. Upon them will be green garments of fine silk and heavy brocade, and they will be adorned with bracelets of silver; and their Lord will give to them to drink of a Wine Pure and Holy.'' (Sura 76, verses 11–21)

Which pleasures are to be sought and indulged in, this world's or the Hereafter's? God, nevertheless, does not forbid all earth's pleasures; He only forbids excess of them. Furthermore, God does not make the pleasures of the Hereafter conditioned by forsaking the pleasures of the earthly life:

"Say Who hath forbidden the beautiful (gifts) of God, which He hath produced for His servants, and the things clean and pure, (which He hath provided) for sustenance? Say! they are, in the life of this world, for those who believe, (and) purely for them on the Day of Judgement. Thus do We explain the Signs in detail for those who understand. Say: the things that my Lord hath indeed forbidden are: shameful deeds, whether open or secret, sins and trespasses against truth or reason, assigning partners to God, for which He hath given no authority, and saying things about God of which ye have no knowledge." (Sura 7, verses 32–33)

Pleasures as pleasures are not at all forbidden by God; rather the degrading and low values attendant to them and which make man practise them in a manner not prescribed by God. On the other side other values exist:

"Those who show patience, firmness and self-control; who are true (in word and deed), who worship devoutly; who spend (in the way of God) and who pray for forgiveness in the early hours of the morning." (Sura 3, verse 17); "The believers must (eventually) win through; those who humble themselves in their prayers, who avoid vain talk, who are active in deeds of charity, who abstain from sex except with those joined to them in the marriage bond, or (the captives) whom their right hand possesses, for (in their case) they are free from blame. But those who desire to exceed those limits are transgressors.

Those who faithfully observe their trusts and their covenants, and who (strictly) guard their prayers. These will be the heirs who will inherit Paradise. They will dwell therein forever." *(Sura 23, verses 1–11)*

Thus differentiation arises, in fact, between values and values more than between pleasures and pleasures; between man's moral values and the values which he shares with animals or with Satan. This moral aspect of life associated with the perpetual and the declining values, the elevated and the degrading values, is closely related to the question of divinity. All the sublime values are conditioned by the belief in God, the One, the indivisible and the peerless, and the Day of Judgement on which the righteous man will be rewarded for his belief. All the degrading values are, likewise conditioned by the rejection of true belief, associating other partners with God and following Satan. Thus we see that the Qur'an has, so far, carried on the discussion on religious doctrine in several fields.

Through all these questions, the Qur'an speaks most elaborately about man and to man. The discourse on divinity is addressed to man to acquaint him with his Lord in order to believe in Him and worship Him truly. In like manner, the discourses on the universe and life are all intended for man to make him know his Lord better, and to familiarize him with God's names, characteristics and deeds in order to worship Him alone without associating other partners with Him. But through all these questions, there is a specialized discourse on man which ought to be included in a special chapter in our treatment of the questions of the Qur'an. We can even say that the whole question is but two questions: the question of divinity, on the one hand, and of servitude, on the other. Both man and universe share in this servitude, each in his own way, according to the innate divinely created nature. But it is evident that the Qur'an devotes the largest part of the discourse to man and his servitude. This is quite natural since the Qur'an addresses man.

The question of man deals with several points and aspects.

First, who is man? What does he consist of? What are his characteristics and the limits of his energies?
Secondly, what is his role, his function on earth, the end of his existence?
Thirdly, what is his fate?
Fourthly, what is the method according to which his life will proceed in this world and the next?

In other words, the Qur'an provides answers to these queries pressing on nature whether consciously or unconsciously, seeking sufficient explanation; where from? where to? why? and how? Where has man come from? Where is he going after death? Why do we live (for what purpose)? How do we live (by what method)? These questions must inevitably haunt man's mind, whether he knows it or not, and he must press for immediate answers. If man was led to the true answers to these queries, he would live a settled, prosperous and righteous life; but if he were led astray, he would be subdued with misery and the feeling of being lost.

Philosophers are not the only people who are exposed to the pressure of these questions. They are not the only ones who endeavour to search for satisfactory answers to those pressing questions even though they are more conscious of them than others. All mankind is subject to the pressure of these questions and they are apt to provide questions for themselves. The answers, astray or guided, will outline the path of life for them.

Modern *Jahilliyya* (Ignorance) is the most illustrative example of this question. Modern people are lost, perplexed, restless, miserable and have strayed away from the straight path of life because they have not worked out satisfactory answers to these pressing questions. Philosophers were not the only people who gave expression to all this. Millions upon millions of human beings, consciously or unconsciously, expressed the wrongs and ills of modern *Jahilliyya*, often miscalled civilization, in their behaviour, thoughts and feelings; in the high percentage of psychological, nervous and intellectual diseases; in the ever increasing number of wine and opium addicts, sex maniacs, football maniacs, cinema and television maniacs, and in the rising crime rates.

The ills and wrongs of contemporary civilization are reflected in the behaviour, thoughts or feelings of modern people in the form of "rejection" or "protest" whether this protest is serious enough to search for drastic solutions or clownish or immodest as was seen in the Beatles, "hippies", and vagabonds. Hundreds of behavioural patterns and proofs emphasize man's unhappiness and his feeling of being lost.

When one of the ancient *Jahilliyyats* (Ignorances) said, "What is there but our life in this world? We shall die as we live, and nothing but Time can destroy us." (*Sura 45, verse 24*), it was providing answers for these pressing questions in a wrong manner and then acting accordingly, sticking to degrading values and forsaking elevated ones, for both have different specific answers. Contemporary *Jahilliyya* (Ignorance), iterating the same statement, is actually acting in the same manner as the ancient one did despite the vast differences between both in time, place, tools of material civilization, scientific achievement and subjugation of the environment. These worldly achievements do not in fact shape man's life; only values shape man's life and these are dependent upon the kind of answers man provides to the pressing questions posed by the innate human nature. These values are human values on the one hand, and animal or Satanic values on the other.

Hence, man's life, irrespective of time, place, environment, tools of human civilization and amount of scientific progress, has been in the common course of history, either guided or misguided, astray or straight: two modes closely connected with belief in God or disbelief in Him.

Let us go back to the whole question right from the very beginning. What is man? What does he consist of? What are his characteristics? What are the limits of his energies? Is he an animal as Darwin wished him to be? Is he a god as he imagines himself to be, particularly in modern *Jahilliyya*, often miscalled civilization? (One of the self-contradictions of modern *Jahilliyya* is that it believes in the two things at the same time: that man is both animal and god at the same time. *Man in the Modern World*, by Julian Huxley.) No, man is *human*, he is not an animal, nor god nor devil. He is unique in the way he has been created, in his energies, in his characteristics and hence in the function assigned to him:

"Behold, thy Lord said to the the angels: 'I am about to create man from clay. When I have finished him (in due proportion) and breathed into him of My spirit, fall ye down in obeisance unto him'." (*Sura 38, verses 71–72*)

Thus man was created: a handful of earth's clay and a breath of divine spirit made up this unique being, unequalled among other creatures. The handful of dust out of which man's body was created in due proportion may resemble, in some degree, the bodies of other animals; but the divine, heavenly breath had proportioned him into a being completely different from the animal even in the sensuous aspect which they both share.

It is an irony of contemporary *Jahilliyya* (Ignorance) that Julian Huxley, a New Darwinist writes in his book previously referred to,

"Modern science has proved that man is unique in his biological structure as well as his psychological and intellectual constitution. Science places man very near to where religion places him; on a different basis altogether." We have no comment on this except to say: Praise be to God, the Most High.

Although man and animal eat, drink and multiply in an apparently similar way, there is, however, a huge, essential, difference between the biological functions of each. This essential difference in the performance of the biological functions of both man and animal lies in the existence of awareness, consciousness, will and the power to choose the required amount of food, drink or sex and the appropriate behavioural approach, and the ability to abstain, willingly, from action even for a period of time. How huge this difference actually is! If this difference exists in the emotional aspect of man which we may imagine at first glance to resemble that of the animal, what about the other aspects of man, the spiritual as well as the intellectual, in which man is absolutely unique?

Man is a unique being not to be compared with an animal. When he regresses, and his insight is veiled, and his soul blinded, he is not only an animal but worse and degraded: "They are like cattle; nay more misguided, for they are heedless (of warning)." (Sura 7, verse 179) An animal possesses an innate nature which guides it and guards it against all endeavours to disable it, but if man loses the spiritual guidance attained through awareness, sensibility and consciousness, he would not only disable himself but inflict utter destruction upon himself, thus becoming more misguided than an animal.

Man, on the other hand, is not God, and never can be. He is one of God's creatures, nothing more. It is true that he is a unique creature, but his uniqueness does not entitle him to be more than one of God's countless creatures. Man must have fallen into the dismal, bottomless, unspiritual abyss out of his own accord when he defied and disobeyed God by committing himself to the worship of other gods, moral or material, or even those emanating from passion which makes man proud enough to rebel against God. "Seest thou such a one as taketh for his god his own passion (or impulse)?" (Sura 25, verse 43) But this does not change the reality of man and transform him into an actual god; it only makes him a slave rebellious against his master. Referring for the third time to Julian Huxley's book entitled *Man in the Modern World*, it is worth quoting what is briefly written in this connection.

Huxley says: "In the ages of ignorance and helplessness, man was fully subjugated to God, but now having acquired knowledge and controlled the environment, it is high time that he shoulder the responsibilities he had once assigned to God, and becomes himself a god." No! Never will man become a god, whatever his fancy or imagination. He cannot make himself by himself as the author of *Man Makes Himself* asserts; neither can he stand alone unsupported by God as Huxley alleges. In all aspects he is only human. When he assumes another character, he is either a believer or a non-believer; a Muslim or a non-Muslim. Therefore, he is in the best of moulds or the lowest of the low: "We have indeed created man in the best of moulds, then do We abase him (to be) the lowest of the low, except such as believe and do righteous deeds." *(Sura 95, verses 4–6)*

Man is undoubtedly unique in his nervous, intellectual and psychological energy: "And He gave you hearing and sight, and intelligence and affections; that ye may give thanks (to God)." *(Sura 16, verse 78)* The hearing and the sight mentioned in this Quranic verse do not indicate the ear and the eye. It is the relationship between the ear and eye and the contemplative in constant search for Truth, that really matters: "They have hearts wherewith they understand not, eyes wherewith they see not. They are like cattle, nay more misguided for they are heedless (of warning)." *(Sura 7, verse 179)*

Man is a conscious, sensible and reasonable being. His senses lead him to know the facts and proofs through which he can attain the ultimate Truth, and following it, he will be in the best of moulds as God had created him. But if he does not use his senses for the attainment of ultimate truth he will still be human, but the lowest of the low, because he will then have betrayed his uniqueness of creation and rejected the honour God conferred upon him. No wonder he degenerates into the lowest of the low and becomes more misguided than all animals.

The ability to learn is one of the energies God gave to man. God already taught Adam the nature of all things and taught the children of Adam thereafter:

"And He taught Adam the nature of all things." *(Sura 2, verse 31)*; "God, Most Gracious. It is He who hath taught the Qur'an. He hath created man. He hath taught him speech (and Intelligence)." *(Sura 55, verses 1–4)*; "Proclaim! And thy Lord is Most Bountiful, He who taught (the use of) the Pen; taught man that which he knows not." *(Sura 96, verses 3–5)*

This learning ability is one of the tools God has provided man with in order to help him accomplish the function for which he was created, namely, to inherit and till the earth. Though endowed with such energies man's ability is eventually limited. Therefore, he cannot, as Julian Huxley wants him to, become a god, for he cannot create out of nothingness nor say to a thing "Be" and it is, nor penetrate the curtains of the unknown except those which God permits him to. Moreover, man cannot sustain himself in all matters; he has to rely upon other objects God has created for him. God describes himself in this verse:

"God! There is no God but He, the Living, the Self-Subsisting, Eternal. No slumber can seize Him, nor sleep. His are all things in the heavens and on earth. Who is there can intercede in His presence except as He permitteth? He knoweth what (appeareth to His creatures as) before or after or behind them. Nor shall they compass aught of His Knowledge except as He willeth. His Throne doth extend over the heavens and the earth, and He feeleth no fatigue in guarding and preserving them, for He is the Most High, the Supreme (in glory)." (*Sura 2, verse 255*)

In addition to man's limited capacity to learn there is a particular point of weakness which is always tested; i.e. the transformation of what is forbidden in the realm of senses from a wish into an unleashed desire, controllable only through self-willed effort.

This is the true significance of the story of the tree which the Qur'an relates and which acquaints man with his own reality. God accommodated Adam and Eve in His Paradise and allowed them to eat all the fruits of Paradise except for those of one particular tree which they were ordered not to approach. Regardless of the identity of this tree it was transformed in the realm of their senses into something desirable simply because it was forbidden. Satan whispered into their ears, alluring them into disobedience of God:

" 'O Adam! dwell thou and thy wife in the Garden, and enjoy (its good things) as ye wish: but approach not this tree, or ye run into harm and transgression.' Then began Satan to whisper suggestions to them, bringing openly before their minds all their shame that was hidden from them (before). He said: 'Your Lord only forbade you this tree lest you should become angels or such beings as live forever.' And he swore to them both, that he was their sincere adviser. So, by deceit he brought about their Fall; when they tasted of the tree, their shame became manifest to them, and they began to sew together the leaves of the Garden over their bodies. And their Lord called unto them: 'Did I not forbid you that tree, and tell you that Satan was an avowed enemy unto you?' '' (*Sura 7, verses 19–22*)

Adam and Eve responded to the machinations of Satan not because the tree was in itself desirable, but forbidden. God pardoned them because they did not purposefully intend to disobey Him out of disbelief as Satan insisted. They said:

"Our Lord! We have wronged our own soul. If Thou forgive us not and bestow not upon us Thy Mercy, we shall certainly be lost." (*Sura 7, verse 23*); "Then learnt Adam from his Lord words of inspiration, and his Lord turned towards him; for He is Oft-Returning, and Most Merciful." (*Sura 2, verse 37*)

The story of the forbidden tree is still the story of the children of Adam after their parents, Adam and Eve. As we have previously mentioned, the earth teems with pleasures and allurements: "That which is on earth We have made but as a glittering show for the earth, in order that We may test them as to which of them are best in conduct." (*Sura 18, verse 7*) Some of these pleasures are good and permissible, and not forbidden by God. Some are too excessive, i.e. exceeding the limits set forth by God, and therefore, forbidden. Man's particular point of weakness which is liable to severe testing throughout his life is this: does man, when tasting the earth's pleasures, confine himself to those God has allowed and made accessible to him? In other words, does he, in all his concerns, resort to God's law and abide by it? Or does he lend ears to the machinations of Satan, exceed all limits of permissible pleasures, and eventually fall into disobedience of God? If he commits himself to God's law, Paradise will be his reward. There he would enjoy immeasurable eternal bliss incomparable with the false, dying, short-term happiness on the earth. But if he exceeds all limits and enjoys what God has forbidden, he will be then worshipping Satan and eternal hell will be his reward.

God forgives all sinners if they repent their sins and do not insist on committing them again:

"And those who, having done something to be ashamed of, or wronged their own souls, earnestly bring God to mind, and ask for forgiveness for their sins, and who can forgive sins except God? And are never obstinate in persisting knowingly in (the wrong) they have done; for such the reward is forgiveness from their Lord, and Gardens with rivers flowing underneath an eternal dwelling. How excellent a recompense for those who work (and strive)!" (*Sura 3, verses 135–136*)

The equation, which is the field of testing, will be as follows: on earth there is bliss and agony; bliss derived from pleasures, and agony caused by deprivation. In the Hereafter there is also bliss and agony: eternal bliss for those who obeyed God and abided by His law, and eternal agony, unendurable, for those who enjoyed pleasures forbidden by God. "Those who reject our Signs, We shall soon cast into the Fire. As often as their skins are roasted through, we shall change them for fresh skins, that they may taste the Penalty." (*Sura 4, verse 56*)

Which of the two blisses is to be sought, and which of the two agonies is to be avoided? Should he give up eternal bliss for the sake of moments of fleeting, desirable and expirable pleasure? Or should he obey God and abstain from excessive pleasure in return for eternal bliss?

Where does he turn to if he disobeys God for the sake of this fleeting, restless pleasure? Does he have a refuge?

"Although, when the sight is dazzled, and the moon is buried in darkness. And the sun and moon are joined together. That day will man say 'Where is the refuge?' By no means! No place of safety! Before the Lord (alone), that Day will be the place of rest. That Day will man be told (all) that he put forward, and all that he put back. Nay, Man will be witness against himself, even though he were to put up his excuses." (*Sura 75, verses 7–15*)

This is the Qur'an's reply to the first question about the identity of man, his constitution, his characteristics, and the limits of his energies. Let us now consider the second question which inquires about man's role, his function on earth and the aim of his existence. Here are three integrated non-contradictory quotations from the Qur'an to elaborate and pin-point man's function and the aim of his existence on earth:

"Behold! Thy Lord said to the angels: 'I will create a Vicegerent on earth.' " (*Sura 2, verse 30*); "It is He Who hath produced you from the earth and settled you therein." (*Sura 11 verse 61*); "I have only created the earth and men, that they may serve Me." (*Sura 51, verse 56*)

Man was created in order to be Vicegerent on earth, its sole and powerful master. The most outstanding aspect of this vicegerency and one of its most significant functions is the tilling of the earth. Simultaneously, God's worship is the sole end of man's creation. At first glance, there seems to be a contradiction or dissimilarity between the third quotation which states that man was originally created on this earth only to worship God, and the other two quotations which speak about vicegerency and the tilling of the earth. This apparently existing contradition springs from our narrow-minded and traditional outlook on worship as being restricted to mere rituals. But if we understood worship, in its Quranic, comprehensive sense, this superficial contradiction would soon be eliminated, and we should discover that the first two quotations are implied in the third and most comprehensive one.

"I have only created the earth and men, that they may serve Me." This quotation, so decisive and final, states that the reason why God created man was only to serve and worship Him, and that God will not accept anything from man but worship, because he was originally created to perform this assigned function. Does the quotation apply to the meaning of worship if we confine it to the mere performance of rituals? How long does the performance of these rituals take during one single revolution of the sun? How long does it take throughout a whole life-time? Where and how does man spend the rest of the hours and days, months and years?

On the other hand, how do the Quranic verses harmonize, one with the other, when we are told that God created us only to worship Him, and in some other verses that He assigned us some functions amongst which are: setting up and abiding by God's law on earth, fighting in His cause, tilling and exploring the earth, eating of God's sustenance, knowledge-seeking, marriage, multiplication and the enjoyment of all permissible and sanctioned pleasures?

Where do all these assignments fall? Do they fall within the purview of worship, or without? If they fall without the purview of worship, how do verses and quotations harmonize? We should understand worship in the wide Quranic sense, and as the Qur'an elaborates and interprets it. "Say: Truly my prayer, and my service of sacrifice, my life and my death, are (all) for God, the Cherisher of the Worlds." (*Sura 6, verses 162–163*)

This is the comprehensive sense of worship according to Islam. Prayer and services of sacrifice are a part of worship. The entire life should be devoted to the worship of God, right from the first life-giving breath to the last life-taking one. Rituals of worship should not be performed all day and night. This is quite impossible for man. They can be effected by obeying God's orders in every aspect of life and devoting every action, feeling or thought to God only in love of Him. Thus the integration and co-ordination between the three previously mentioned quotations from the Qur'an will be self-evident. All combined, they will give a clear cut definition of man's role in life.

Man's function, as has been previously iterated, is the worship of

God. God has systematized this worship in a way that suits man's nature and soul; and because He is the Merciful and the Most High, has made the natural activities of the body, mind and soul, if devoted and committed to God, forms of true worship. His food, drink, multiplication and searching for sustenance by exerting tremendous muscular efforts will all become worship. Man's intellectual investigation into the ways of the universe, the properties of the matter and the extraction of all energies found in the heavens and the earth and exploiting them for the benefit of mankind, will all become worship. The spiritual journeys of his soul and their illuminating consequences will also become worship. All duties of worship will integrate and co-ordinate until man becomes a true and devout servant of God, worshipping Him in every single moment of his life. Tilling of the earth will become worship.

But which tilling? Are all forms of the earth's tillage forms of worship? And what is the difference between the tilling done by a believer and a non-believer? If we understand tilling to be the material tilling of the earth, i.e., the material production and all scientific and technological achievements needed for it, one may rightly ask: what is the relationship between science and technology and religion? Would the properties of the matter change if religious doctrine changed? Would the manufacture of a car, a plane, a bomb or a rocket suffer any change if a believer or a *Kafir* (non-believer) manufactured them?

Any person asking these questions will be rightly entitled to do so as long as we understand the tilling of the earth as a purely material process connected with extracting the physical world energies and adapting them to the use of man.

But the situation changes if we look into the basis upon which this process, the tillage of the earth, is built and the end it endeavours to accomplish. When the end of human existence on this earth is, as illustrated in modern *Jahilliyya* (Ignorance), the excessive indulgence in earthly pleasures regardless of their vanities or limits, the methods and aims of tilling the earth will, undoubtedly, be different from when the end of human existence becomes the worship of God in its comprehensive sense previously referred to, i.e., abiding by and adhering to God's orders and laws in all concerns of life. Then the tillage of the earth on capitalist or communist lines will be basically wrong because it does not conform to the divine method set for the activities of man on earth, and because it is based on injustices done to the rest of people by a group of individuals. It is a truth universally acknowledged that capitalism extracts the energies of the universe and adapts them to the use of man. But capitalism does not care in the least about using some or many of these energies in excessive and harmful luxury leading to moral corruption and taking man from the true and straight path of God and the bliss promised him in the Hereafter, in breaking up the family, urging children to rebel against their parents and the inherited traditions of the society, and in propagating unhealthy habits very destructive to the human body. Furthermore, capitalism, in the actual process of industrialization, inflicts enormous political, economic, social, spiritual, intellectual and moral oppression on the workers in the interest of capital. Capitalism is based on profit, no matter how it comes; it is not based on what is deemed allowable or forbidden, which constitutes the core of God's *Sharia* (legal system).

It is a truth equally universally acknowledged that communism extracts the energies of the universe and adapts them to the use of man. But it does not care in the least about using some or many of these energies to impose undignified and dehumanizing humiliation on the mass of the people, to deprive them of their natural rights, to persecute and extinguish religious belief, to legalize and organize moral corruption, to break the social and natural ties of the family by forcing the man and woman to work and practise destructive espionage which eliminates confidence between husband and wife, father and son.

In addition to the above mentioned, the two camps, the capitalistic and communist, store up tools of destruction and devote enormous amounts of money and effort to manufacture, possess and accumulate such destructive devices which are definitely not for the good and service of mankind. Statistics prove that had those amounts of money and effort been spent to till the earth, not a single poor or hungry man would have remained on the surface of the earth.

It is not the material tillage of the earth that matters, even though it is part of man's function on the earth. The values upon which the tilling of the earth is based are the more important. In this respect, setting up material civilization on earth in accordance with God's divine curriculum differs from the material civilization achieved through the curricula of the *Jahilliyyats* (Times of Ignorance and Darkness).

Tilling the earth, though it involves a material aspect, is an act of worship, according to Islam. But it is not so unless it is based on God's curriculum which permits the exploitation of the energies of the heavens and the earth on condition that man should maintain himself "in the best of moulds", in the sense that he should cherish the human values based on his belief in God and the Hereafter. It will not be an act of worship if it is based on a curriculum which debases man "in the lowest of the low" as modern *Jahilliyya*, in the east and west alike, does. A true Muslim should till the earth and contribute toward the establishment of material civilization upon it, otherwise he will be considered, in the eyes of Islam, inefficient and incapable of performing the function assigned to him. But he does not till the earth by excessive and harmful luxury, by corrupting morals or religious belief, or by incurring social, economic and political oppression. This will not be tillage but corruption and contamination of the earth:

"Call on your Lord with humility and in private for God loveth not those who trespass beyond bounds. Do not mischief on earth, after it hath been set in order, but call on Him with fear and longing (in your hearts), for the Mercy of God is (always) near to those who do good." (*Sura 7, verses 55–56*)

This is the divine method for tilling the earth which breeds genuine civilization and goodness.

The third question bearing on human existence is the one related to the fate and destiny of man. It is a question of paramount importance in man's life, his aims and values, behavioural patterns, morals and thoughts. If, in answer to this question, death without return is man's fate, and that death is the inevitable, inescapable and everlasting end of man, this will definitely and violently be reflected in the entire life of man and all its details.

If man conceives life as a single opportunity offered to him and limited to his age on this earth which is short, and which no matter how long it lasts, cannot absorb all his aspirations, ambitions or desires, what then will be the suitable logic for this conception? Naturally, all pleasures available on this earth will be exhausted in every possible manner since life is man's only opportunity, and if he lets it escape it will never come back.

Hence, all the *Jahilliyyats* (Ignorances) which do not believe in the Hereafter hang over and clutch at the pleasures of life. Consequently, individuals and groups, peoples and countries will fight relentlessly over these pleasures allowing conflicts to rise among all mankind. The 20th-century *Jahilliyya*, no doubt, offers the best example of this life.

Let us introduce another conception and witness its impact on the life of man. Let us conceive a man who believes in the Hereafter, the resurrection, the Day of Judgement, reckoning and reward, and let us ask: "How does he feel about all this?" Surely, his attitude towards life will be completely different in manner and outlook. Life is not the only available opportunity offered to him; nor will never come back if he lets it escape. Life will everlastingly extend after death. In the life after death, man will be granted the complete opportunity to taste all imaginable pleasures. There, are things no mortal eye had ever seen, no mortal ear had ever heard and no mortal mind had ever thought of. Any man having this conception will not abstain from enjoying the good and pleasurable things on the earth, because God has given him strong urges and instincts which always clamour for their share in worldly pleasures. Even if man gave up the enjoyment of worldly pleasures he would not be a true Muslim.

"Three men went to one of the homes of the Apostle of God (Peace be on him) and asked how he worshipped God. When they were told of it they thought it was far less than they had expected. One of them said, 'I fast every day until the last day of my life'; the second one said, 'I pray all night and never sleep or slumber'; the third one said, 'I do not marry women'. When the Apostle of God, (Peace be on him) was informed of that, he summoned them in his presence and said: 'Is it you who said so and so? By God I am more devout in my worship than you, but I fast and eat, awake and sleep and marry women. He who rejects my Sunna (the Prophet's words and deeds) is not one of my followers.'"

If man knocks off the shackles that bind his soul to the earth, he will be more competent to control his wishes and desires within the limits prescribed by God; for he knows that for every excessive pleasure he had forsaken on earth to please God he will be doubly and trebly rewarded on the day of Resurrection when he will stand in the presence of God and enter God's Paradise, where he will enjoy eternal bliss for not disobeying Him.

Man's energy which he had saved and which would have been spent on fighting over earthly pleasures will have to be spent for a completely different cause. It will be spent in consolidating supreme values among people; values which could never be consolidated or even maintained in an atmosphere of conflict. It will be spent in establishing divine justice on earth which could never be established when people are busy seizing the opportunity offered to them. It will also be spent in fighting in the cause of God, not to gain supremacy and power, just for the sake of power.

On earth, there will be a conflict, but of a different kind altogether; it is a conflict more sublime and valuable than the dismal, ugly-looking conflict which exists among all mankind in their *Jahilliyya*. It is a conflict between right and wrong, good and evil, justice and injustice. Only then will a nation emerge so vividly and truly described in this Quranic verse: "Ye are the best of peoples evolved for mankind, enjoying what is right, forbidding what is wrong, and believing in God." (*Sura 3, verse 110*) This nation did not race for the accumulation and possession of earthly pleasures, but for something else:

"Be ye foremost (in seeking) forgiveness from your Lord, and a Garden (of Bliss) the width whereof is as the width of heaven and earth, prepared for those who believe in God and His apostles. That is the Grace of God which He bestows on whom He pleases; and God is the Lord of Grace abounding." (*Sura 51, verse 21*)

Nevertheless, this nation did not neglect the tilling of the earth because it is part of man's worship of God. They tilled the earth in accordance with the divine law otherwise their worship would not be accepted by God. Proceeding with the last question in our discussion and scrutinizing study of man, we should ask: "What is the curriculum according to which man's life in this world and the next will become straight and righteous?" The Qur'an provides a sufficiently clear answer to this question: it is the divine curriculum revealed by God, and which was completely and finally embodied in the message God sent down of Prophet Muhammad, (Peace be on him) the day when this Quranic verse was revealed, "This day have I perfected your religion for you, completed my favour upon you, and have chosen for you Islam as your religion." (*Sura 5 verse 3*) The Qur'an explains why this particular curriculum should be followed and not any other one made by man for mankind. There are two reasons why no curriculum conceived and devised by man should be adhered to by all mankind:

(1) This is polytheism: "Follow (O men!) the revelation given unto you from your Lord, and follow not, as friends or protectors, other than Him. Little it is ye remember of admonition." (*Sura 7, verse 3*)

Worship, which is the end of human existence, cannot be genuine and complete if it is restricted to the mere performance of rituals while man, in all his life concerns, abides by orders other than God's. In this case he will be, in fact, believing in two gods instead of one. He will be worshipping one god inside the temple, fasting and praying for him, and another outside the temple, closely following his instructions: "God has said: Take not (for worship) two gods: for He is just One God; then fear Me (and Me alone)." *(Sura 16, verse 51)* Worship will be entirely and sincerely devoted to God, and man will be able to fulfil the end of his existence, only if he worships God, the Only One, by performing religious duties and carrying out His orders at the same time. Man will then become truly righteous and will deserve to be God's vicegerent on earth to till it according to the divine curriculum.

(2) God's *Sharia* (laws) is better than any other one conceived and formulated by man in times of *Jahilliyya* (Ignorance): "Do they then seek after a judgement of (the Days of Ignorance)? But who, for a people whose faith is assured, can give better judgement than God?" *(Sura 5, verse 50)*

Human legislation, as we have previously mentioned in the introduction to this chapter, must be characterized by inconsistency, inadequacy and incomprehensiveness. Any legislator must be neutral and his vision must be clear and inclusive. He must, of necessity, know man's past, present and future, in order to formulate legislation that will meet all his needs and be applicable in all cases. No human being, whatever he is, can be so highly qualified or possess these characteristics.

The history of mankind is laid before our eyes. The works of philosophers and thinkers are kept and read. Which one of them could acquaint himself with everything? Which one of them was not wronged by others? Which one of them tried to experiment practically on his philosophy to find out whether it would succeed or fail? How often had mankind been misled while engaged in formulating legislation in times of Ignorance; shifting from extreme right to extreme left and back again to extreme right? How often had mankind over-valued the individual until society disintegrated, and over-valued society until the individual was crushed, and back again? How often had mankind robbed the rulers of their power, and then raised them to the stature of gods and destroyed them? How often had human relations shrunk until the vitality was drained out, expanded to restore the lost vitality and then shrank again? How often had mankind used *reason* until they were agonized, and shifted to *intuition* and back again to *reason*?

Throughout all its phases humanity was perverted, agonized and misguided, though it believed at every stage that it had assimilated all experiments, and that it would never be misled.

God's revealed *Sharia* was laid down by Him, the All-Knowing,

Who created man and knows all the innermost secrets, the ins and outs of his soul. He also knows all that man needs: "Should He not know He that created. And He is the One that understands the finest mysteries (and) is well acquainted (with them)." (*Sura 67, verse 14*)

This *Sharia*, as we have referred to in the introduction to this chapter, is comprehensive, integrated and balanced. So is Islam.

Islamic *Sharia* comprises all man's activities, political, economic, social, intellectual and spiritual. Every single human activity or action is regulated in Islam. *Sharia* has a particular attitude towards it: it rejects, accepts, favours or dislikes it.

God's *Sharia* is integrated; this is a matter of considerable importance in any life governing system. Any system may comprehend all aspects of life but handle it as if it were a set of independent disconnected pieces. Modern *Jahilliyya* (Ignorance) acts in this manner assuming that economics is economics only and has nothing to do with morals, that politics is politics only, not related to morals, and that interest, not morals, is the basis upon which commercial transactions in the society are built. Modern *Jahilliyya* also asserts that art is just art and has nothing to do with anything else at all.

The human being is a self-integrated unit. All human activities emanate from this self-integrated whole which is man. How are we to tear this whole into pieces and study every piece in isolation? The true and faultless curriculum should comprehend all the physical and spiritual aspects of man, bind them together in one bond, so that, when putting this curriculum into practice, the human soul will not be torn out and fragmented in all directions. This is the distinctive feature of Islam and Islamic *Sharia*. Islamic *Sharia* is coherent because it is based on the belief in one God, the Creator and Legislator of unified and consistent laws.

When all is said and mentioned, Islamic *Sharia* is also balanced. This is another characteristic extremely important in man's life. It is not sufficient that *Sharia* is comprehensive and integrated, for it can be so without necessarily being balanced, in the sense that it emphasizes one particular aspect of the human soul or life more than the other. Modern *Jahilliyya* stresses the economic element and assumes that it is life or at least the most significant aspect of life. The two opposed camps, capitalism and communism, hold the same belief. Both underestimate, ignore or fight the moral and religious aspects of the human soul. Both give priority to material production over any other production accomplished by man. The individual will inevitably suffer loss of balance; so will the whole society. The human soul will be perverted and all mankind will be miserable.

Islamic legislation is characterized by this balance lost in all the legislations of the *Jahilliyya*. Islam gives every aspect of human life its due significance without over-emphasizing one aspect at the expense of the other.

If Islamic *Sharia* attaches the most considerable importance to the religious aspect it is because upon the religious aspect only, the whole structure of life is set up. The whole structure of human life will stand fully erect and balanced because it rests, in an even degree, on this religious basis, which comprehends the individual and the society, the physical and the moral, the present and the future, the natural and the supernatural, the function of man and the worth of God; this world and the next, in one self-contained system. In reality, there is no man-made system so comprehensive, coherent or balanced. There is not even one single conception so wide and so inclusive. In this cursory glance where we cannot cite examples of the justness of this *Sharia* or its actual effects on man's life, we will mention two historical facts:

1. The least number of crimes on earth are committed in communities which apply Islamic *Sharia*.

2. All *Jahilliyya* legislations have failed to fight one particular crime, wine-drinking; whereas, in the Muslim society, people abstained from drinking wine once they were told it is forbidden.

This is the difference between a system based on religious belief and a system based on something else whether it is interest or fear.

When Islam gives answers to these questions it, in fact, furnishes man with a guidebook which will guide him through his entire journey on earth from beginning to last, and into the world of eternity. A traveller armed with a guidebook to tell him where to go in order to reach his destination, is, no doubt, different from a traveller lost in the wilderness because he does not carry a guidebook with him. We cannot say that a traveller having no guidebook does not get tired. Every traveller toils painfully: "O thou man! Verily thou art ever toiling on towards thy Lord, painfully toiling but thou shalt meet Him," (*Sura 84, verse 6*); "Verily We have created man into toil and struggle." (*Sura 90, verse 4*) But there is a huge difference between one toil and another. It is true that a traveller having a guidebook to guide him throughout his journey toils, but he knows his aim and that every effort he makes will bring him nearer to his aim and destination. But the traveller who does not have a guidebook and who walks aimlessly adds to the inevitable toil, restlessness, confusion and the feeling of being lost. Satisfaction is given to those who believe in God: "Those who believe, and whose hearts find satisfaction in the remembrance of God; for without doubt in the rememberance of God do hearts find satisfaction." (*Sura 13, verse 28*)

Modern *Jahilliyya* is the best illustrative example of those who rejected the worship of God and worshipped Satan instead. People are suffering from countless psychological, nervous and intellectual diseases. Millions of people have become lunatics, criminals, sex maniacs, wine and opium addicts. Restlessness, confusion and the feeling of being lost prevail in modern *Jahilliyya*.

The only salvation from the evils in which mankind has fallen is Islam which preaches the belief in God, the One, the Indivisible; in Muhammad, peace be on him), the Apostle of God and the last in the wilderness of modern *Jahilliyya* and who suffer the scorching heat and the freezing cold.

Today, mankind has had enough of its perverted experiments, and has begun to awaken. They have begun to understand that the worst of their experiments was the rotten material civilization which we rightly call the 20th century *Jahilliyya* (Ignorance) and that this contemporary civilization has made them more miserable than any other civilization in history. Throughout their entire history mankind had never disbelieved in God so openly, defiantly and fearlessly as they do in this contemporary crazy *Jahilliyya*. Nevertheless, they have begun, as we believe, to get fed up with this *Jahilliyya*, and have begun to feel their way. Nothing but Islam will guide them to the straight path, to God. "The Religion before God is Islam (submission to His Will)." (*Sura 3, verse 19*)

The day will soon come when all mankind will return to the true religion and reject the beliefs, conceptions, thoughts and curricula which have driven them headlong into confusion, misguidance and loss. The dawn of this day has already risen, and tomorrow, all Mankind will believe and abide by this religion.

Intellect and Intuition
their Relationship from the Islamic Perspective
Dr Seyyed Hossein Nasr

In a world in which the intellect has become synonymous with reason and intuition with a "biological" sixth sense concerned with fore-telling future events, it becomes difficult to understand what intellect and intuition, these two key faculties upon which knowledge is based, can mean in the context of Islamic thought. To understand the meaning of these terms in the traditional Islamic universe where the light of the One dominates all multiplicity, and multiplicity is always seen in the light of Unity, it is necessary to examine the actual terminology em-ployed in Islamic languages, particularly Arabic and Persian, to denote the concepts of intellect and intuition.

In modern Western languages the fundamental distinction between intellect and reason is usually forgotten and the term intellect is used as the equivalent of reason. In Arabic and other Islamic languages a single term, *al-'aql*, is used to denote both reason and intellect, but the distinction between the two as well as their inter-relation and the dependence of reason upon the intellect is always kept in mind. *Al-'aql* in Arabic is related to the root *'ql* which means basically to bind. It is that faculty which binds man to God, to his origin. By virtue of being endowed with *al-'aql*, man becomes man and shares in the attri-bute of knowledge, *al-'ilm*, which ultimately belongs to God alone. The possession of *al-'aql* is of such a positive nature that the Holy Qur'an refers over and over again to the central rôle of *al-'aql* and of intellect (*ta'aqqul* or *taffaqquh*) in man's religious life and in his salva-tion.[1] But *al-'aql* is also used as reason, intelligence, keenness of per-ception, foresight, common sense and many other concepts of a related order. Moreover, each school of Islamic thought has elaborated in great detail certain aspects of the meaning of intellect as it pertains to its perspective and inner structure.

As far as the word intuition is concerned, such terms as *hads* and *firasah* have usually been used. These terms imply a *participation* in a knowledge which is not simply rational but not opposed to the intellectual as the term is understood in its traditional sense. Another set of terms more prevalent in texts of philosophy, theology and Sufism are *dhawq, ishraq, mukashafah, basirah, nazar* and *badihah*. These terms are all related to the direct vision and participation in the knowledge of the truth in contrast to indirect knowledge upon which all ratiocination is based. This contrast is emphasized also in the usage of the term *al-'ilm al-huduri*, or *presential knowledge*, as opposed to *al-'ilm al-husuli*, or *attained knowledge*,[2] but these terms refer to the difference between intuition as a form of a knowledge based upon immediate experience and ratiocination as indirect knowledge based upon mental concepts. In no way, however, do all these terms, as used in traditional Islamic languages stand opposed to *al-'aql*; rather, they serve as its complement in its profoundest sense. Islam has never seen a dichotomy between intellect and intuition but has created a hierarchy of knowledge and methods of attaining knowledge according to which degrees of both intellect and intuition become harmonized in an order encompassing all the means available to man to know, from sensual knowledge to the *knowledge of the heart*.

To understand fully the relationship between intellect and intuition in Islam, it is necessary to turn to those Islamic intellectual perspectives which have brought to actualization various possibilities inherent in the Islamic revelation. They include, as far as the present discussion is concerned, the purely religious sciences such as Quranic and Shari'ite studies, theology, various schools of philosophy and finally Sufism.

In the religious sciences the function of the intellect is seen only in the light of its ability to elucidate the verities of revelation. It is revelation which is the basic means for the attainment of the truth, and it is also revelation which illuminates the intellect and enables it to function properly. This wedding between revelation and the intellect makes it in fact possible for the mind to *participate* in the truth by means of that *act* or *leap* which is usually called intuition and which is inseparable from the faith which makes knowledge of the truth possible.

Some of the more esoteric commentators of the Holy Qur'an have emphasized the complementary nature of revelation and intellect which in fact has been called particular or partial revelation (*al-wahy al-juz'i*) while objective revelation which causes a new religion to become established is called universal revelation (*al-wahy al-kulli*). Only through the objective and universal revelation do the potentialities of the intellect become actualized. It is only by submitting itself to objective revelation that this subjective revelation in man which is the intellect, becomes fully itself, capable not only of analysis but also synthesis and unification. In its unifying function the intellect is salvatory and is able to save the soul from all bondage of multiplicity and separateness. The instrument of revelation, the Archangel Gabriel, is also the Holy Spirit which illuminates the intellect and enables it to possess the faculty of intuition. In the light of revelation, the intellect functions not merely as reason but as intellectual intuition which, wedded to faith, enables man to penetrate the meaning of religion and more particularly God's word as contained in the Holy Qur'an. Man must exercise his intelligence in order to understand God's revelation, but in order to understand God's revelation, the intellect must be already illuminated by the light of faith[3] and touched by the grace issuing from revelation.

As far as Islamic theology of *Kalam* is concerned, it is engaged more with the understanding of the will of God than reaching the universal dimensions of the intellect. This is especially true of the dominant school of Sunni theology founded by Abu'l-Hasan al-Ash'ari. The Ash'arite school is based on a voluntarism which reduces the function of the intellect to the purely human level and remains nearly oblivious to the aspect of the Divinity as objective Truth and Knowledge.[4] For this school, truth is what God has willed and the intellect has no function outside the external tenets of the religion. Although the extreme form of voluntarism found in the earlier school of Ash'arism was somewhat modified by the later school (*al-muta'akhkhirun*) of such men as al-Ghazzali and Fakhr al-Din al-Razi, Ash'arism has remained throughout its history as a school of theology in which the intellect is made subservient to the will of God and not considered in its function of returning man to the Deity and penetrating into the heart of *tawhid*.[5]

In other schools of *Kalam*, whether it be Mu'tazilitism and Maturidism in the Sunni world or Twelve-Imam Shi'ite theology, a greater role is given to reason in its interpretation of God's will as manifested in His revelation without, however, leading to the type of position known as rationalism in the modern Occident. Nor do these schools of theology envisage, any more than Ash'arism, the role of the universal function of the intellect which includes what is known as intuition as a means of attaining true knowledge. The function of *Kalam* has remained throughout Islamic history to find rational means to protect the citadel of faith (*al-imam*). It has not been to enable the intellect to penetrate into the inner courtyard of faith and become the ladder which leads to the very heart of the truth of religion. In fact it is not so much in theology but rather in religious philosophy and gnosis that we must seek for an explanation of the full meaning of the intellect and intuition and a complete methodology of knowledge in Islam.

In Islamic philosophy we can distinguish at least three schools which have dealt extensively with the methodology of knowledge and the full amplitude of the meaning of the intellect in its relation to intuition: peripatetic (*mashsha'i*) philosophy, illuminationist (*ishraqi*) theosophy and the "transcendent theosophy" of Sadr al-Din Shirazi.[6] Although the *mashsha'i* school in Islam drew most of its teachings from Aristotelian and Neoplatonic sources, it is not a rationalistic school as this term is usually understood in Western philosophy. The *mashsha'i* school is based on a view of the intellect which is properly speaking metaphysical and not merely philosophical and distinguishes clearly between the reflection of the intellect upon the human mind which is reason and the intellect in itself which transcends the realm of the individual.[7]

A complete treatment of the intellect and *a theory of knowledge* is to be found in the writings of the master of Muslim Peripatetics, Ibn Sina. Basing himself upon the treatises on the intellect (*al-Risalah fi'l-'aql*) by al-Kindi and al-Farabi,[8] Ibn Sina gave an extensive analysis of the meaning of the intellect in several of his works especially *The Book of Healing* (*al-Shifa'*), *The Book of Salvation* (*al-Najat*) and his last masterpiece *The Book of Directives and Remarks* (*Kitab al-isharat wa'l-tanbihat*). Basing himself upon the Alexandrian commentators of Aristotle such as Themistius and Alexander Aphrodisias and with full awareness of the Quranic doctrine of revelation, Ibn Sina distinguishes between the Active Intellect (*al-'aql al-fa'al*) which is universal and independent of the individual, and the intellectual function within man. Each human being possesses intelligence in a latent form. This is called material or potential intelligence (*bi'l-quwwah*). As the human being grows in knowledge the first intelligible forms are placed in the soul from above and man attains to the level of the habitual intelligence (*bi'l-malakah*). As the intelligibles become fully actualized in the mind, man reaches the level of actual intellect (*bi'l-fi'l*) and finally as this process is completed, the acquired intelligence (*mustafad*). Finally above these stages and states stands the Active Intellect (*al-'aql al-fa'al*) which is Divine and which illuminates the mind through the act of knowledge.[9] According to Ibn

Sina every act of cognition involves the illumination of the mind by the Active Intellect which bestows upon the mind the form whose knowledge *is* the knowledge of the object in question. Although Ibn Sina denied the Platonic ideas, he stands certainly closer to the realists of the mediaeval West than to the nominalists. It is not accidental that the followers of St Augustine were to rally around the teachings of Ibn Sina once his works were translated into Latin and that a school was developed which owed its origin to both St Augustine and Ibn Sina.[10]

The *mashsha'i* doctrine concerning the intellect and intuition can be summarized by saying that there are degrees of intellect which are attained as man advances in knowledge with the aid of the Active Intellect. As the intellect grows in strength and universality, it begins to acquire functions and powers which are identified with intuition rather than intellect in its analytical function connected with the act of ratiocination. The means of acquiring metaphysical knowledge is, according to Ibn Sina, intellectual intuition by which *ta'aqqul* should be translated rather than mere ratiocination. But by intuition here we mean not a sensual or biological power which leaps in the dark but a power which illuminates and removes the boundaries of reason and the limitations of individualistic existence.

In traditional Islamic sources the *mashsha'i* school is usually called *hikmah bahthiyyah* (rational philosophy or more precisely argumentative philosophy) in contrast to the *ishraqi* school which is called *hikmah dhawqiyyah* (intuitive philosophy). Although *mashsha'i* philosophy is by no means merely rationalistic as shown above, it is in the *ishraqi* or illuminative school of wisdom founded by Shaykh al-ishraq Shihab al-Din Suhrawardi that the intuitive aspect of the intellect is fully emphasized and a ladder described reaching from sensual to principial, metaphysical knowledge. Suhrawardi, like such Western metaphysicians as St Augustine and St Thomas, emphasizes the principle of adequation or *adaequatio* (*adaequatio rei et intellectus*) according to which to each plane of reality there corresponds an instrument of knowledge adequate to the task of knowing that particular level of reality. But what characterizes and distinguishes *ishraqi* epistemology is that according to this school every form of knowledge is the result of an illumination of the mind by the lights of the purely spiritual or intelligible world. Even the act of physical vision is possible because the soul of the beholder is illuminated by a light which in the very act of seeing embraces the object of vision. In the same way, the knowledge of a logical concept is made possible by the illumination of the mind at the moment when the very form of the logical concept in question is present in the mind. As for higher forms of knowledge reaching into the empyrean of gnosis and metaphysics, they too are naturally the fruit of the light of the spiritual world shining upon the mind. In *ishraqi* wisdom, therefore, there is no intellection without illumination and no true knowledge without the actual *tasting* (*dhawq*) of the object of that knowledge, that tasting which is none other than *sapientia* (whose Latin root *sapere* means literally to taste) or intuitive knowledge at its highest level of meaning.[11]

As for the third school associated with Mulla Sadra, the views of both the Peripatetics and Illuminationists are incorporated by him along with the Sufi doctrine of the "knowledge of the heart", into a vast methodology of knowledge in which all the diverse faculties of knowing are to be found in hierarchy leading from the sensual to the spiritual.[12] Each act of knowledge, according to Mulla Sadra, involves the being of the knower and the hierarchy of the faculties of knowledge corresponds to the hierarchy of existence. Of particular interest is Mulla Sadra's insistence on the importance of the power of imagination (*takhayyul*) as an instrument of knowledge corresponding to the "world of imagination" ('*alam al-khayal*) or *mundus imaginalis* which has an objective reality and stands between the physical and purely spiritual realms of existence.[13] Corresponding to this world, man possesses an instrument of knowledge which is neither sensual nor intellectual but which fills the domain in between. This power of creative imagination which is only perfected in the Universal Man (*al-insan al-kamil*), is able to create forms in the imaginal world and know these forms ontologically. According to Mulla Sadra, the very existence of these forms is the knowledge of them in the same way that according to Suhrawardi, God's knowledge of the world is the very reality of the world. In any case the harmony and balance between intellect and intuition is perfected by Mulla Sadra through his recourse to this intermediate domain and the intermediate faculty of knowing his domain, the faculty which is none other than the power of *imagination* (*takhayyul*) residing in the soul and integrally related to the rational, intellectual and intuitive faculties of the soul.

The fullest meaning of the intellect and its universal function is to be found in the *ma'rifah* or gnosis, which lies at the heart of the Islamic revelation and which is crystallized in the esoteric dimension of Islam identified for the most part with Sufism. There are verses of the Holy Qur'an and a *Hadith* of the Holy Prophet which allude to the heart as the seat of intelligence and knowledge. The heart is the instrument of true knowledge as its affliction is the cause of ignorance and forgetfulness. That is why the message of the revelation addresses the heart more than the mind as the following verse of the Holy Qur'an reveals:

"O men, now there has come to you
an admonition from your Lord, and
a healing for what is in the breasts (namely the heart)
and a guidance, and a mercy to the believers."
(*Sura 10, verse 57*)

In the same way, it is the knowledge gained by the heart which counts before the Divine. Again, to quote the Holy Qur'an:

"God will not take you to task for a slip in your oaths; but He will take you to task for what your hearts have earned; and God is All-forgiving, All-clement." (*Sura 2, verse 225*)

Likewise, the knowledge of the heart, at least at some levels, is considered as essential for salvation, for those who refuse to identify themselves with the heart or centre of their living forfeit the possibility of entering into Paradise which already resides at the centre of the heart as the famous dictum of Christ "The Kingdom of God is with you" testifies. The Holy Qur'an asserts:

"We have created for Gehenna many jinn and men; They have hearts, but understand not with them." (*lahum gulub un la yafqahunabiha*) (*Sura 8, verse 178*)

In the *Hadith* literature there are also numerous references to the knowledge of the heart, a knowledge which is principial and essential and identified with faith as the following *Hadith* quoted by both Bukhari and Tirmidhi demonstrates: "Faith descended at the root of the hearts of men, then came down the Qur'an, and (people) learnt from the Qur'an and from the example (of the Prophet)."[14]

Also, that heart is considered praiseworthy which grasps for knowledge, for as the Holy Prophet has said: "Blessed is he who makes his heart grasping."[15] It could in fact be said that in the language of the Holy Qur'an and *Hadith* the heart means essentially the seat of knowledge or the instrument for the attainment of knowledge. It is upon this foundation that the Sufis have developed the doctrine of *the knowledge of the heart* which has occupied so many of the great masters of Sufism.

The Sufis speak of the *eye of the heart* (*'ayn al-qalb* in Arabic and *chishm-i dil* in Persian) as the "third eye" which is able to gain a knowledge different from that gained by the physical eyes yet direct and immediate like physical vision.[16] As the famous Persian poet Hatif states:

"Open the 'eye of the heart' so that thou canst see the spirit
And gain a vision of that which is invisible."

This knowledge which is identified with the heart is principial knowledge gained through an instrument which is identified with the heart or centre of being of man rather than the mind which knows only indirectly and which is a projection of the heart. The heart is not simply identified with sentiments which are contrasted in modern philosophy with reason. Man does not possess only the faculty of reason and the sentiments or emotions which are contrasted with reason. Rather, he is capable of an intellectual knowledge which transcends the dualism and dichotomy between reason and emotions, or the mind and the heart as they are usually understood. It is the loss of gnosis or truly intellectual knowledge in an operative and realized manner in the modern world that has caused the eclipse of the Islamic conception of *the knowledge of the heart*, a knowledge which is at once intellectual and intuitive in the profoundest meaning of these terms.

To understand fully the intellectual knowledge identified with the heart, it is necessary to return to the distinction between *presential* (*huduri*) and *attained* (*husuli*) knowledge. All rational knowledge related to the mind is made possible through concepts which are *attained* by the mind. All mental knowledge is *attained* knowledge. Mentally and rationally man can only know fire or water through the concept of fire or water abstracted through the senses and made available by the various mental faculties for the analytical faculty of the mind identified with reason. But there is another type of knowledge, possible for all men, but in practice attained only by the few. It is a knowledge which is direct and immediate without the help of any intermediary concepts or ideas. It is *presential* knowledge identified with the heart. The knowledge of the heart has the immediacy and directness of sensual knowledge but concerns the intelligible or spiritual world. When man gains knowledge of the perfume of a rose through direct experience of the olfactory faculty, he does not gain knowledge of the concept of the perfume of the rose but a direct knowledge of it. For most men this kind of knowledge is limited to the sensual world, but for the gnostic whose eye of his heart is opened through spiritual practice there is the possibility of a knowledge which has the directness of sensual experience but concerns the supernal realities. From the point of view of this presential knowledge, this supreme form of knowing in which ultimately the subject and object of knowledge are the same, the most concrete of all realities is the Supreme Principle. Everything else is relatively speaking an abstraction. To know in an ultimate sense is to know God through a knowledge which is both intellection and intuition in the highest meaning of these terms. It is to know the fire by being burned and consumed in it; it is to know water by being immersed in the ocean of Universal Existence.

In the Islamic perspective, therefore, one can speak of a hierarchy of knowledge ranging from the sensual, through the imaginary and the rational, to the intellectual which is also intuitive and identified with the heart. But just as the rational faculty of knowledge is not opposed to the sensual, the intellectual and intuitive are not opposed to the rational. Rather, the mind is a reflection of the heart, the centre of the microcosm. The Islamic doctrine of Unity (*al-tawhid*) has been able to embrace all modes of knowing into complimentary and not contending stages of a hierarchy leading to that supreme form of knowledge, that gnosis of the purified heart which is ultimately none other than the unitive and unifying knowledge of the One and the most profound realization of Unity (*al-tawhid*) which is the Alpha and Omega of the Islamic revelation.

Notes

1 See for example "They also say: If we had only heard, and had understood (*na'qilu*) we would not have been of the inhabitants of the Blaze." (*Sura 18, verse 10*) In this verse the refusal to understand or literally *intellect* is equated with the loss of paradise.

In many other verses various forms of the verb *faqaha* are used with the same meaning as *'aqala*, for example "We have distinguished the signs for a people who understand (yafqahun)." (*Sura 8, verse 98*)

2 Concerning *al-'ilm al-huduri* and *al-'ilm al-husuli* see S. H. Nasr, *Islamic Science-An Illustrated Study*, London, 1976, p.14.

3 On the relation between faith and intellect or revelation and reason see F. Schuon, *Stations of Wisdom*, trans. G. E. H. Palmer, London, 1976. "If 'no man cometh unto the Father but by Me', this truth or this principle is equally applicable to the pure

Intellect in ourselves: in the sapiential order – and it is only in this order that we may speak of Intellect or intellectuality without making implacable reservations – it is essential to submit all the powers of the soul to the pure Spirit, which is identified, but in a supra-formal and ontological manner, with the fundamental dogma of the Revelation and thereby with the *Sophia Perennis*.'' F. Schuon, *Dimensions of Islam*, trans. P. Townsend, London, 1970, p. 76.

4 On Ash'arite voluntarism see F. Schuon, *Logic and Transcendence*, trans. P. Townsend, New York, 1975.

5 On Ash'arism and its views concerning the intellect see L. Gardet, *Introduction à la théologie musulmane*, Paris, 1948.

6 On these schools see H. Corbin (in collaboration with S. H. Nasr and O. Yahya) *Histoire de la philosophie islamique*, Vol. I, Paris, 1964; Nasr, *Three Muslim Sages*, Albany (N. Y.), 1975; Nasr, *The Transcendent Theosophy of Sadr al-Din Shirizi*, London, 1978.

7 Classical philosophy, before its decadence, cannot itself be reduced to profane philosophy and is not merely of human inspiration. Rather, it is based on a wisdom of Divine origin. It is only the rationalism of modern thought that has reduced the whole of ancient philosophy to a "harmless" antecedent of modern philosophy and refused to see in a Pythagoras or a Plato anything more than somewhat more intelligent professors of philosophy as one would find in any contemporary Western university. It must be remembered that the Muslims called Plato the "Divine Plato" (*Aflatun al-ilahi*). Concerning intellectual intuition as it functions in the context of traditional wisdom or the *philosophia perennis* and ratiocination in modern philosophy, F. Schuon writes, "Intellectual intuition communicates *a priori* the reality of the Absolute.

"Rationalistic thought infers the Absolute by starting from the relative; thus it does not proceed by intellectual intuition, though it does not inevitably exclude it.

"For philosophy (in the profane sense) arguments have an absolute value; for intellectual intuition their value is symbolical and provisional." *Spiritual Perspectives and Human Facts*, trans. D. M. Matheson, London, 1953, p. 106.

8 These treatises had a profound influence upon Western Scholasticism and were well known to the mediaeval masters such as St Thomas and Duns Scotus.

9 See Ibn Sina, *Le livre des directives et remarques*, trans. A. M. Goichon, Beirut, 1951, pp.324–326; and Nasr, *An Introduction to Islamic Cosmological Doctrines*, London, 1978, chapter 14; also F. Rahman, *Prophecy in Islam*, London, 1958, pp.11–29, which contains the translation of the relevant sections from the *Shifa'*.

10 See E. Gilson, *Les sources gréco-arabes de l'augustinisme avicennisant*, Archives d'Histoire Doctrinale et Littéraire du Moyen-Age, Paris, Vol. 4, 1929, pp. 5–149.

11 Suhrawardi's epistemology is expounded in the second book of his *Hikmat al-ishraq* but cannot be fully understood without the commentaries of Qutb al-Din al-Shirazi and Shams al-Din al-Shahrazuri. See the prolegomena of H. Corbin to Vol. II of Suhrawardi, *Oeuvres philosophiques et mystiques*, Tehran-Paris, 1977.

12 Concerning Mulla Sadra see S. H. Nasr, *Sadr al-Din Shirazi and His Transcendent Theosophy*; the introduction of H. Corbin to Mulla Sadra, *Le livre des pénétrations*

métaphysiques, Tehran-Paris, 1964; and F. Rahman, *The Philosophy of Mulla Sadra,* New York, 1975, which, however, gives a somewhat excessively rationalistic interpretation of the master of the transcendent theosophy.

13 The impoverished modern vision of reality did not only banish the angels from the cosmos after Leibnitz, but also reduced the *mundus imaginalis* to pure whim and fancy with which the word imagination is identified today. Perhaps with H. Corbin, one should use the term imaginal to distinguish the traditional *"imaginalis"* from all that the word imaginary brings to mind. Concerning this imaginal world see H. Corbin, *Creative Imagination in the Sufism of Ibn 'Arabi,* trans. R. Manheim, Princeton, 1969; and also Corbin, *Spiritual Body and Celestial Earth: from Mazdean Iran to Shi'ite Iran,* trans. H. Pearson, Princeton, 1977.

14 Quoted in *Sayings of Muhammad,* ed. and trans. Mirza Abu'l-Fadl, Allahahad, 1924, p.51.

15 *Ibid,* p.229.

16 On the symbolism of the "eye of the heart" see F. Schuon, *L'Oeil du coeur,* Paris, 1976.

Islam and the Pillars of its Faith

Dr Ebrahim M. A. El-Khouly

In the name of God, the Merciful, the Compassionate. By this expression Islam is visualized as a building borne on five pillars. The primary pillar is testification to the unity of God, which is the foundation and source of Islamic principles, values, provisions and systems that direct society and all affairs in life. Other pillars surround this basic centre point: prayer regulates the believer's relationship with his Lord; community wealth tax (*zakah*) regulates his relationship with his society; fasting trains him and strengthens his will; and the pilgrimage shows him in true submission to his Creator, being an enactment of the principles of unity, equality and peace.

All five pillars stand on the firm foundation of God's being the Lord of all creation, and men being His servants: in this lies the completeness of their humanity, while the deficiency of their humanity lies in their rebellion against the requirements of service to Him. He declares in the Qur'an: "I have created *jinn* and mankind only that they might serve Me." (li:56)

The First Pillar

The *Shahada* (Oneness of God and Prophethood of Muhammad) (peace be upon him). The Islamic belief in the pure oneness of God rectifies man's attitude towards his Creator (glory to Him!) when he admits to singularity in Godhead and His Lordship of all the universe, as declared in the Qur'an: "He it is Who in heaven is God, and on earth is God" (xliii:84); "Say: He is God, One, God, the Everlasting Refuge, Who has not begotten and has not been begotten. None is equal to Him." (cxii). It also rectifies man's attitude towards the universe in which he and other human beings amongst whom he lives exist.

His servanthood to God frees him from servitude to anything other than God. In his awareness that God is greater than everything, a believer does not and should not submit to any king or ruler, or be enslaved to a human need or controlled by a human passion. His awareness of the greatness of God protects him from falling from the high station to which his service to God has raised him, for his byword in life becomes, "My prayers and my sacrifice, my life and my death, are all for God, Lord of all Being. No partner has He. Thus I am commanded, being the first of those who surrender (to Him). Say: 'Should I seek any but Allah for my God, when He is the Lord of all things?'" (vi:162–4)

Conversely, a man who refuses servanthood to God loses the real immunity that protects him from falling into servitude to men. Thus he becomes enslaved by a system, a party, a ruler, an employer or a state – or even to himself in being controlled by whims, appetites or sexual passions. The Qur'an described such a man as "he who makes his desire his god" (xlv:23) and the Prophet (peace be on him) said of such a man, "May he become wretched, the worshipper of the dirham, the worshipper of a dinar and the worshipper of a rich garment." (related by Bukhari). On the other hand, a believer's worship of God ensures his strength, for "might belongs to God, to His Messengers, and to the believers." (lxiii:8)

Admitting the pure unity of God is the meaning of the first half of the *Shahada*: admitting the prophethood of Muhammad (peace be upon him) is the meaning of its second half: "I bear witness that Muhammad is the Messenger of Allah", which is naturally dependent upon the first. When one believes in the unity of God and is aware of His attributes one is consequently prepared to receive His teaching in order to lead one's life according to the requirements of divine decree. Thus "the Messenger" and "the *Sharia*" (Islamic law) become indispensible for protecting men from the blind alleys to which their whims would lead them.

Committing oneself sincerely to the One God entails committing oneself to adherence to His law, which can only be obtained through His Messenger. Consequently in obeying the Messenger (whose prophethood has been proved by the Qur'an) we obey God: "Muhammad is the Messenger of Allah." (xlviii:29); "And whatsoever the Messenger gives you, take it; and whatsoever he forbids, abstain from it." (lix: 7); "Whosoever obeys the Messenger thereby obeys God." (iv:80)

By his *Shahada*, then, a believer declares that belief in the unity of God has taken full possession of his soul and that he adheres to the *Sharia*, the system of laws laid down by God. He also testifies to the prophethood of Muhammad, the Seal of the Prophets whom God has sent with His final message of Islam. The *Shahada* is thus the creed of the believer, the basis of his attitude to life and philosophy, and the source of his commitment to God's system with all the religious observances, ethics, principles, and provisions it entails. It is the behaviour of the true Muslim that, in the end, embodies his adherence to this system, since it is the living manifestation of his belief in God and his abiding by the *Sharia*. Hence, in defining belief the Prophet (peace be on him) said, "It is that which is firmly established in the heart and is attested to by actions," and in answering someone who said to him, "Tell me something about Islam which I can ask of no-one but you," he said, "Say: 'I believe in Allah' and thereafter be upright."

The choice of the word *Shahada* (testification) to express belief in God and the prophethood of Muhammad means that the believer must declare his belief, just as a witness declares his testimony. Concealing a testimony in worldly matters is sinful: concealing the *Shahada* deprives a person of being regarded as a Muslim until he declares it.

The Second Pillar

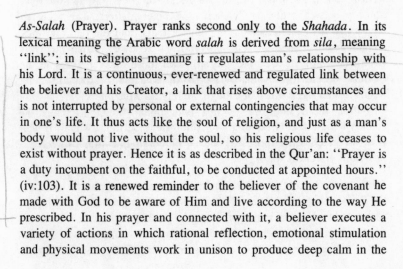

As-Salah (Prayer). Prayer ranks second only to the *Shahada*. In its lexical meaning the Arabic word *salah* is derived from *sila*, meaning "link"; in its religious meaning it regulates man's relationship with his Lord. It is a continuous, ever-renewed and regulated link between the believer and his Creator, a link that rises above circumstances and is not interrupted by personal or external contingencies that may occur in one's life. It thus acts like the soul of religion, and just as a man's body would not live without the soul, so his religious life ceases to exist without prayer. Hence it is as described in the Qur'an: "Prayer is a duty incumbent on the faithful, to be conducted at appointed hours." (iv:103). It is a renewed reminder to the believer of the covenant he made with God to be aware of Him and live according to the way He prescribed. In his prayer and connected with it, a believer executes a variety of actions in which rational reflection, emotional stimulation and physical movements work in unison to produce deep calm in the soul and limbs, and complete submission to their Creator, whose meanings are made clear in such expressions repeated by the worshipper as, "Greater is God", "Glory be to my Lord, the All-Mighty" (in the *ruku'* (kneeling)), "Glory be to my Lord, the Highest" (in *sujud* (prostration)) and "My face is bowed to Him Who created and shaped it and split open its sight and hearing, blessed be Allah, the best of Creators!" (a tradition of the Prophet related by Muslim and Abu Dawud, Al-Tirmidhi and al-Nasa'i). When a worshipper surrenders his face to God in this way we see the effects of this on him and on his relations with people and things around him, and in such effects we can perceive the functions of prayer:

(a) *a spiritual function*, shown in fulfilling the rights of servanthood to God, by endeavouring to draw nearer to Him and submitting to His Might and Glory and seeking His guidance: "So pray to your Lord and sacrifice" (cviii:2); "O, you who believe! Bow down and prostrate yourselves and worship your Lord and do good." (xxii:77); "Be guardians of your prayer, and the middle prayer and stand up with devotion to Allah" (ii:238); and "Guide us to the straight path." (i:6)

(b) *an educational function*, seen in the Quranic readings used in the prayer, remembrance of God, in His glorification and in devotional formulae: prayers are thus like daily lessons on the faith, on ethics, on what is lawful and unlawful, on the system of governing and the relationship between ruler and nations and other matters. The repeated recurrence of these lessons at appointed hours, and the fact that they contain fixed elements (in all prayers) and renewed varied elements (from the whole text of the Qur'an) – all these make prayers in the Islamic system an invaluable means of education, especially with regard to the basic unity of thought among all Muslims.

Within the framework of this educational function comes the weekly lesson of *Khutbat al-Jum'a* (the Friday Sermon) which, if well planned in content, form and means of communication can have a profound effect on society.

(c) *a psychological function*, since prayer is a great source of safety for the worshipper in times of fear, of strength in periods of weakness, of hope when he despairs of strength: it links him to the Supreme Power that reigns over the whole universe and enables him to rise above his present condition and circumstances, believing that God is with him with His help and guidance: "Seek help in steadfastness and prayer." (ii:153); "You alone we worship and to You alone we turn for help. Guide us to the straight path." (i:5–6); Prayer also offers protection from sicknesses of the soul and a cure for them: "Indeed Man was created impatient. When evil befalls him he is despondent; but blessed with good fortune he grows niggardly – save the worshippers who are steadfast in prayer." (lxx:19–23); Prayer is a regular training for the believer as he performs it with a calm and humble attitude before God.

(d) *a moral function*, since prayer reminds the believer of his convenant with God and makes him aware of the greatness of his Creator and by the Quranic recitation it contains, prayer strengthens within the believer his inner self-control and engenders in him awe and a sense of shame before his Lord which help protect him from falling into sin: "Recite what has been revealed to you of the Book, and perform the prayer; prayer forbids indecency and dishonour. God's remembrance is greater and God knows all that you do." (xxix:45)

(e) *a social function*, since the social spirit of Islam vibrates in prayer and spreads into the soul of the worshipper to make him an altruistic person who puts others before himself. He does not see himself as separate from society but as a brick in a building or an organ in a body that responds to the state of other organs. He begins his prayer by magnifying his Creator: "Greater is God", then as a part of the universe he praises "the Lord of all beings"; then he declares himself as part of the believing community: "You alone *we* (not I or me) worship and to You alone *we* ask for help. Guide *us* to the straight path"; then he goes further to declare himself part of all those who believed, believe or will believe in God and His Messengers: "Peace be on us and all the righteous worshippers of God." This enhances the believer's awareness of being related to the community. This is further strengthened by the congregational prayer and the meeting and affection held between worshippers who come together five times a day in the house of God and in response to His call.

The main principles of Islam which shape the rightly-guided life are contained in prayer and by living them daily in practice they become part of the fabric of his psychological life and of his behaviour in life from day to day. Thus equality in its complete manifestation appears in congregational prayer in Islam when all shoulders and feet are on a par; king and commoner, rich and poor, are all alike. It is true equality that brings a person whose social position has led him to vanity or snobbery back to what behoves a Muslim: to consider all men brothers of his, equal before their Creator in their human value, a value which is not affected by any social position. It also brings anyone whose social position causes a sense of humility and lowliness back to the sense of dignity of the believer, whatever his circumstances may be.

The congregational prayer is a continual training in leadership and obedience: the Imam is the leader and the congregation follow him, not preceding nor delaying in following him. But in following him they are responsible for the proper performance of their joint prayer. If he does anything that impairs the prayer they draw his attention to it and if anything occurs to him that prevents him from continuing his leadership he should retire and depute a suitable person to lead. If he persists in actions that spoil the prayer they should not feel bound to follow him, since his leadership has been nullified. It is a responsible, undictatorial leadership calling upon a responsible, enlightened and limited obedience.

Prayer, moreover, is a good training for Muslims to unite towards one common objective. Facing the direction of the Qibla in Mecca is a condition for sound performance of the prayer and is a symbolic direction for Muslims that they may have one common purpose and objective and that no consideration of time or place should stand in the way of their unity. In facing the Qibla wherever they may be Muslims overstep geographical, racial, linguistic or other barriers to be united to one God, one religion and faced towards one direction, the House of God, which He made a resort and sanctuary for men, in response to the Quranic directive: "Whichever way you start forth, turn your face towards the Holy Mosque, and wherever you are, turn your faces towards it." (ii:149)

(f) a bodily function, for prayer offers integrated training for the character of the Muslim which includes physical movements and positions that train the limbs in addition to the spiritual training of the person. Hence the Prophet's emphasis on the form in its details, up to the perfect levelling of the lines in congregation, which he considered part of the proper performance of prayer: "Pray in the way you have seen me pray" (related by al-Bukhari); "I have been commanded to prostrate on seven bones" (related by Muslim).

Timing the prayer and distributing the five prayers throughout the timetable of daily activity from dawn until evening means regulating periods of rest from work for the Muslim twice or three times – at noon, mid-afternoon and sunset – for physical relaxation and psychological recreation and for the Muslim to seek help and guidance from his Lord. Such periods thus offer the worshipper compulsory rest from toil, as no-one is entitled to prevent him from praying, and it is an obligation on society to organize its activities in a way to allow every individual times for prayer. The length of the periods in which each prayer may be offered allows sufficient flexibility in determining times for different individuals in a way that does not affect work and production planning under whatever system may be followed.

The Third Pillar

Zakah (Community Wealth Tax). The Muslim contribution to life is open, without limits: he gives of his effort, his mind, his knowledge, his status and his money. The Prophet (peace be on him) said, "Every Muslim must perform a charity." They asked, "Messenger of God, what if a person cannot find anything to give?" He answered, "He should work with his hands to benefit himself and give in charity." "And what if he could not find that?" they asked again. "He should assist an aggrieved person in need." "And what if he could not do that?" "Then he should do good and refrain from evil – that would be his charity." (related by al-Bukhari)

Zakah regulates the wealth contribution in its minimum, making it a religious obligation from which the individual cannot free himself or take concessions, since it is the right of society to be devoted to the benefit of the needy and disabled individuals and classes.

In its proper sense, *zakah* is a practical manifestation of the brother-hood between the faithful and establishes mutual solidarity between them by the firm bond it creates between rich and poor, in a way that strengthens the individual's sense of relation to the community and the community's awareness of the value of the individual, and that it is strengthened by his strength and weakened by his weakness.

An analysis of *zakah* in the Islamic system reveals its various functions in a Muslim society:

(*a*) *a religious function:* In this respect *zakah* is a manifestation of the faith that affirms that God is the sole owner of everything in the universe, and what men hold is a trust in their hand over which God made them trustees to discharge it as He has laid down: "Believe in Allah and His Messenger and spend of that over which He made you trustees" (lvii:7). It is also an expression of gratitude towards the Bestower Who said: "If you give thanks, I will give you more." (xiv:7) In this respect *zakah* is an act of devotion which, like prayer, brings the believer nearer to his Lord, and being one of the pillars of religion, avoidance of payment is a manifestation of *shirk* (serving other gods besides God): "Woe to the idolaters, who do not pay *zakah*." (xli:6–7)

(b) *an economic function:* Its economic function is revealed in many ways: firstly, *zakah* gives a strong incentive for investing wealth for the benefit of society and makes us refrain from hoarding it. When the amount reaches the taxable minimum (not exceeding £1000 now) and has been possessed for a whole year, *zakah* falls due on it whether it has been invested or not. Those who do not invest their wealth expose it to continuous reduction of at least 2.5% annually. Gradually it will be removed from their possession to be used for the benefit of society.

Apart from this, *zakah* is a means of compulsory redistribution of wealth in a way that reduces differences between classes and groups, thus preventing the many social disorders from which Communist and Western societies alike suffer, no less than contemporary Muslim societies that have neglected *zakah*. Moreover, *zakah* is a means of establishing justice indirectly. It rectifies whatever wrongs, injustices or means of exploitation in trading and industrial relations that have arisen. This may explain the fact that it is called a "right" rather than "charity", or an act of beneficence. *Zakah* also facilitates the proper direction of purchasing power in society. It transfers part of the power of consumption which may be used extravagantly to fulfil a proper function in the lives of those who need it.

(c) *a social function: Zakah* makes a fair contribution to social stability. By purging the soul of the rich of selfishness and the soul of the poor of envy and resentment against society, it stops up the channels leading to class hatred and makes it possible for the springs of brotherhood and solidarity to gush forth. Such stability is not merely based on the personal feelings of the rich: it stands on a firmly established right which, if the rich denied it, would be exacted by force if necessary.

Zakah is not used merely to meet the present needs of the poor and needy, but serves other functions that deeply affect social life. As the

Qur'an laid down, it solves the following problems:

(i) The problem of freedom, by assisting slaves seeking their freedom to attain it (slavery was an established system in the world at the time the Qur'an was revealed).

(ii) The problem of indebtedness which threatens an individual with bankruptcy, hardship, stress, humiliation or loss of good name, whether caused by the necessities of life or fluctuation in the market resulting in hardship to a good producer or an honest merchant. The Qur'an allots a portion of the *zakah* fund to solving such problems of indebtedness – a better solution than any contemporary system of insurance, as it is more positive and more in line with true co-operation and social solidarity.

(iii) The problem of defence and security of Muslim land against external threat and such matters as may be related to struggle in the cause of God.

(iv) The need of those who are away from their home seeking knowledge or a lawful livelihood and have not attained a settled life yet – the Qur'an devotes a portion of the *zakah* fund to meeting their need.

All this is contained in the Quranic verse that specifies the items upon which *zakah* should be expended, and recipients of the fund: "The alms are only for the poor and the needy, and those employed in collecting them, and those whose hearts are to be reconciled, and to free the slaves and the debtors, and for the cause of Allah, and (for) the wayfarer, a duty enjoined by Allah; Allah is All-Knowing, All-Wise." (ix:60)

In its lexical definition *zakah* means "purity" and "growth", in both of which we can perceive its religious connotations: it purges society of destructive afflictions and causes human and social virtues to grow, leading to sound social relations, peace and stability.

In this light we can understand the position taken by Abu Bakr, the first Khalifa (may God be pleased with him) in the face of the first attempt to suspend payment of *zakah* by those who refused to pay it. He used the Muslim army to uphold this social right and compelled the recalcitrant faction to pay the community wealth tax, asserting a principle in which he was following the Prophet (peace be on him), "I swear by God, if they refuse to pay to me even a small piece of robe which they used to pay to the Messenger of God, I would fight them for it." (related by al-Bukhari).

The Fourth Pillar

Siyam (Fasting during the month of Ramadan). In an Islamic society the individual carries great responsibility and many duties and obligations towards God and society are expected of him. It requires a strong, unwavering will and resolution to meet such responsibility and fulfil such duties and obligations. Since "there is no compulsion in religion" (ii:256); "Whosoever will, let him believe, and whosoever will, let him disbelieve" (xviii:29); and "To those amongst you that have the will to be upright" (lxxxi:28) – and since the intention of the individual is vital for the validity of his acts, as the Prophet said, "Actions are but by intention and every man shall have nothing but what he intended" (related by al-Bukhari and Muslim) – the will of the individual and training it to enable him to control himself and succeed in the endless choice he faces between right and wrong, good and evil, fair and ugly, and to carry out his religious obligations is of paramount importance in Islam. Fasting is the foremost means of educating the will of the individual. It provides the individual with the capacity that enables him to stand firm in the face of crises and challenges in his life, and to curb his soul's desires when faced with testing experiences and enhances his strength to carry out his obligations.

In this light we can perceive the following functions of fasting in Islam:

Firstly; the Islamic way of life which a Muslim (whether by upbringing or conversion) is required to follow demands that he free himself from beliefs, ideas and habits that contradict Islam. This requires a high degree of ability to free oneself from the hold of the familiar, of habits and of the inability to change. A strong, resolute will is needed for the attainment of such freedom, a will that enables the individual to make the right decision, unhindered by fear or desire. Thus the main function of fasting is to make the Muslim free from "within" as other aspects of the *Sharia* make him free from "without". By such freedom he responds to what is true and good and shuns what is false and evil. This is what we can perceive in the Quranic verse: "O you who believe, fasting is prescribed for you as it was prescribed for those before you, that you may guard yourselves against evil" (ii:183), and also in a holy utterance it is said of the fasting person: "He suspends eating, drinking and gratification of his sexual passion for My sake." (related by Al-Bukhari and Muslim).

Fasting, then, awakens the conscience of the individual and gives it scope for exercise in a joint experience for all society at the same time, according to the same system, thus adding further strength to each individual. A fasting person by his own choice deprives himself of what is necessary and lawful at other times. Fasting thus creates an inner control in the Muslim which raises him to the rank of *ihsan*, which the Prophet (peace be on him) defined as: "It is to worship God as though you are seeing Him, for if you do not see Him, nonetheless He sees you." (from a long tradition related by al-Bukhari)

Secondly; the human body is a living machine which gets exhausted by continuous work and fatigued by charging it to overcapacity. In operating this machine we do not always adhere to what suits it. Some of us can abide by this directive of the Prophet (peace be on him): "The worst type of container-filling a man can do is filling his own stomach. It is sufficient for a human being to have a few morsels to keep his back-bone upright, but if he has to fill it, then a third should be for his food, a third for his drink and a third for his breathing."

Human self-indulgence makes it possible only for a few to abide by this and not always! Does this over-worked human machine not deserve a rest during which the body can free itself from the consequences of excessive consumption? Fasting offers it a compulsory rest for the duration of one full month.

Thirdly; fasting, with the hunger, thirst and deprivation of other lawful enjoyment the individual experiences through it reminds him of those who are deprived throughout the year, or throughout life. Fasting wrenches him from his rich or comfortable life to make him experience what other, less fortunate, brothers in religion suffer. They have been tried by poverty and he has been tried by wealth, so let him show his gratitude to God and pay the dues of the brotherly bond that joins him to them. Thus the joint experience of fasting that takes place at the same time and according to the same system purifies the souls of those partaking of it, engenders tender emotion, deepens the sense of unity and brotherhood and renews the sense of solidarity between them.

The saying of the Prophet, "He that feeds a fasting person at the end of the fast will be given a reward similar to his without any decrease in the reward of that person" is an invitation to Muslims to share together during Ramadan the fortune God has bestowed on them. The effect of doing this with an understanding of its objectives will appear in all aspects of their life. The brotherly caring, the necessity of which they were made to feel by the fast, will make them understand better the saying of the Prophet (peace be on him), "He that spends the night with a full stomach while his neighbour is hungry and he knows it, is not one of us."

The Fifth Pillar

Al-Hajj (Pilgrimage to the House of God in Mecca). Belief in the Oneness of God is the most fundamental principle of Islam; Prayer regulates the believer's relationship with God; *Zakah* controls his relations with society; fasting exercises and strengthens his will: the *Hajj* offers Muslims, as one nation, the opportunity to exercise the high principles, values and objectives upon which Islam bases the shaping of the individual and the nation. It is the climax of the individual's spiritual life and an embodiment of the unity of the nation which is based on a brotherhood in the faith that towers above narrow considerations or race, nationality, colour or tongue. In this light we can see the following functions of the *hajj* which complement the functions of the other pillars of Islam:

(*a*) *a psychological and spiritual function:* the hajj is an exercise of the will of the believer at its height, where he rises above day-to-day preoccupations and casts off what men ordinarily cherish. Thus we can understand the deep symbolic meaning of the clothes he wears during *ihram* (the state of consecration). They symbolize his inner state which makes him leave behind his family, home, wealth, position and everything dear to him. With his free choice he leaves the good things that were lawful to him and enters a spiritual *haram* (sanctuary) which he sets up within himself before he enters with his body into the *haram* in Mecca. The stations at which pilgrims must stop to enter the state of *ihram* serve to remind them of the inner renunciation of worldly preoccupations so that their pilgrimage may produce its desired effect.

(*b*) *a moral, behavioural function:* the stations of the *hajj* are entrances through which pilgrims pass coming from every distant quarter, repairing to the sacred House, whither the message of Truth was imparted to Muhammad (peace be on him). In this blessed land the Muslims meet to live a spiritual life on a special level, enacting a rite that exposes the exalted value of Islam and where equality, brotherhood and unity among the faithful is embodied, where response to the call of God comes before that to any other call: "And proclaim among men the pilgrimage: they shall come to you on foot and upon every lean beast; they shall come from every deep ravine." (xxii:27) The *hajj* is an unique gathering that gives the pilgrims an experience unavailable to them at home in their usual life. In *hajj* there is an exercise of strict self-discipline and control where sacred things are revered and the life of even plants and birds is made inviolable and everything lives in safety: "And he that venerates the sacred things of God, it shall be better for him with his Lord" (xxii:30); "And he that venerates the waymarks of God, it surely is from devotion of the heart" (xxii:32); "And when We made the House (at Mecca) a resort for men and a sanctuary." (ii:125)

The *hajj* is a rigorous training in self-control: "The pilgrimage is in the well-known months. He that undertakes the duty of the pilgrimage during them must abstain from coition, ungodliness and acrimonious dispute, and whatever good you do, Allah is aware of it. Take provision (from it) for yourselves, for the best provision is piety." (ii:197) "Take provision" indicates that the effects of this experience should extend to the conduct of the Muslim in his normal life afterwards, and that he should live and conduct himself by the values that manifest piety, "the best provision".

(*c*) *a social function:* this has many aspects and dimensions in the life of Muslims as a nation. The Qur'an points to this function in the *hajj* verse cited above: "And proclaim among men the pilgrimage: they shall come from every deep ravine; they shall come to witness things of benefit to them and mention the Name of Allah." "To witness things of benefit to them" is a general expression that covers benefits to individuals and groups in the religious and worldly spheres. The fact that it is placed in the verse before mentioning God's Name (which is the foremost objective in the devotional act of *hajj*) is intended (I think, but God knows best) to dispel any thought that acquiring benefit from trade, for instance, necessarily contradicts the spirit of the *hajj*. What we deduce from this verse was explicitly stated elsewhere in the Qur'an: "It is no sin for you to seek the bounty of your Lord." (ii:198). The expression, "seeking His bounty" covers, in other usages, benefits from trading, as in "and others travel in the land in search of the bounty of Allah." (lxxiv:30). The only condition is that such worldly benefits remain a secondary objective and not a diversion of the spiritual meaning of the *hajj*. The desired balance is maintained in the verse by using the concessionary expression, "It is no sin for you . . ."

In all events, the "benefits" the pilgrims could derive from the experience of the *hajj*, for themselves, their countries, and the Muslim nation as a whole could, with good planning and guarantees for effectiveness and continuity, bring about enormous changes in the life of Muslims of which they are in dire need. The benefits are numerous, perennial and capable of increase from age to age and of taking various forms to suit different individuals, groups or countries. We understand this in the Arabic expression from the use of the indefinite plural in the word, "benefits". Within the limited scope of this paper I will give one example of the benefits Muslims could derive from the *hajj*, properly understood.

The *hajj* gives an opportunity to all Muslims from all groups, classes, organizations systems and governments from all over the Muslim world to meet annually in a great congress. The time and venue of this congress has been set by their One God. Invitation to attend is open to every Muslim. No-one has the power to bar anyone. Any such attempt would amount to the crime of debarring Muslims from the House of God which He has made "a resort for men and a sanctuary". Every Muslim who attends is guaranteed full safety and freedom as long as he himself does not violate its safety: "Whoever enters it is safe." (ii:97). Such a congress is a miniature of the Muslim nation and offers an unique opportunity for discussion of all Muslims' problems and issues whether related to the system of government, economics, culture, education, military and defence matters, industry, trade or commerce and the condition of Muslims in every part of the Muslim world. Such discussion could take place on the level of the layman, or at specialist level, in the *hajj* atmosphere of detachment, inspired by the sense of unity instead of self-seeking individualism, and enriched by a multiplicity of ideas and experience. It could also take place on the level of Muslim decision-makers and rulers whom the *hajj* calls from the towers of authority to mingle together and with ordinary Muslims in complete equality before their One Lord. What a tremendous assembly that should be, and what great "benefits" the Muslim could derive from it!

We do not, in fact, go too far when we ask for the unity of the Muslims to be the first issue to which all efforts should be directed during the *hajj* season: the efforts of rulers, politicians, economists, thinkers, jurists and all efforts of the media. Let the unity of the Muslim *ummah* and work for it be "the provisions" Muslims take from the *hajj* when they make for the House of God from every corner in their lands, and let this unity be their starting and finishing point when they seek the "benefits" to which God has invited them on the *hajj*. If this happens (and we pray to God to open the Muslims' hearts, eyes and ears to it) it would restore to the *hajj* its foremost function, and realize the message of this devotional act which, alas, appears nowadays to be devoid of it: yet "God prevails in His purpose, but most men do not know it." (xii:21)

Islam: its Political and Legal Principles

A proglomena to the Theory and Practice of Politics and Law

Allahbukhsh K. Brohi

"Man in relation with his Creator is sublime, and his action is creative: on the contrary, as soon as he separates himself from God, and acts alone, he does not cease to be powerful, for this is a privilege of his nature; but his action is negative, and tends only to destroy."

"Withdrawn, by his vain sciences, from the single science which truly concerns him, man has believed himself endowed with power to create. He has believed, he who has not the power of producing a single insect or a sprig of moss, that he was the immediate author of Sovereignty, the most important, the most sacred, the most fundamental thing in the moral and political world; and that such a family for example, reigns, because such a people wills it: while there are numerous and incontestable proofs that every sovereign family reigns because it is chosen by a superior power. He has believed that it was himself who invented languages; while, again, it belongs to him only to see that every human language is learned and never invented. He has believed that he could constitute nations; that is to say, in other terms, that he could create that national unity by virtue of which one nation is not another. Finally, he has believed that, since he had the power of creating institutions, he had, with greater reason, that of borrowing them from other nations, and transferring them to his own country, all complete to his hand, with the names which they bore among the people, from whom they were taken, in order, like those people to enjoy them with the same advantages.

"If the formation of all empires, the progress of civilization, and the unanimous agreement of all history and tradition do not suffice still to convince us, the death of empires will complete the demonstration commenced by their birth. As it is the religious principle which has created everything, so it is the absence of this same principle which has destroyed everything."
(Joseph de Maistre)

An attempt will be made in the pages that follow to present the essentials of theory and practice of politics in Islam with a view to enabling the reader to appreciate the peculiarities of the lines of thought along which Muslims have solved the problems of politics and the extent to which they, in principle, seem to have contributed significantly to the development of those socio-economic institutions which we associate with and are sanctioned by their religion.

1 Paradoxes of secular constitutions

Politics may be broadly defined, for the purpose of this essay, as the art and science of organizing a political society. The nature, purpose and processes of a political society are themselves the concern of the science and art of politics, but stated concisely, a society that claims to be politically organized, when viewed from the juridical point of view, becomes a *state* and the machinery that is set up to administer its affairs becomes the *government* of that state. In order that a state should come into being, there should be a basic law (otherwise known as the constitution) which must sanction its creation and also set *limits* upon the exercise of powers by those who are to be in charge of its political affairs. In this context, it should be noted that three principal questions become important: (1) What is the *nature* of the political process by which the authority to administer the state is constituted? (2) What is the *extent* to which that authority is accountable and, if so, to whom, for the way in which it evolves and projects its policies and operates the machinery of administration? (3) What is the methodology and technique by resort to which the validity of the constitutional authority of those who are in actual charge of the affairs of the state is to be tested, so that, should inadmissible deviations take place, they can be made to give up power in order to enable others to take their place? All these questions are answered having regard to the law and customs of the constitution of a country.

Here, as any one can see, there is a paradox involved, which must be faced. As is well known, ordinary or constitutional law can only be sanctioned by the sovereign authority that is reposed in the state, and unless the state exists, there can be no law, ordinary or fundamental! And if as has been said above, the state itself is the creation of law, the question which remains to be resolved, would be: How can a state be established by law if there be no state which to begin with could be said to have sanctioned the making of such a law?

Sovereignty considered both as a term of political science and jurisprudence is somewhat of a vague kind and the meaning which in fact is assigned to it has a great deal to do with the context in which the concept is invoked. The politician and the jurist both utilize the concept of sovereignty, but each seems to accord to that term varying shades of meaning, so much so, that it is widely held by political theorists and jurists alike that no term is so extravagantly ill-defined as sovereignty. From Austin down the ages indeed right up to the jurists of our own time, (for instance, Hans Kelsen,) we have been regaled with ponderous discourses on sovereignty, but it must be said, in all sad sincerity, that in all the literature that has been made available to us the subject of sovereignty does not make a student any wiser. Indeed, he, at the end of his labours, is likely to feel more confused than enlightened.

A people must be sovereign to be able to establish a state, and the current opinion on the subject is that sovereignty is essentially a legal concept and that it has a reference to the *rules* which identify the sovereign and prescribe its composition and functions. And furthermore, it is to be insisted that these rules are logically prior to it. Then there is a distinction drawn between rules which govern, on the one hand, the composition and the procedure and define, on the other hand, the area and extent of power of a sovereign law-making authority. It is said Courts of law have the jurisdiction to question the acts of the legislature in case the acts passed by it are in disregard of the composition of the sovereign authority and the procedure required for the passage of the bills into laws, but not until the constitution expressly affirms it, have they the competence to question the extent of power exercised by the legislature. (See R. F. V. Heuston's Essay on "Sovereignty" in Oxford Essays in Jurisprudence, Oxford University Press, 1961.)

The paradox that arises while considering the relative priority of the legal and political meanings of the term "sovereign" has reference to the way in which the meanings of the word "sovereign", when qualified by the words "legal" and "political", are understood. If constitutional law is to be regarded as a body of those legal principles which determine the constitution of the state – that is to say, the rules that determine the essential and fundamental portions of the state's organization, its structure and the relationships between the principal organs of its sovereign powers – then, it must follow, that the constitution of a state can never be determined by law; for, as has been pointed out earlier, to establish a state, the law establishing it must have been sanctioned by the state itself. In other words, there can be no law unless there is already a state whose law it is. And what is more, there can be no state without a constitution. A leading authority on jurisprudence in the western world resolves the problem thus:

"The state and its constitution are therefore necessarily prior to the law. How then does law determine the Constitution? Is not the constitution the pure matter of fact with which law has no concern? The answer is that the constitution is both a matter of fact and a matter of law. The constitution as it exists *de facto* underlies, of necessity, the constitution as it exists *de jure*. The constitutional law involves concurrent constitutional practice. It is merely the reflection, within the courts of law, of the external objective reality of the *de facto* organization of the state. It is the theory of the constitution as received by the courts of justice. It is the Constitution, not as it is in itself but as it appears when looked at through the eye of law. The constitution as a matter of fact is *logically prior* to the constitution as a matter of law. In other words, constitutional *practice* is logically prior to the constitutional *law*. Here there may be a state and a constitution without any law, but there can be no law, as I have stated, without a constitution. No constitution therefore can have its source and basis in the law." (See Sir John Salmond's *Jurisprudence*.)

Thus the priority of *de facto* existence of the state is a condition precedent to there being any law at all.

In *secular society*, where somehow law emerges from the continuity of a pre-existing historical process as a kind of customary response which a given people makes to the problem of organizing affairs of their society politically, this paradox undoubtedly arises. All the revolutionary constitutions, on the other hand, such as that of France of the 18th century or that of the Soviet Union that has more recently been established in the second decade of the 20th century, can be said to be constitutions that come into being as a result of the operation of the principle of *volenti generale* at a certain point of time. That is because revolution by its very definition means a sort of rude interruption which breaks up historical continuity of the life of a nation. As is well known, these revolutionary constitutions are set up by revolutionaries themselves – that is to say, men who have brought revolution into being. This is generally done by setting up the constituent assemblies which are invested with the *constituent power* to draw up a charter providing for the creation of the new state as also the limitations on the power of its principal organs among which the sovereign power of the people is to be distributed.

Thus, revolution necessarily means the disruption of the old legal order and the creation of a new one. A constituent assembly is set up to redefine the very concept of state to be established and to redistribute its sovereign power into its various principal organs. A constitution drawn up by such a constituent assembly has first to be acknowledged by the courts that will be set up under it before they will undertake to construe the provisions of the constitution that it enacts and also the laws that are passed by the legislature set up by it.

But the important question to consider is: how can a constitution drawn up by a few people be binding for all time to come upon posterity? This is a question that raises yet another paradox.

But this paradox can have no relevance where the sovereign lawgiver is not merely eminent in the historial community that is to organize itself politically, but is to be traced to the operation of a transcendent principle or in the language of religion, *Will of God*. In Islam the real sovereign is and can only be God. He alone is the Ruler and the real Legislator. His Will alone sanctions the law. And there can be no Islamic state unless it is regarded as the manifestation of the Divine Will on earth and is acknowledged as such by the community. Such a state, no doubt, manifests itself through institutions which are manned by the believers in their capacity as recipients of a delegated authority from God, an authority which they exercise subject to the limitations imposed upon them in the *Holy Writ* (Al-Qur'an) and as enjoined by that *writ* by the *practice* of the Prophet. The *secular* constitution as well as *theocratic* dispensation which sanctions the constitutions of religious societies ultimately converge upon one and the same focal point – which is to enable the people to organize themselves politically.

The aim of the exercise of politics is to enable the people to organize themselves for the purpose of administering their affairs, for securing the good of the individual citizen and also the welfare of the people composing a given community or any other purpose which appeals to those who mean to live together and work together for the satisfaction of their common needs. But precisely what it is that constitutes the real good for man, the good life which the state ought to promote, is a question to which the secular and religious modes of returning answers are different. Secular societies are based on the *philosophic* conception of the nature of man and his destiny; religious societies, such as the one which is inspired by Islam, are based on the view of the nature of man as has been unfolded by the *revealed law* – a law that is brought by a Prophet who is inspired to deliver it to a people.

Philosophers like Aristotle have said that the state exists to promote a good life and that it must use its coercive power to enable its citizens to reach a high water-mark of human excellence. But what human excellence consists in is an issue upon which no two philosophers seem to agree. Hegel said that the state is the Divine idea as it exists on earth and he argued that precisely to the extent to which a citizen participates in its activities he derives his worth, his status and his station in life. (See his *Philosophy of History* Eng. tr. p.41.) Per contra "state", said Marx, avowedly a disciple of Hegel, is nothing more than the apparatus of coercion improvised by the *bourgeoisie* to deny to the workers what is due to them in the productive process in a given society. The state is, in short, an engine of oppression, tyranny and exploitation of the working classes by the owners of the means of production and the controllers of the distribution of wealth. Marx was, right up to his dying day, proud of the fact that he was a disciple of Hegel, but having regard to his actual teaching, it would appear, no disciple has been so far away from the teachings of his master as is Marx from Hegel. After all, from the state being regarded in the Hegelian image as an incarnation of the divine idea to the state being considered as an apparatus of coercion, which is what Marx taught, there is a long way to traverse. Hegel saw in the flowering of the state the *fulfilment* of the destiny of man; Marx saw the *summum bonum* of man in its withering away.

The postulates of political theory that underlie the foundation of state in a secular society, thus, upon examination, turn out to be the expression of value judgements which are born of the experience of the individual philosopher who makes them. So it is said by Professor H. Laski:

"Hobbes's immense edifice is built, in the last analysis, upon the dual foundation of a belief that human nature is evil and that only an irresistible sovereign can maintain order against its inherent tendency to evil. Locke starts with a belief in the goodness of human nature and the danger of any government which could act without regard to the wishes of its subjects. Rousseau sought a formula of state which in its operation would secure an equal basis for all citizens in the result of the social process. From Plato onwards, the more we know of a thinker's personal history, the more fully can we explain the causes which led to the assumptions upon which he bases his work; and those assumptions are always the result of the view he takes of what a society should be like. (See his *The State in Theory and Practice*, pages 43–44.)

The escape from this relativism of which Laski rightly complains is possible only if we can erect the edifice of political theory upon some transcendental norm, a norm which is capable of being regarded as *independent* of human speculation and which is in a significant sense autonomous in its own right as having come from some source higher than mere conceptual thought and therefore one which compels recognition from all those who claim to apply its deliverance to the task of organizing a political society. Mere philosophers' findings upon the way in which a society is to be organized politically will simply not do – considering that these vary from one philosopher to another – if the *whole* of mankind is to be brought within the ambit of an enduring political process by which its affairs are to be regulated.

If by a state is to be understood a political society which is to function by reason of possessing supreme coercive authority, whether it be in respect of any individual or any group of individuals which is a part of a society, this coercive authority, the existence of which is a *sine qua non* of a state, is identifiable by its ability to coerce and enforce its will upon the subjects of the state, regardless of whether or not the will thus enforced is based on some moral basis, wisdom or justice. The. only source of obligation which may justify obedience to such a will is the conventional one of saying that we have to have an ordered society and that, unless we have a sovereign who is capable of absolute and unconditional authority to enforce his mandates, there would be no security and no social progress in the realm.

Today the world is divided into about 139 nation-states, each claiming to be sovereign. This is what is meant by the expression "sovereign equality of all nations, large and small" in the Charter of United Nations. The expression implies that no one of them will acknowledge any authority higher than its own, and yet it is expected that somehow out of the competing and conflicting wills of these sovereign nation-states humanity would be capable of organizing peace and security on earth and also establish conditions in terms of which the prospect of its continued progress and prosperity can be contemplated.

These are some of the paradoxes that vitiate all attempts to evolve and apply political constitutions which have no reference to any transcendent principle – a principle which goes beyond the reach of mere speculative thought. The position was summed up by Joseph de Maistre who, in his famous essay, *The Generative Principle of Political Constitutions*, summed up the position thus:

"The more we examine the influence of human agency in the formation of political constitutions, the greater will be our conviction that it enters there only in a manner infinitely subordinate, or as a simple instrument; and I do not believe there remains the least doubt of the incontestable truth of the following propositions, (1) that the fundamental principles of political constitution exist before all written law (2) that a constitutional law is, and can only be, the development or sanction of an unwritten pre-existing right (3) that which is most essential, most intrinsically constitutional, and truly fundamental, is never written, and could not be, without endangering the State (4) that the weakness and fragility of a constitution are actually in direct proportion to the multiplicity of written constitutional articles.''

Any one who is familiar with the modern constitutions and the way they are interpreted by courts of law knows precisely how very real are the difficulties which beset the way of those who are called upon to work, to apply and to interpret these constitutional provisions. The principles that are generally invoked, such as the *due process, natural rights, law of nature, inherent and inalienable rights of human beings*, are so ill-defined that they mean many things to many people. It is said, for instance, that sovereignty belongs to the people, and the government, being the creation of a sovereign will, has to have limits imposed upon it and limits are to be spelled out from the written word as it is seen in the light of principles such as are embodied in *due process of law* clause contained in the Constitution of the U.S.A. The too frequent invocation of those principles is a pointer to the various inadequacies that vitiate man-made models upon which constitutional governments are patterned and fashioned. The paradox of the relative priority of the state and the law, the difficulties inherent in the concept of the sovereignty of the people (viz. if the people are the sovereign, as must be the case in a democratic constitution of a secular society, then the question is, who are the subjects?), the relativity involved in the formation of the goals and purposes (which must vary from time to time having regard to the changing conditions of society) which are to be realized within the framework of secular constitutions – all these exhibit the utter futility of relying on mere words written on a parchment drawn up by people who claim to lay down, even for ages unborn, the fundamental law, when, as creatures of time, they themselves cannot see, as the metaphor has it, beyond their noses. Such merit as may be discovered in a secular constitution would, upon careful examination, appear to be traceable to the inspiration its authors have derived from those *eternal verities*, the knowledge of which is brought to mankind by the Prophets of universal religions.

2 The general character of the Constitution of religious societies

It is now time to turn to the next section of our essay and to deal concisely with the grammar of religious constitutions or, what comes to the same thing, the constitutions inspired by religion. It is the contention of the present writer that the religious constitutions are, speaking comparatively at any rate, free from the difficulties touching and concerning secular constitutions which have been pointed out above. In religious constitutions such as those that are inspired by Islamic faith the sovereign is the Transcendental Presence who is a source of all law. He is the creator and ruler of the universe and also of man. He is the abiding presence; He is the first, He is the last; He is the hidden operative principle lying behind all that one sees in nature, history and in oneself; He is also the outer warp and woof, the garment of nature, whether it is to be conceived of as nature in the conventional sense or regarded as the form in which man has been cast and the law by which he has been brought into being and guided. God, in the conception of revealed religion, has created man as His vicegerent on earth and man is bound by that primeval contract referred to in the Holy Book ''Am I not your Lord? the Lord enquired from the souls of men before man was created and they said indeed 'Thou art'.'' (*Sura 7, verse 172*) Out of that primeval contract in which the soul of man has acknowledged his Lord and Master, who is also the Creator and Ruler of the Universe, flow his obligations to obey God and to submit to His Will, which takes on the form of law for him. The earthly state exists to enable mankind, which has been created, *ka nafsin wahidatin*, that is to say as one *indivisible self*, to do its appointed task here below. The state is thus an instrument improvised by man to respond to the basic human need of organizing mankind to the end that they co-ordinate their activities with a view to establishing order on earth. It also establishes conditions for securing the realization of the goals for which mankind has been created. Indeed man is, according to the Qur'an, called upon to obey God, His Prophet and *Olil amr minkum*, – those who are the constituted authorities charged with the administration of his affairs. This expression necessarily excludes usurpers, who, by nefarious means, turn up as base pretenders to the noble calling of managing the affairs of mankind. And further, that when they, that is, the believers, proceed to decide matters between themselves, they have to do so by mutual consultation in the light of what is revealed in the

Qur'an and what is enjoined by the *sunnah* (practice) of the Prophet.

It is essential to point out in this context that the Muslim society which is to be organized politically has, to begin with, to subscribe to belief in the unseen, even as in the divine origin of the Creation. It views the life of man within the framework of a supra-individual and supra-physical dispensation. Believers acknowledge the Divine Presence or the creative principle which is eminent in the Creation but which is all the same independent of it. The *rights* and *duties* of the believers will therefore be determined by the extent to which this divine principle is allowed, by the free choice of man to operate in his individual and collective life. The Qur'an says, *"You would not see change in God's law (Wa Lan Tajida Lesunnatallah Tabdila)."* Further, human nature itself is fashioned on the divine pattern (*Fit-ratallah alti Fitrannasi alaha, La tabdila lekhaliqillah zalika deenul qayyim*). Islam treats nature itself as God's Revelation (*Ayat*). Human nature is made in the Divine mould and it is guided by the divine word (*Sura 30, verse 30*). Man is called upon to assimilate or absorb divine attributes in himself. The attributes of God are to be regarded as transcendental and eternal values (*"Takhalaku bi Ikhlaquillah,"* said the Prophet). Man, as an individual, taken by himself, is not complete; he draws his nourishment from diverse sources including a larger synthesis of mankind. The creation of mankind is likened to the creation of one indivisible self – and each individual is to be conceived as an integral part of that larger single self. The status and dignity of man does not depend upon the quality of blood that circulates in his veins, nor upon the language he speaks, much less does it depend upon the geographical territory he is tenanting or comes from. Indeed, he is the best and nearest to God who is more self-controlled, that is to say, more of a *muttaqi*. Man is called upon to enjoin justice because justice is the fundamental foundation upon which the operation of the whole creation of man and nature has been grounded by the divine dispensation. Economic disparities which contribute to the formation of classes and generate conflicts between masters and slaves, haves and have-nots, between the owners of the instruments of production and the workers in society are, to begin with, all artificial, and justice demands that there should be equal opportunities for all the sons and daughters of the human race. They all have, within the framework of a political society, to make a living and to secure the development of their moral, mental and intellectual faculties. There is only one Master and Lord of the Universe and there is no such thing as the ruler and the ruled in the Muslim society. Indeed, in Islam he who is in charge of the affairs of a political society is to be viewed only as the managing director of public affairs rather than as a ruler. He derives his very right (or rather duty) to manage these affairs after consultation with, and therefore as a consequence of, the consent of the people. He is accountable to them for seeing to it that he obeys God's Law, and *sunnah* of the Prophet. He conducts their affairs with a view to advancing the cause of the spiritual unity of mankind – and thus fulfils the purpose for which mankind itself has been created. The purpose of man's life which has been fashioned on the divine pattern, is none other than the securing of his awareness of his true nature – which is suffused with the divine breath as is suggested by such expressions appearing in the Holy Qur'an as "God has instilled His spirit unto Adam" and He has created human beings in the best of forms. Man is to *freely* realize the best of which he is capable. He can only worship God in *freedom* – all obstructions that lie in his way and deny him that freedom (*Yassadun anas Sabilillah*) are to be removed. Man is called upon to choose the path of righteousness, and he must choose freely. Since the Qur'an considers man's life on earth to be a prelude to a life to come in the Hereafter (*Akhrat*) which is better and eternal, righteousness is enjoined as a discipline since it prepares man for the high reward which is reserved for him. All the duties that religion enjoins upon man have reference to this and to prepare man to transcend the grip which animal Nature, with which he is endowed, has over him. Man must strive hard to grasp the Divine helping Hand to be able to reach the angelic state. He must consciously choose to obey the call of duty and act righteously. This gift of freedom is of course not absolute. To begin with, it is hemmed in primarily by the limitation imposed upon man by the Law Divine and those suggested by the *sunnah* or practice of the Prophet and, secondarily, by the demands which his fellow-men make upon him – for unless those demands are met, there can be no such thing as the realization of the Muslim ideal.

Every Islamic state is a reflection in political parlance of the way in which the Muslim ideal has to be realized on Earth. Lest what has been said so far may sound somewhat dogmatic for those who are nurtured in the secularistic way of thinking, a mode of thinking which has somehow become fashionable in these Godless times in which we live, it becomes necessary to cite certain well-known observations from western writers in support of the view advanced in this essay.

(a) It is necessary once again to refer to Joseph de Maistre's argument, viz., *that man is the instrument of God and unless God plays on that instrument and man submits to God's Will, he cannot fulfil himself*. Maistre says:

"We are deceived on this point by a sophism so natural, that it entirely escapes our attention. Because man acts, he thinks he acts alone; and because he has the consciousness of his liberty he forgets his dependence. In the physical order, he listens to reason, for although he can, for example, plant an acorn, water it, etc., he is convinced that he does not make the oaks, because he witnesses their growth and perfection without the aid of human power; and moreover, that he does not make the acorn; but in the social order, where he is present, and acts, he fully believes that he is really the sole author of all that is done by himself. This is, in a sense, as if the trowel should believe itself the architect. Man is a free, intelligent, and noble being; without doubt; but he is not less an instrument of God, according to a happy expression of Plutarch, in a beautiful passage which here introduces itself of its own accord; 'We must not wonder,' he says, 'if the most beautiful and greatest things in the world are done by the will and providence of God, seeing that in all the greatest and practical parts of the world there is a soul: for the organ and tool of the soul is the body, and the soul is the Instrument of God. And as the body has of itself many movements, and as the greater and more noble are derived from the soul, even so it is with the soul; some of its operations being self-moved, while in others it is directed, disciplined, and guided, by God, as it pleases Him; being itself the most beautiful organ and ingenious instrument possible; for it would be a strange thing indeed that the wind, the water, the clouds, and the rains, should be instruments of God, with which He nourishes and supports many creatures, and also destroys many others, and that He should never make use of living beings to perform any of His works. For it is far more reasonable that they, depending entirely on the power of God, than that the bow should obey the Scythians, the lyre and flute, the Greeks.' (Quoted from Plutarch's *Banquet of Seven Sages*.)

"No one can write better; I do not believe that these beautiful reflections could be more justly applied than to the formation of political constitutions, where it may be said with equal truth that man does everything and does nothing."

(b) The practical value of managing political society in the light of revealed word of God in contra-distinction to that which can be ascribed to some pseudo-philosophical speculation having no other foundation than the mere cerebral activities of the thinkers of the world, has also been adverted to by no less a writer than De Tocqueville who in his famous book *Democracy in America* says:

"There is hardly any human action, however particular it may be, that does not originate in some very general idea men have conceived of the Diety, of his relation to mankind, of the nature of their own souls, and of their duties to their fellow creatures. Nor can anything prevent these ideas from being the common spring from which all the rest emanates.

"Men are therefore immeasurably interested in acquiring fixed ideas of God, of the soul, and of their general duties to their Creator and their fellow men; for doubt on these first principles would abandon all their actions to chance and would condemn them in some way to disorder and impotence.

"This, then, is the subject on which it is most important for each of us to have fixed ideas; and unhappily it is also the subject in which it is most difficult for each of us, left to himself, to settle his opinions by the sole force of his reason. None but minds singularly free from the ordinary cares of life, minds at once penetrating, subtle and trained by thinking, can, even with much time and care, sound the depths of these truths that are so necessary. And, indeed, we see that philosophers are themselves almost always surrounded by uncertainties; that at every step the natural light which illuminates their path grows dimmer and less secure; and that, in spite of all their efforts, they have discovered as yet only a few conflicting notions, on which the mind of man has been tossed about for thousands of years without ever firmly grasping truth or finding novelty even in its errors. Studies of this nature are far above the average capacity of men; and, even if the majority of mankind were capable of such pursuits, it is evident that leisure to cultivate them would still be wanting."

Having thus explained the need for having those fixed ideas about God and human nature, without which mankind would find it difficult to do their day's work here below, De Tocqueville proceeds to advance the thesis that this need is adequately satisfied by religion. In his words:

"The first object and one of the principal advantages of religion is to furnish to each of these fundamental questions a solution that is at once clear, precise, intelligible, and lasting, to the mass of mankind. There are religions that are false and very absurd, but it may be affirmed that by religion which remains within the circle that I have just traced without pretending to go beyond it (as many religions have attempted to do for the purpose of restraining on every side the free movement of the human mind), imposes a salutary restraint upon the intellect; and it must be admitted that, if it does not save men in another world, it is at least very conducive to their happiness and greatness in this.

"This is especially true of men living in free countries. When the religion of a people is destroyed doubt gets hold of the higher power of intellect and half paralyzes all the others. Every man accustoms himself to having only confused and changing notions on the subjects of most interest to his fellow creatures and himself. His opinions are ill-defended and easily abandoned; and, in despair of ever solving by himself the hard problems respecting the destiny of man, he ignobly submits to think no more about them. Such a condition cannot but enervate the soul, relax the springs of the Will, and prepare a people for servitude.''

(c) The foundation of modern democratic form of governance as analysed by L.T. Hobhouse in his famous book *Elements of Social Justice* would seem also to point unmistakably towards the paramount importance of organizing society politically by appeal to *spiritual principle*. His argument takes, broadly speaking, the following form:

For any workable democracy, he says, we may agree that there must be some sense of community. Without it democracy simply will not live. It will break up into anarchy, faction, lynch law, terrorism, or some kind of tyranny – whether the tyrants be many or few. Let us then postulate a certain sense of community, but recognize that along with it there may be permanently or temporarily a feeling of what we may call "discommunity". Something like this we may consider to be the normal situation, even in a reasonably well-ordered State, and we have therefore to consider normal means of dealing with it. Let us first remark that the traditional theory of the sovereign state, particularly of the sovereign people, ignores the problem. For this theory, when the people has spoken that is law. What is worse, it is not only the law, but also the Prophet's. It has not only *legal* sanction, but *moral* authority. Every one on this principle is entitled to his voice and his vote; but when these are cast and and the majority ascertained, the rights of the individual and the section sur-cease. *One will must prevail*.

Having said that, L. T. Hobhouse goes on to refer to the historical causes which have brought about the inter-mixture of the rule of law with moral authority. He says:

"Historically the theory of the sovereign State arose from the authoritarian conception of kingship, when the cosmic spiritual authority was removed. In the Middle Ages, government was barely distinguished from territorial owner-ship; but, conversely, territorial ownership was based on allegiance and func-tion and behind and over all was a spiritual power, which was the ultimate judge of political right. With the rise of nations and the religious schism the king stood out as the tangible flesh and blood head of the State. There was none above him but God, and God was further off than Rome. In Protestant countries he was the spiritual as well as the temporal Lord. From him the law hung as a chain from its support, and he himself was above it. True, there were limits, the old Estates or the budding Parliament; but these could either be regarded as his advisers, or incorporated with him as a definite body of persons who together constituted the recognizable sovereign. The essential was the conception of law and government, flowing from a superior, and that an ultimate superior possessing moral authority backed by physical force. Democratic theory, in one form, took over this conception with a single modification. The sovereign became servant: the people master. The whole was sovereign over the parts. The people knows no master, and is its own authority. This doctrine was always combated by an opposite theory to be found in different forms from Paine and the American constitutionalists to Mill, according to which the individual only gives up to the State as much as is necessary to collective organization, and in the partition of territory retains a private demesne for himself. But with the rise in Socialism, this opinion became less popular with advanced thinkers. When schemes of reconstruction were afoot, personal liberty became a bore. And it must be admitted that the word was misused often enough to justify the apostrophe of Madam Rolland. [Hobhouse is referring to the French writer, who had said, 'Oh liberty, how many crimes are committed in thy name.'] Hobhouse then goes on to show that in reality. the theory of sovereignty is rooted in conditions which are obsolete, and as applied to democracies involve confusion in ideas, and some consequent evils in practice.''

It would take the present writer too far afield to traverse the whole argument. Suffice it to say that if the modern theory of sovereignty is followed strictly in the setting up of political and economic institutions by modern nation-states then, in the words of Hobhouse, patriotism would have to be put above humanity and political action would be uprooted from its real habitat, namely the moral law. The remedy lies in substituting for a number of independent sovereign states claiming absolute allegiance and enforcing it by absolute power, the spiritual principle embracing all humanity and finding organized expression in diversity of forms. It would, however, be necessary to quote as a *finale* to what has been said above, the following which is taken from the last paragraph with which Hobhouse's book ends:

''For social philosophy the firm conclusions are that the democratic community must be international; that in the whole every part whether we divide by functions or localities, requires its own organ, has its own sphere of self-government and its own right to maintain and enforce its views; that conversely there must be organs of adjustment maintaining the whole as a whole; that as a question of order, if it comes to physical force, the last word lies with the whole, or that which is its nearest and best representative; but that beneath all physical force there is a deeper spring of justice, and the ultimate supre-

macy rests with no organization whatever, but with the spiritual forces imper-
fectly apprehended in the minds of the wisest, and for that very reason legitimately appealed to, even by the humblest. Of all the retrograde movements
threatening us, the most serious is the loss of grip on the hard-won conception
of liberty – a loss typified in the prevailing belief that to fight Bolshevism it is
necessary to kill Bolsheviks and even cut off their supplies of chloroform for
their hospitals. Perhaps the history of this adventure will teach the world once
again that the spring of progress is spiritual and that this spirit is not aided by
the secular arm. Perhaps alternatively, a true spiritual authority will arise out
of the present welter of bald knowledge and conflicting dogmatisms; but it
must be an authority true to its own spiritual principle, governing by the light
of reason and through the convictions of men, indifferent to place and power,
an organization, not of officials and monarchs, but of knowledge, wisdom and
righteousness: the bodiless church of humanity in which the federated democracies of the world may find their soul.''

It would appear to the perceptive student of politics that Hobhouse has
virtually paraphrased in the vernacular of modern thought the teaching
of Islam as it is to be applied to give shape to the political order in
terms of which the life of humanity is to be organized. There is one
God; there is one mankind and there is for it one goal to pursue. When
mankind is created as one and is decreed to reach one and the same
goal of scaling the high water mark of spiritual life, all that ministers
to this process of the spiritual flowering of the mankind, whether it be
within the framework of the nation-state or any other social synthesis,
would be acceptable and anything which divides the house of mankind
against itself will be eschewed.

Islam would not subscribe to the establishment of a *territorial state*
of the kind which has become fashionable in our time and which gives
rise to the slogan ''My country, right or wrong'' and which advances the
same claim as ''Patriotism is higher than humanity'' as adverted to by
Hobhouse in the passages that have been quoted above. Islam provides
for spiritual *nexus* between man and man and aims at organizing the
life of humanity on a spiritual basis. Iqbal while talking of *Principle of
movement in the structure of Islam* dealt with the very same question
in the following words:

''To my mind these arguments, if rightly appreciated, indicate the birth of an
international ideal which, though forming the very essence of Islam, has been
hitherto overshadowed or rather displaced by Arabian Imperialism of the earlier centuries of Islam. This new ideal is clearly reflected in the work of the
great nationalist poet Zia whose songs, inspired by the philosophy of Auguste

Comte, have done a great deal in shaping the present thought of Turkey. I reproduce the substance of one of his poems from Professor Fisher's German translation: 'In order to create a really effective political unity of Islam, all Muslim countries must first become independent: and then in their totality they should range themselves under one Caliph. Is such a thing possible at the present moment? If not today, one must wait. In the meantime the Caliph must reduce his own house to order and lay the foundations of a workable modern State. In the International world the weak find no sympathy; power alone deserves respect.'

"This line of thought clearly indicates the trend of modern Islam. For the present every Muslim nation must sink into her own deeper self, temporarily focus her vision on herself alone, until all are strong and powerful to form a living family of republics. A true and living unity, according to the nationalist thinkers, is not so easy as to be achieved by a merely symbolical over-lordship. It is truly manifested in a multiplicity of free independent units whose racial rivalries are adjusted and harmonized by the unifying bond of a common spiritual aspiration. It seems to me that God is slowly bringing home to us the truth that Islam is neither Nationalism nor Imperialism but a League of Nations which recognizes artificial boundaries and racial distinctions for facility of reference only, and not for restricting the social horizon of its members." (See his *Lectures on the Reconstruction of Religious Thought in Islam*.)

The basic proposition which seems to call our attention when we meditate upon the texts of the various verses (*Ayats*) of the Qur'an and we set out to establish what may be called an Islamic State is that the Qur'an does not give us any fixed and unalterable system or machinery of government – instead, it provides us with the spiritual perspective in which operations of government, regardless of its form and structure, have to be conducted. Some of the verses of the Qur'an which furnish a clue to us for the organization of an Islamic State are the following:

1. And their rule is by counsel amongst themselves. (*Sura 42, verse 38*)

2. Pardon them and seek protection from them and take counsel from them in the affairs of the State. (*Sura 3, verse 158*)

3. Allah commands you to make over trust to those worthy of them and when you judge between people, you judge with justice. (*Sura 4, verse 38*)

4. Oh! David, we have made thee a Khalifa in the land, so judge the people with justice and do not follow thy desires. (*Sura 38, verse 26*)

5. Obey Allah and Obey the Messenger and those in authority from among you and if you quarrel about any thing, refer it to Allah and the Messenger. (*Sura 4, verses 58 and 59*)

6. You are the best *Ummah* sent out to the rest of mankind to enjoin what is right and to forbid what is prohibited, and you believe in Allah. And if the People of the Book had believed, it would have been better for them. Some of them are believers but most of them are transgressors, (*Sura 3, verse 109*)

7. Those whom we establish on Earth with Authority, organise Prayers and the paying of poor rate. (*Sura 22, verse 41*)

Verses listed as items (1) and (2) highlight the necessity of having a democratic Constitution and the duty of taking counsel between the believers: items (3) and (4) create the obligation on the people to repose their trust in those who are worthy of their trust and to abide by the duty to do justice when it comes to judging the relative claims of various persons; item (5) lays down the unconditional obedience which is to be shown to the Word of God and the *Sunnah* of the Prophet and those who are in authority over the affairs of believers. Some of the commentators of the Qur'an somehow believe that this verse implies the duty of showing obedience to any and every authority, no matter how appointed to manage affairs of the believers. But it appears to the present writer that since obedience to the Messenger is really the obedience to God according to the Qur'an and he was an authority in charge of the affairs of the State while he lived, but when he passed over, his place is taken by the duly constituted authority of the *Ummah*. For obedience can, at all events, only be to one True God. Now suppose the Amir enjoins a rule of conduct, obedience to which brings the believer into conflict with the law of God, would such a rule be binding? The answer must clearly be in the negative. Similarly, suppose a usurper claims to be in authority over the believer – would his commands be binding? Obviously not. Thus, in any case, there is, it would appear, no unconditional obedience to the earthly authority because the later clause of the same verse which enjoins, ''if you quarrel about anything refer it to Allah and the Messenger'' would ordinarily seem to exclude the reference of dispute to the *de facto* authority *simplicitur* — as though he were the last court of appeal and a law unto himself. The authorities in charge of political affairs too are bound by the demand that they obey Allah and the Messenger and anyone who flagrantly violates these limitations on his freedom of choice forfeits his right to being obeyed. For instance, if the Amir refuses to decide all disputed cases with reference to the commandments of God, and the *Sunnah* of the Holy Prophet, he forfeits the right of obedience. *What the Qur'an enjoins upon the believer is only conditional obedience to the orders of an Amir.* This is the foundation of all constitutional governments – where you have the government of law and not of a ruler. An Amir exists to give effect to the law. Negatively stated, in the theory of Islam, the law does not derive its validity from the mere fact that it purports to be the command of an Amir.

The last item in the list has reference to the paramount duty of the Muslim community to enjoin the right and to prohibit what is forbidden. All operations of the Islamic State will have to comply with this demand because fundamentally the Muslim *Ummah* is there to proclaim and promulgate the law of the Lord, to secure unity of mankind and to demolish internecine warfare which may be raging between various nations and to bring them to one spiritual platform – so that they may be able freely to worship one true God, and march in formations in the *Dinullah* (Way of God) on earth.

It is with reference to these ideas that Muslim polity is to be organized and any polity which conforms to these limitations on its power to administer public affairs can be justifiably called an "Islamic State". There is no fixed form or specific structure of polity which is prescribed in this regard so that conformity with it may make a state an Islamic State. By their participation in the value system of Islam shall we be able to say whether or not a state is Islamic. How could it be otherwise? A religion that claims to be universal and therefore valid for all epochs could not very well have given us a fixed formula for designing the machinery or actual structural form of Government.

3 General character of Islamic polity reflected in the establishment of the "Khalifat" during the period of Khulfa-i-Rashdin

The account relating to the establishment of the caliphate (*khalifat*) as an aftermath of the passing over of the Prophet in Islam is too well known to be recounted in any measure of detail. As long as the Prophet lived he was the religious and political head of the community of the believers and the believers obeyed him implicitly as the Qur'an had made it plain that they were to obey God and his Prophet – and obedience to the Prophet is described by the Qur'an as obedience to God. By obedience to God was necessarily meant obedience to the mandates contained in the Holy Book that was revealed to the Prophet of Islam and by showing obedience to the Prophet was meant obedience to whatever he commanded the believers to do. With the death of the Prophet on 8th June, AH 632, the Prophetic channel of receiving further revelations ceased to be available for the guidance of the *Ummah* but the body of revelations that had by then been received by the Prophet was available to it. With the passing over of the Prophet the secondary source of guidance for the *Ummah* was also interrupted but the guidance was still available in the form of the sayings of the Prophet and deductions to be drawn from the acts he performed during his life time. All this compendiously is known as the *Sunnah* of the Prophet.

It should be recalled that when the Prophet of Islam came to Medina he was accompanied by the *Mohajiruns*, the fellow migrants from Mecca, and was received by the *Ansars*, who were his helpers, from Medina. Over and above these two groups there were the non-believers who remained hostile towards him and his religion and in this class the Jews were in a majority.

The first state established by the Prophet of Islam was at Medina where, soon after his arrival from Mecca, he drew up a charter defining the position with regard to the rights and duties of each party or group in the new state. Some of the provisions of the Charter that have a bearing upon the problem of state-craft may be reproduced.

"This is a charter of Muhammad, the Prophet, applicable amongst the believers and muslims of the Quraysh and to Yathrib (Madina), and amongst those who follow them and attach themselves to them and fight along with them.

They are one Ummah (community) over against mankind.

The Muhajirun of the Quraysh remain in their former (tribal) constitution. They pay in common any blood-wit, etc., incurred by any members of theirs and they ransom their own prisoners – aided by what is considered right and equitable amongst believers.

The five groups forming the Khazraj tribe and the three forming the Aws were similarly to preserve their old constitution and be responsible each for the same collective payments as before and for redeeming their own prisoners."

Amongst the guarantees given to the Jews were the following:

"Any one of the Jews who follows us has our support and aid. They are not to be wronged nor their oppressors supported. The Jews shall pay the cost of war with believers. The Jews of Banu Awf and other tribes are a community alongside the believers; however, the Jews keeping their faith and the Muslims theirs; that they with their clients except anyone of them who has committed a wrong or an offence – and he does not involve anyone but himself and his household in destruction.

The friends of the Jews stand on the same ground as they themselves.

None of them shall take the fief in war except with Muhammad's leave. None shall be hindered from avenging a wound."

The comment of Professor Levy on the charter of the first Medanite state makes it clear that he regards it as containing:

"the germ of Islamic State if that can be called a state in which organisation is so entirely haphazard and in which the machinery for carrying out the functions of government is left in such a rudimentary condition." He goes on to add, "Of these functions the legislative one alone was adequately provided for and even then so long as Muhammad himself remained alive though Allah stands behind the Prophet to provide guidance for the community when necessary. So far, however, the other functions such as judicial and executive are concerned the Charter provides no better organisation than that already existing in the tribes. The old chiefs are left with some part of their internal authority; law and order are still maintained within the family group by its being held liable to pay, as before, for the delinquencies of its members and for the ransom of kinsmen who are prisoners. But there is now the important addition that the tribe is required also to produce, for vengeance to be exacted, any one of its members who has committed a wrong against a member of another group."

So far as regulation of the conduct of the Muslims was concerned a vital change immediately affecting their lives was introduced by the Charter. The decisive declaration was: if you dispute over any matter then your recourse is to God and to Muhammad. This, as any one can see, was a new idea totally foreign to the pre-existing mode of securing the organization of the tribal society of the pagan Arabs. They were now all made subservient to divine authority as members of a community of God in a state in which the political power was held by Allah and his apostle Muhammad. There could be no distinction here of church and state. The *Ummah* (community of believers) partook of the nature of both and the purposes of one were the purposes of the other. Similarly the Prophet derived his political power from his divine office and from nowhere else.

With this as a historical background of the political arrangements (a sort of confederal type of Governance established at Medina), one can see the magnitude of crisis that overtook the community of believers when their prophet lay dead. The choice of the leader was a must but neither the Qur'an nor any of the specific directions of the Prophet contained in his utterances was there to enable the believers to choose their leader. Was he to be elected and if so by whom? On the day when the Prophet died, after a short period of illness covering roughly 13 days, the community stood leaderless and virtually paralyzed – Omar refused to let anyone say that the Prophet was dead and not until the calm and sedate Abu Bakr referred to the following verse of the Qur'an was he brought back to his senses:

"Muhammad is only an apostle: Apostles before him have passed away. When he cometh to die or is killed, will ye turn back on your heels. The man who so turneth will not harm God, but God will reward those who acknowledge Him." (*Sura 3, verse 143*)

The fledgling Muslim community was called upon to face the grave emergency that had arisen and the choice of the leader got somewhat complicated by the rival claims that were being put forward on behalf of the *Mohajiruns* (those that left Mecca for Medina) and the *Ansars* (the helpers). But despite the furious disagreement that occurred between the Mohajirs and the Ansars in the hall of Banu Sa'ad, Abu Bakr was elected in a democratic manner in line with the tradition of the pagan Arabs. The crisis was overcome by the resolute stand of three men, Abu Bakr, Umar and Abu Ubaida – the latter two more or less left no option with Abu Bakr but to accept the leadership of the community as the sole successor of the Prophet. He was designated as *Khalifa* or successor of the Prophet and on the following day when the Mohajirs and Ansars met in larger numbers in the mosque they ratified his election to that highest office.

Many have relied upon the admitted fact that the Prophet of God had, during the course of his illness, directed Abu Bakr to lead prayers on his behalf and this circumstance amounted to more or less a direction to the believers to choose Abu Bakr as the successor; yet some others have referred to the saying of the Prophet that the leadership was to fall on one of the *Quraysh* and suggested that it is this that prevented the *Ansars* from putting forward their claim of having one of themselves elected or selected as their leader. But to the impartial student of the history of Islam those considerations do not appear to be sufficient to explain the choice of Abu Bakr – much less the manner in which he was chosen. The significant fact remains that so important and more or less an inevitable step which the community of believers was to take after the passing away of the Prophet, namely the selection of the leader, turns out to be a matter as to which both the holy writ and the words of the Prophet do not provide any specific answer. The Prophet also had grown weak during his last illness and ought to have known that he was not going to live long; he had even hinted in his farewell address when he had performed the last Hajj of his life that he might not be with the believers on the occasion of the succeeding Hajj and that, what is more, the Qur'an had provided to him clear indication that Prophets before had died and in this case he, that is, Muhammad too was fated to die; were those who were the followers of the religion of Islam going to abandon the work that had been assigned to them? It is, therefore, idle to contend, as some western writers on Islam have attempted to do, that the Prophet of Islam left no clear guidance as to who his successor was going to be because somehow he felt that he was immortal and was not going to die. The observation of Professor Levy to the effect that:

"The fact would appear to be that, since neither Muhammad nor his people seem to have envisaged the possibility of his dying, no provision was made for the continuance of government in the community and no successor was appointed to the man who was the head of the State as well as the spiritual guide of the community. He had, moreover, constantly proclaimed himself to be the direct and only agent of God upon earth, the last of the prophets and without heir,"

could not possibly be accepted as being in accord with what the Prophet's own attitude with respect to the question of leaving guidance for the community as to the mode or manner in which their leader was to be chosen after him. Indeed, his silence upon so important a question must be construed as a result of a definite decision on his part not to interfere with the right of the community to decide for itself by resort to whatever means or method, whether by selection, nomination or election how their future leader had to be chosen. *Ummah* at all times is to be treated as autonomous and is to carry on its duties in accordance with its own judgement.

The *Ummah*, after all, had to carry on the work entrusted to it by the Qur'an; as we know it is described there as the best of *Ummah* that was sent to mankind to enjoin upon them what was right and to dissuade them from doing that which was forbidden. If that task had to be tackled successfully, the *Ummah* must be regarded as being implicitly invested with the authority to take a final decision with respect to the person who was going to be its leader for doing all that which it was necessary for it to do. A great deal was to be done not only to guard the heritage of Islam left by the Prophet but also to consummate the purposes for which the Prophet of Islam had inaugurated the Muslim era in history. Nor again is it at all possible to take seriously the position that the *Imam* or *Khalifa* in the Muslim community, either by reason of any mandate contained in the Qur'an or utterance of the Prophet, existed by rights traceable to divine will – in the sense that the selection or election of such an *Imam* or *Khalifa* by the *Ummah* was not necessary. *Per contra* the following verse of the Qur'an is too clear upon this subject to admit of any serious controversy. In Sura 33, verse 40 the Qur'an has proclaimed:

"Muhammad is not the father of any one of your men but he is the messenger of Allah and the seal of Prophets and Allah is knower of all things."

By saying that "Muhammad is not the father of any of your men" it is clearly implied that no one man can possibly claim any inheritance from him, that is to say, from Muhammad regarded as a person. But only such link is possible as the believer can establish with Muhammad in his capacity as messenger of Allah, viz. the relationship of any one believer, which is capable of being sustained in principle is to view Muhammad as the messenger of Allah and establish a direct link with that which is enjoined in the message brought by him – a link which can be established only by obeying the mandates of the Qur'an and the Sunnah of the Prophet. The sincere believer is linked with the messenger of Allah only to the extent to which he claims to follow the message that the Prophet of Islam has brought and the example he has furnished of the way in which it is to be obeyed and any claim that can be advanced by any one man upon the legacy or heritage of Muhammad apart from that which he left in his capacity as a messenger of Allah for the *Ummah*, is foreclosed by the divine revelation to which reference has been made earlier. What is more, what was left behind by the Prophet could not be other than the legacy of the word of God revealed to him and what he did to implement that word. The message of Islam is the heritage of all believers but the question of choosing the person who should be the guardian of that heritage and manager of the affairs of the *Ummah* of Muhammad (on whom be peace) is a question which, from the nature of the case, must be left to be decided each time it arises by the body of believers, not only those who were with him and have survived him but all those who are comprised in the *Ummah*. They alone had the right to inherit that legacy and they had therefore to select, elect or nominate one by any way that recommended itself to them to appoint their leader.

There is also in the Qur'an a reference to *Muhammadur Rasul Ullah*, *Wallazina Mahahu* indicating that the Prophet is being mentioned conjointly with those who were with him (Sura 48, verse 29). The full import of this concept of the Prophet being addressed along with those who are with him has not been sufficiently appreciated by writers on Islam. The point that seems to have been made plain by this reference is that Islam is after all a historical movement of world-wide proportions. It was inaugurated by the prophetic call and had to be carried on till the last day of reckoning. Thus the movement, to begin with, was to be carried out by the Prophet and by those "who were with him" and after his passing over by those that survived him, as inheritors of his message and mission. If the reference is to those who were with the Prophet in flesh and blood, the implication is that it is they, who are, when the life of the Prophet comes to an end, at all events expected to carry on the work assigned to the total body of believers – the latter being viewed as a sort of a juristic corporation in which men enter and pass away. And if that be so then, when the Prophet lay dead and those who were with him (his companions) had to carry on the tasks that lay ahead, they could not have very well done so without choosing a leader. Now the question whether they, as a matter of fact, happened to choose their leader by appeal to one method or another, their choice, regardless of the justification or plausibility of the method in the judgement of posterity, was a matter solely for them to decide. This unfettered competence to decide the issue is the foundation of *Ijma* in Islam. *Ijma* is the process of making a bye-law, consistently with the letter and spirit of the *Qur'an* and *Sunnah* and this authority to make the bye-law is vested in the *Ummah* that is supposed to carry on the movement for the propagation of Islam. For any one to say that the *Ummah's* exercise of *Ijma* proceeded on a wrong principle or was determined by conforming to an indefensible norm, which in the considered opinion of the present writer, is hardly relevant; surely, the believers had the authority to choose their leader as is done in all movements after the founder of the movement disappears from the scene. The movement is not allowed to die down but in order to continue it they are entitled to choose their leader and the question whether that choice was right or wrong is hardly a matter that arises for critical examination by men of later times and this for the simple reason that in the exercise of the authority to choose, they had the full freedom to choose rightly or wrongly and for that matter the issue is incapable of being reopened on the plane of a mere speculative argument based on some fanciful ideas that might commend themselves to subsequent writers or thinkers.

The moral to be drawn from the admitted facts is that neither the Qur'an nor the Prophet left any clear-cut guidance as to how succession to the state-authority after the death of the Prophet was to open up. This is tantamount to virtually giving a mystical hint that it was not a matter upon which any guidance could have been given to the *Ummah* of the Prophet of Islam – it being their task to decide for themselves how best they were going to choose their leader.

The expression quoted above (*Muhammadur Rasul-Ullah Wallazina Mashu*) appears in the following Quranic context:

"Muhammad is the Messenger of Allah, and those with him are firm of heart against the disbelievers and compassionate among themselves. Thou seest them bowing down, prostrating themselves, seeking Allah's grace and pleasure. Their marks are on their faces in consequence of prostration. That is their description in the Torah – and their description in the Gospel – like seed that puts forth its sprout, then strengthens it, so it becomes stout and stands firmly on its stem, delighting the sowers that He may enrage the disbelievers on account of them. Allah has promised such of them as believe and do good, forgiveness and a great reward."

In the context in which this expression occurs marks of identification of "those who are with Muhammad" are also indicated, and if we were to identify those marks within the class of believers who answer the description that is given concerning them, we can define the franchise for the electors who are to choose the leader or leaders that can be entrusted with the task of seeking the fulfilment of historical mission of the Prophet of Islam. The marks that identify the community of believers are assimilated to even pre-Muhammad religious manifestations – in that the believers in Taurat (Tora) and the Gospel (Avangeel) are mentioned alongside those who, historically considered, were with the Prophet of Islam as his companions and who were committed to advancing the programme for fulfilling the purpose for which the religion of Islam had been founded. Similar argument can be supported by yet another expression in the Qur'an viz. *Assabukumul Awaloon minal mahajrin wal Ansar* (See also Sura 2, verse 214 where there is reference to *Hata Yakul Rasul Wallazin Amino ma'hu*).

There are references in the Qur'an to the concept of *Khalifa* and some of these are:

"It is He(God) who has made you successors (Khalif) on the earth and exalted some of you in rank above others that He may try you by the test of that which He has given you. Surely thy Lord is Quick in requiting (evil), and He is surely the Forgiving, the Merciful." (*Sura 6, verse 465*)

Here the reference apparently is to the general mass of believers. Similarly in Sura 38, verse 26 one gets the following:

"O David, surely, We have made thee a ruler Khalifa in the land; so judge between men justly and follow (thy) desire, lest it lead thee astray from the path of Allah, for them is surely a severe chastisement because they forgot the day of Reckoning."

Yet in another place (Sura 2, verse 30) Adam and David (Dawood) are given the designation of *Khalifa*. The actual verse runs as follows:

"And when thy Lord said to the angels, I am going to place a successor Khalifa in the earth, they said: 'Wilt Thou place in it such as make mischief in it and shed blood? And we celebrate Thy praise and extol Thy holiness.' He said: Surely I know that you know not.' "

If right to be successor to his mission was given to the messenger of God's heritage then all believers were entitled to it and no one man could claim it, for no one man could be referred to as a person to whom Muhammad, as the one sent down, can be considered as father. This reference rules out the concept of there being a successor to Muhammad as a person in the conventional sense. The believers know him as *Rasul-Ullah*, as a messenger of God, and no man that lived, moved and had his being in the sphere of this belief could go legitimately beyond this permissible limit so as to redefine in his own way his relationship with the Prophet of God.

The subsequent selection of the three other *Khalifas* from Khulfa-i-Rashdin was, each time when the occasion arose, made by appeal to a different principle. Abu Bakr nominates Umar and Umar in his turn sets up a council of six persons charging them with the duty of electing one of themselves as the *Khalifa* by appeal to the majority principle. And after Hazrat Usman was so chosen, Usman in his turn could furnish no guidelines how this was to be done as quite suddenly he was assassinated. But then Hazrat Ali was chosen to be the caliph by those who were then in Medina. Thus Ali was elected as *Khalifa* by the majority of those qualified as *Assabaquoon ul Awalone minul mahajirin wal Ansar*. By common consensus, these four are considered to be the right guided *khalifa* and one cannot seriously question the validity of the authority they wielded by reason of any defect that might have vitiated their claim to being appointed as *Khalifa*. The very fact that each *Khalifa* was appointed with reference to a different method of selection is consistent with the contention put forward in this essay viz. the right to choose a *Khalifa* belongs to the whole body of believers and each time it is confronted with the option as to whom it should choose and appoint from amongst themselves as *Khalifa* it is entitled to do so by resort to any method it sees fit. If those who chose Hazrat Abu Bakr had chosen Hazrat Ali by appeal to any consideration no one would have been competent or qualified to question that choice. In other words, there is no such thing as common law of succession in Islam which could be said to have been established upon the precedents that refer to the mode in which the first four "right-guided" *khalifas* came to hold their offices – all we get, however, is the right to choose being vested in the *Ummah* and that they could proceed in any manner to choose their leader.

The authority exercised by the Prophet of Islam was total in the sense that no believer had the right to question him. The believers are called upon unconditionally to obey God, His Prophet and those who are constituted authorities over them. (See Sura 4, verse 59.) Elsewhere, it is provided that he who obeys the Prophet obeys God. (See Sura 4, verses 80–81.) But this is not to say that the Prophet was an Absolute Ruler. For instance, the Qur'an had enjoined on the Prophet to take *shura* Counsel (*Shawarhum fil Amr*) from his companions, that is, counsel for the management of the affairs of the administration and surely to that extent even he sought counsel from those who could be trusted to advise him properly and some times, it is known, such advice was accepted by him contrary to his own initial inclination to act otherwise than the course subsequently suggested. So far as the authority of the *Khalifa* was concerned it was, relatively speaking, far more limited. He was bound by the Qur'an and by the traditions of the Prophet and indeed the first sermon that Abu Bakr delivered when he was elected as *Khalifa* of Islam shows his consciousness as to his limitations as a ruler. He said:

"O people now I am ruler over you, albeit not best amongst you. If I do well support me; if ill then set me right. Follow the True wherein is faithfulness. Eschew the False wherein is treachery. The weaker amongst you shall be as stronger with me until I shall have redressed his wrong; and the stronger shall be as the weaker until, if the Lord Will, I shall have taken from him that which he hath wrested. Leave me not off to fight in the ways of the Lord alone

Obey me as I obey the Lord and his Prophet, wherein I disobey, obey me not.
Now arise to prayer, and the Lord be with you.''

The assembly stood up for prayer and Abu Bakr for the first time as
Caliph filled the place of Muhammad and became *Khalifatur Rasul*.

It shall be remembered that the Prophet in his last farewell address
had conspicuously pointed out that Arabs had no superiority over the
non-Arabs nor did the non-Arabs have any superiority over the Arabs –
except to the extent to which any one of them was more of a *muttaqui*
(*illa bittaqwa*). He had also said: "If there be a deformed Abyssinian
slave and he has authority over you and chooses to conduct your
affairs according to the Book of God, I ask you to follow him." The
Qur'an too had declared that all believers are brethren (Sura 49, verse
13) and there is also the authentic tradition of the Prophet to the effect
that: "There is no priority of one Muslim over another except by
piety." In view of these declarations, every believer is a potential
Khalifa and whether he does become one or not depends on the extent
to which he receives support from the body of believers who constitute
the *Ummah* at the time when the occasion or the opportunity comes up
for choosing a leader.

There is that famous letter of Khalifa Umar to Moosa, then Governor of Basra, which incidentally states the approach with which the
ruler should look upon the ruled ones. He said in that letter:

"People have an aversion for their rulers, and I trust to Allah that you and I
are not overtaken by it, stealthily and unexpectedly, or by hatreds conceived
against us. See to the execution of the laws even if it be for only one hour in a
day and if two matters are present before you, one Godly and the other one
worldly, then choose as your portion the way of God. For the present world
will perish and the other world remains. Strike terror into wrong-doers and
make heaps of mutilated limbs out of them. Visit the sick among Muslims,
attend their funerals, open your gate to them and give heed in person to their
affairs, for you are but a man amongst them except that God has allotted you
the heaviest burden.''

The authority of the *Khalifa* of Islam, though limited, was, all the
same, fairly extensive in its range in the sense that he was not merely
the head of the community, in the conventional sense, but he was also
the *Imam* who led the prayers and was a watchman and guardian of the
religious law. He possessed executive powers and an army and since
the need of the hour was such that political and military action was
demanded of him he also assumed political and military authority. The

judicial authority steadily got vested in the *Qadis* so much that even the *Amirul Mo'minin* (Commander of the Faithful) had no immunity from the judicial process as he could be summoned in a judicial forum to answer the charge should it be brought against him, at the instance of anybody who felt aggrieved by what he did or had failed to do. Apart from the authority of law, the *Amir* has no authority.

In what has been said so far an attempt has been made to outline the elements of early Islamic political history and present it in a generalized form to enable the reader to grasp the significance of the mass of facts and ideas that form the warp and woof of Islamic political theory. And it is from that perspective that he has to perceive the significance of Islamic political thought and then proceed either to appraise it or criticize it – all depending on the view he takes of the primary principles upon which the institution of the Islamic State, in theory at least, is grounded.

4 Reflections on the factors responsible for the deviation of practical politics in Islam from its general theory of law and constitution.

There is no scope in this essay to consider the implications of the developments that are taking place today in the various Muslim states that have emerged in our own time. Nevertheless in order to assist the reader to recreate for himself the picture of the past, as suggested by an impartial examination of historical evidence relating to the Theory and Practice of Islamic State, a few observations, be they even of a rather desultory and disconnected character, are called for and unless these are kept in mind, full justice cannot be done to the labour of those theoreticians of Islamic Polity whose ideas upon the subject have been presented by the author of the present essay.

(i) It is true that the period of the Khulfa-i-Rashdin which covers thirty years after the passing-over of the Prophet of Islam is a golden era in Muslim history and we must pay our tribute to the enlightened fervour with which the first four caliphs took upon themselves the task of consolidating the Muslim community and of furthering the cause of Islam. But the point that is often missed by the historians when they proceed to deal with this period has reference to the undeniable fact that right up to the assassination of Usman, the third Khalifa, there was hardly any dissension of a significant sort in the camp of the believers, or any conflict amongst them upon any important issue concerning religious belief and practice. Whereas it is true that the first four *Khalifas* have, considered as persons, been regarded as shining symbols of the institution of *Khalafat* in action it is equally true that the believers to whom they provided their captaincy were themselves united on all the major issues and there was hardly any internal dissension for them to contend against. Dissensions broke out only after the assassination of Hazrat Usman. And it was this feature of *Khalafat* that really created major difficulties for the fourth *Khalifa* of Islam, namely, Hazrat Ali to whom *baiyyat* (formal acceptance of his authority) was refused by Amir Mua'aviya, who was then Governor of Damascus, upon a wholly unjustifiable and practically indefensible plea that Hazrat Ali must, in the first instance, bring the murderers of Hazrat Usman to book before *baiya* can be made to him. Hazrat Ali rightly insisted that unless, to begin with, allegiance was shown to him by Mua'aviya and his hands strengthened, it would be difficult for him to expose the conspiracy and bring the offenders, who were responsible for the murder of Usman, to justice.

(ii) Be that as it may, the factors responsible for the falling away and switching off from the high standard of political probity and wise conduct exhibited by Khulfa-i-Rashdin by the successive *Khalifas* thereafter (with the possible exception of Umar bin Abdul Aziz) is also in part attributable to the peculiar situation that arose by about the time of which we are speaking. With the passage of time came the expansion of the Muslim territories and this development brought in new peoples with their own distinct historical backgrounds and political attitudes, and, what is more, the control of the expanding Muslim empire from its distant capital at Kufa and elsewhere having regard to difficulties posed by lack of adequate means of communication and travel, created problems which were practically insurmountable. Hazrat Ali when he succeeded to the caliphate found himself opposed by the very party whose candidate he had himself at one time been, and this party had gathered strength in the interval. With the rapidly expanding Muslim empire pagan ideas, particularly of racial pride and tribal arrogance infiltrated the body-politic of Islam and a strong resurgence of Arab Nationalism took place which hitherto had somehow been pushed into the background due to the intensity of the light of the faith which had blessed the hearts of earlier converts to Islam. It was inevitable that this development had to take place: many conquered nations had embraced the faith of Islam, and as Muslims, they had become the equals of their conquerors – so that what elements of pride had existed in them found their gratification in the ideas of race and birth (rather than in those of religious fervour and piety which conquered races could not assimilate) which were of special importance to the people of pagan Arabia.

There is an episode in the life of Al Mamun, an Abbasid Caliph, which highlights the difficulties that beset the way of those who were anxious to secure the succession of one Caliph by the next on the basis of the consensus of the community. It is related that a Beduin Arab walked into the Court of Al Mamun somewhat unceremoniously without even having secured from the guards on duty formal permission to enter. The guards ventured to stop him but the Caliph having noticed his aggressive behaviour, asked the guards to allow him to enter. The Beduin walked straight up to the throne of Al Mamun and without so much as referring to his honorific titles, simply called him by his first name and asked him who had appointed him as the head of Muslim state; had he stepped up to the throne by his own will or had he been elected to that office by the consensus of the community? Al Mamun replied: "Neither is the fact: the actual position is that my father happened to be the chief of the State and when he died, leaving a large realm to be administered, his mantle naturally fell upon me and I had to shoulder responsibility in the absence of any one who could be elected by consensus of the Islamic Community. Plebiscite of the learned is the right method but it was not easy to secure it. Now I appoint you an agent for this purpose: go through the Islamic Realm and secure a consensus in favour of someone, whoever he be, and I will abdicate in his favour." The Beduin went away completely nonplussed by the answer he got from the Caliph. The moral of the story is that it was simply not possible, such was the situation, to find out what was the consensus of the community with respect to the election of a particular person as the Caliph.

All this is not being said in an endeavour to justify the false attitude of racial pride and tribal arrogance that was being adopted by some of the succeeding Caliphs and, what is worse, the way some crude sort of apologia was being offered by the doctors of Islamic law in support of those false attitudes. But it is also clear that no government can maintain a quality of administering the affairs of its people which, somehow, is far above the quality of life of those it is called upon to guide. We are all cognizant of the trite saying which has it that "the people, in the last resort, get the government they deserve''. Any impartial student of history must, therefore, keep an eye on the difficulties that had beset the way of those who were anxious to secure orderly transfer of power to the successor-in-office before he sets out to judge the matter before him.

(iii) Such experiments in the art and science of governing the affairs of the country, regarded as a territorial state, as the early history of the development of polity in Islam familiarizes us with, have to be viewed in the light of the conditions under which they came to be improvised. It would appear that the approach of the early administrators of Islam to the problems of statecraft was conditioned by two main factors.

(a) All around the nascent community of believers lay, scattered about, close-knit and well-organized religious groups like those of the Jews and the Christians and other 'non-believer' groups who, taken in their totality, were viewed by the early administrators of Islam as constituting a grave source of danger to the continued existence of the fledgeling Muslim community which was growing under their care. The Muslim society of the time was in a state of rapid growth and was surrounded on all sides by rival religious communities that could not conceivably have contemplated its existence with equanimity. There was a suppressed sense of indignation on their part against the Prophet of Islam and his band of believers who had, by their crusade against idolatry, superstition and pernicious pagan practices, questioned the very foundations of a form of society that pre-dated the advent of Islam. There were, on all sides, to be seen the forces of hostility, threats of aggression and visible symptoms of subversion – and all these had to be counteracted if the community of believers was to survive. Every precautionary measure had, therefore, to be taken to fortify the frontiers of the territories in which the Muslim administrators had undertaken to establish the law of God, and firm steps had to be taken to ensure that the Muslim community was not harassed or destroyed by the scheming villainies and machinations on the part of the non-believers. Seen in this light, many of the provisions of the covenants drawn up by the early statesmen of Islam between themselves and the non-Muslim communities could be seen and appreciated as reflecting this anxiety on their part to secure, by all appropriate means, the stability of the growing community of believers and to safeguard it against all the possible assaults from the non-believers. It was thus, from the point of view of our early statesmen, a state of emergency that they had to deal with, and the code of political behaviour prescribed by them had reference to their understanding of the practical methods whereby that emergency could, under those extraordinary circumstances, be faced by them.

(b) All the early administrators of Islam were profoundly convinced that the religion of Islam was bound, at a not very distant day, to girdle the whole of the globe, thus encompassing within it the whole of humanity; they felt that until such time as the whole world actually came under the banner of Islam they could afford to wait: they therefore proceeded to make what might be described as *ad hoc*, interim and make-shift political arrangements to continue the administration of the countries that came under their authority – these arrangements were provisional and were to continue till such time as they felt free to devise ways and means of providing a well-considered framework of governance on a world-wide scale.

(iv) As to the rationalization of the authoritarian and monarchical trends which came to menace the orderly growth of the Islamic State, there is not much that could be said here: suffice it to state that the great doctors of law and writers on politics have ruthlessly analyzed some of the stratagems of *Mufties* of the time. They had undoubtedly taken totally indefensible positions to accommodate the whims of the ruling elites. But care should be taken to remember they were no more than creatures of the time and were operating in circumstances which hardly left them with any option except to toe the official line and pander to the whims of the ruling princes. Care should also be taken to remember that the pressure of public opinion was not as great as it is today. Even some of the judges of our own time have not been loyal to the oath of their office and have become party to rendering dishonest judgements to support the *status quo* in order to placate petty tyrants who occupied high and responsible offices. Even today the pressure of enlightened opinion is not available to operate as a brake upon the reckless and immoral designs of some of the authoritarian and dictatorial regimes which are seen operating in the world of Islam. It must be said to the credit of the classical and neo-classical writers, however, that in whatever they said they at least attempted to preserve the unity of *Ummah*. Invincibility of the Holy Word contained in the Qur'an was upheld by them as were the binding values of the traditions of the Prophet. Such stratagems as were resorted to by them, to reconcile the maintenance of the *status quo* with the perennial needs of spiritual institutions such as the *Khalafat*, were attributable less to their love of mischief or their disposition to act as sycophants than we are wont to accept. It was more out of a desire to moderate the rigour and designs of those who, as a measure of retaliation, would undoubtedly have endangered the solidarity of the *millat* that these stratagems were resorted to.

Of course, there is the other view, to which the present writer sub-
scribes: when a ruler ceases to be loyal to the demands which
a higher law makes upon him and degrades his noble calling to
manage the affairs of mankind by making it a means for securing
the satisfaction of his petty ego, it is for the scholar, the *mujtahid* of the
time, to fearlessly and forthrightly expose his pretensions by pointing
out the deviations and aberrations from the traditional path of political
rectitude to which he becomes party, thereby destroying the sanctity
of his office. For, in the last resort, believers must know that the role of
the martyr is highly honoured by Islam; so much so that it is a point of
high excellence with the believer, as the saying of Imam Ghazali has it,
that he should speak the truth before a tyrant ruler. This is precisely
because by exposing the false practices of the deviationists he becomes
a valiant crusader in the cause of truth. By offering his life, if necessary, to defend the perennial truth of God's revealed word, he performs
the duty of responding to the call of honour by showing a daring
disregard of the consequences. The history of Islam is there for any
one to read and it shows quite clearly many heroic figures who have
been prepared to offer their lives to uphold God's law. But it is
equally true that as intensity of belief in the truth of Islamic teaching
diminished many professional doctors of the law gave convenient
opinions to placate the whims of the rulers of the day, and it was
largely because of this cowardly approach by them to the performance
of their sacred duties, as interpreters of the law, that much mischief
spread in the land.

(v) All human institutions, the institution of the *Khalifat* included,
are manned by men, and men without the right belief as an informing
principle of their life's conduct cannot provide effective leadership to
handle the problems that crop up while one is engaged in the task of
handling the affairs of state. Removed in time by many centuries from
the day the Prophet of Islam, after his migration to Medina, established
the first state, the intensity of belief and the extent of conviction in
the inviolable word of God has undergone a great deal of change;
for those who move away from the centre of the circle along its radius
to the circumference, the light radiated by a lamp situated in the centre
gets diffused. Maybe it was for this reason that the Prophet of Islam
said: "If men of my time fail to abide by even one tenth of the
teachings of Islam they will be condemned but as to men of later
times, they will be saved if they abide by even one tenth of that
teaching". Unless men believe, with the fire of their soul, in the call of

the Holy Spirit, they are not capable of transforming their "animal self" into becoming an expression of the divine. Only those whose lives offer to God's light a transparent medium and who believe in His word revealed to the Prophet of Islam can provide genuine leadership. And the moral and mental regeneration of Muslims is still possible if only because the Holy Book is still with us and, we can, if we like, return to it. The Holy Book is the visible embodiment of the Divine Presence in our midst. He who is immersed in the refreshing waters of the divine truth is likely to impart a new impulse to history and take mankind from darkness to light.

(vi) Islamic legal doctrine, considered from a standpoint of the theory of knowledge may be regarded as an interaction of revelation and reason and, so regarded, the conflict between unity and diversity in the Islamic legal doctrine is a natural and inevitable consequence. The Divine revelation is without doubt a fixed and immutable foundation upon which human competence to understand and apply that revelation must work in the light of the feeble powers of perception and discernment with which human beings are endowed. Human reason has perforce to look at the revelation in the light of the concrete situation which presents itself to it for solution, and it necessarily arrives at different conclusions as to what the verses of the Qur'an or the tradition of the Prophet really mean in a given epoch of history. This happens also when, for instance, a constitutional instrument is subjected to judicial interpretation. The American constitution has been interpreted by the judges of the U.S. Supreme Court for the course of the last 200 years and anyone who has examined the course that the judicial interpretation of that document has taken in various epochs of American history is struck by the variations of the theme of the U.S. constitution that are reflected in the diversity of views that have been presented in respect of one and the same constitutional instrument which can be printed in a bare fifteen pages, the size of an ordinary book.

Muslim jurisprudence is without doubt built upon the belief that *Sharia* law exists in its own right, supplying a body of principles which could be invoked at any time to work out a complete and uniform code of behaviour for man as it is prescribed by God – such that if it could be adequately perceived, it would be available for solving all problems with which mankind is confronted for all time to come. But in their endeavour to perceive that all-embracing law, human powers of comprehension, which must from the nature of the case be regarded as deficient and fallible, are not able to do more than touch the outer fringes of the matter. The differences that are decipherable in the juristic speculation as to what *Sharia* enjoins are therefore to be attributed to the grammar of the human mode of comprehending the import of the Divine Word. Here as elsewhere, the play of relativity, like friction in the physical world, could be minimized but not completely eliminated.

In practically the same way, Muslim political theory down the ages has rested upon the ideal of a universal Muslim community or *Ummah*, united under a common Caliph as ruler, while the actual state of affairs in Islam has steadily moved away from that ideal. The community of believers has been splintered into a vast variety of denominations and schisms and what is worse even the locus of the political power in the Muslim world has been vagrant. Unity of *Ummah* has got diffused into different princely states and while the capital of the Muslim world moved from Medina to Kufa, to Damascus, to Baghdad, to Bukhara, to Ghazni, to Delhi, there were also *Khalifas* contemporaneously operating Muslim states in Egypt and Spain independently of allegiance to central Muslim authority.

5 Schools of Islamic jurisprudence -, their unity and diversity

The four principal schools of *fiquah* that have grown up in regard to the interpretation of the actual contents of the ideal *Sharia* law – the *Hanafi*, the *Maliki*, *Shafi* and *Hanbli* – all owe allegiance to one and the same revelation and the *Sunnah* (tradition) of the Prophet but the diversity in their approach and results, although not very conspicuous, all the same recalls the saying attributed to the Prophet, "Difference of opinion within my community is a sign of the bounty of Allah" (or as some other reporters say, ". . . is the sign of the health and vigour of my *Ummah*"). Subsequent scholarship in the world of Islam has regarded these four schools of *fiquah* as equally authoritative; stemming as they do from one and the same source they all the same constitute creative expression of one and the same essence. The strange thing, as the present writer sees it, is not that these schools of *fiquah* should have flourished but that they themselves should have become the constricting bottlenecks that choked the free growth of other schools of law – indeed, their existence seems to have displaced the perennial fountain source, viz. revelation and the tradition of the Prophet, as the source of law. Thus, by about the 12th century the door of *Ijtihad* by the exercise of which the four renowned schools of jurisprudence had emerged was itself closed on posterity – and this despite the cautionary warning administered in this respect by no less an authority than Imam Shafi himself, who is regarded as father of Islamic Jurisprudence, when he is reported to have repudiated the notion of a new school of law growing upon a passive acceptance of his teaching. And yet it was nothing more than a personal allegiance shown to him by his immediate followers that eventually crystallized his teaching into the *Shafi* School of law – with the concomitant result that it, in its turn, foreclosed the possibility of the future growth of law.

According to the present writer, these schools of law represent no more than an attempt to frame bye-laws under the mandate of the Qur'an and *Sunnah* to enable the *Ummah* of Muhammad to cope with the actual task of resolving practical problems of statecraft and also of regulating the legal relationships that were to prevail between believers *inter se* and between believers and non-believers. They have been conditioned by the existence of special circumstances of the age in which they came to be evolved and were applied. They are of course entitled to be shown all the reverence which is due to their founders for the way they showed of solving the actual difficulties with which the community of believers were from time to time confronted. But then each generation must undertake the duty of solving its own problems in the light of the *Sharia* as a universally valid system of legal doctrines and this attempt to do so could not be allowed to be thwarted on the specious plea that our four schools of *fiquah* have said the last word upon what the law of Islam is with respect to all questions for all times to come. To do that would be to make the law of Islam static and unprogressive.

Now that the world has been transformed by the industrial and technological revolutions of our time, revolutions that have radically enhanced the capacities of mankind and given it greater control over its environment, man's individual and collective life can be more easily organized than ever before in the light of the Muslim ideal. But here too the precedent is that man must believe and the quality of his belief, like the quality of mercy in the Shakespearean phrase, is not strained. Here, as elsewhere, you can take the horse to the water but you cannot make him drink. God's mercy and grace are constantly surrounding humanity. But if one were not to open his interior depths for God's light to enter, one would not be able to reach that high degree of personal perfection which is required before one can become the recipient of God's grace. In many places rain falls on God's earth in profuse abundance but flowers do not grow everywhere. Whether they do or they do not, must, in the last resort, depend in part at least on the receptivity and the preparedness of the soil. The same thing holds about the human soul also: without endeavouring to meet the Holy Spirit halfway, man cannot transform himself into becoming a means for playing a serviceable role in the shaping of the course of history.

The present writer would like to bring these reflections on the nature, structure and character of the Islamic State to a close by reproducing the following passage from Sir Mohammad Iqbal's *The Reconstruction of Religious Thought in Islam*, if only because in his considered opinion it is the best that has ever been said in our own time in pointing out not merely the essence but the quintessence of the Islamic State:

"The state from the Islamic standpoint, is an endeavour to transform these ideal principles into space-time forces, an aspiration to realize them in a definite human organization. It is in this sense alone that the State in Islam is a theocracy, not in the sense that it is headed by a representative of God on earth who can always screen his despotic will behind his supposed infallibility. The critics of Islam have lost sight of this important consideration. The ultimate Reality, according to the Qur'an, is spiritual, and its life consists in its temporal activity. The spirit finds its opportunities in the natural, the material, the secular. All that is secular is therefore sacred in the roots of its being. The greatest service that modern thought has rendered to Islam, and as a matter of fact to all religions, consists in its criticism of what we call material or natural – a criticism which discloses that the merely material has no substance until we discover it rooted in the spiritual. There is no such thing as a profane world. All this immensity of matter constitutes a scope for the self-realization of spirit. All is holy ground. As the Prophet so beautifully puts it: the whole of this is only an effort to realize the spiritual in a human organization. But in this sense all State, not based on mere domination and aiming at the realization of ideal principles, is theocratic."

The Economic System of Islam

Dr Sadiq Al-Mahdi

Fourteen centuries ago a new fraternity was established, which salvaged Arab society from the idiocy of polytheism and tribalism by faith in Allah, of whom Muhammad is His apostle who conveyed the Qur'an, His last revealed message to mankind.

The Qur'an and the leadership of the Prophet provided the basis of guidance and policy for the new regime. Economic, political and social policies and regulations were knit together with moral and spiritual injunctions in a global whole. Rulings which could supply us with a moral law, would also provide the directives for recommended economic behaviour. Thus in the words of the Qur'an:

"(They) show their affection to such
As come to them for refuge
And entertain no desire
In their hearts for things
Given to the latter
But give them preference over themselves,
Even though Poverty was their lot."
(*Al Hashr verse 9*)

In the words of the Prophet: "Your faith is incomplete unless you desire for your fellow brother what you desire for yourself."

Notwithstanding the comprehensive nature of social policy in Islam, the specifically economic aspects practised by the regime at Medina were:

1. The Qur'an and the Prophet took a positive attitude to economic enterprise. The Qur'an: "It is He who hath produced you from the earth and settled you therein to develop it." (*Hud verse 61*) The Prophet: "There is a reward for anyone who cultivates land whose produce feeds a living being."

2. All types of unearned income were prohibited: usury, gambling, monopolistic trade practices, speculation, and the meddling of middle-men were ruled out by Quranic and prophetic directives. Thus, the Prophet said: "Monopoly is unlawful, do not trade outside the marketplace, and allow no go-between in urban and rural trade . . ."

3. A tax on the agricultural produce of Muslims, their animal possessions, their merchandise, and their possessions in precious metals, was collected as *Zakah* (which has a double meaning: purification and increment – in a moral sense). Eight categories of deserving people were the recipients of *Zakah*. This established a welfare system.

4. Before Omar's ruling on the black soils of the river valleys, land tenure was as follows: land conquered by force was distributed on the same basis as other spoils of war, with a fifth for the state and the rest for the warriors. Land which came under Muslim control without war was not divided but became state property. The state could, and did, allocate land to individuals who could, therefore, own land in the following ways: by allocation, as a share in spoils, and – if they cultivate it – dead land which no-one else possessed. Individuals could then exploit their land either directly or indirectly through rent (*Ijara*), water partnership (*Musagah*), or crop partnership (*Muzarah*).

5. State revenue was supplied by its share in war spoils, the land tax instituted by Omar after his refusal to divide up the black soil lands (*Kharaj*), and the head tax (*Jizya*) – which is a scaled tax per head on the able-bodied non-Muslim citizens of the State. The State employed its revenue from these taxes to finance the administration and defence. The surplus was distributed as income to all members of the community – Abu Bakr even included slaves and divided it equally between the recipients. When some people appealed to him not to equate people whose contribution to Islam and the community was unequal, he replied: "Those matters will be rewarded by Allah, but peoples' needs for material sustenance are similar."

This ruling of Abu Bakr was later acceded to by Ali Ibn Abi Talib. But Umar, followed in that by Usman, abrogated the equal pay rule saying: "I shall in no way equalize the pay of those who fought against the Prophet with that of those who fought with him."

Payments were then meted out according to what was considered the status of each category of persons. Abu Yousuf narrates that in the last year of his reign Umar regretted the outcome of this unequal distribution and vowed to change it. He died before he could do so.

6. Islam recognized the importance of material well being. When the Prophet was asked whether the evils of deprivation equalled those of polytheism, he answered in the affirmative. This recognition did not, however, lead to a materialistic outlook because it was integrated in the complex of spiritual and moral values. Your worth, according to Islam, is not a function of your wealth but of your piousness. Further, the urge for material enjoyment was constantly tempered by the need for moderation. Thus says the Qur'an: "O, you who believe, do not forbid yourself the good things which Allah made lawful for you, and do not exceed the limits."

7. Finally, the Islamic system revolutionized the economic status of women. They were not entitled to inheritance. Islam rectified that. Marriage payment was given to the woman's guardian as a purchase price – Islam made this payment her property, to act as a type of social insurance. Islamic policy cements the family as the building brick of the community. Every moral pressure was directed to that end. Many times in the Qur'an belief in Allah is directly followed by the need to respect paternal and maternal duty. The *Qudsi Hadith* of the Prophet said: "I am Al Rahman, the term for family relation (Rahim) is carved out of my name. I am pleased with those who honour it and I reject those who fail to do so." This is backed by material muscle as follows:

1. The man in the family is given the function of bread-winner. This ensures the continued financial viability of the family because women inevitably pass through periods of disability.

2. The amount inherited is contingent upon the degree of relationship with the deceased.

3. The male was given a double share in inheritance to go with the function of bread-winner. This is by no means a financial disqualification of the female as she has her unburdened share of inheritance, her right to work, and her dowry. In some cases, e.g. the case of foster brothers and sisters, the male and female shares are equal in the inheritance of the deceased mother. Further, if circumstances change in a way which leads to burdening women with more financial liability, people are free to will a third of their bequest in a way which would change the sum total of what their sons and daughters receive.

The morality, the spirituality, the prosperity, the fraternity, and the social justice of that system earned for Islam glowing praise as an oasis of compassion in a desert of human injustice and callousness.

The following words are by non-Muslims:

W. C. Smith: "Surely the Islamic enterprise has been the most serious endeavour ever put forward to implement justice among men."

H. G. Wells: "Islam has created a society more free from widespread cruelty and social oppression than any society had ever been in
the world before."

The overthrow

Certain factors conceived in the womb of Islamic society destroyed
that system and proceeded to develop a hybrid economic system which
is Islamic only in the loose sense of belonging to Islamic civilization.
Those factors were:

1. The inequalities of distributing the revenue from the land tax
(*Kharaj*) which Umar decided upon, and then lamented, have consolidated other factors, e.g. the enrichment of senior officials which Umar
checked by reprimanding Abu Huraira, Khalid, Abu Musa and others
and confiscating half their newly acquired wealth. Checks which were
discontinued after Umar led to acute inequalities.

2. Sometime during his reign, Usman found that some of the black
soils of the river valleys could be better exploited by allocating them to
individual Muslims, and this was what he actually did. Another practice ascribed to Usman by Al Mawardi was that he made extensive
private hand-outs to individuals from the Treasury.

3. Islam's contact with the ancient civilizations of the Middle East
has enabled it to reshape them in the most historically decisive way.
Consequently the world of Islam was exposed to new influences. To
avoid instability, Muawya introduced the system of dynastic succession and his successors made a habit of studying the dynastic heritage
of ancient Persia and Byzantium to perfect their regimes. The same
channels of opening up to a different world which led to the introduction of monarchy in the political field, led to the establishment of
capitalism in the economic field. And just as the new political regime
had little to do with the democratic nomocratic institutions of Islam,
the new economic system effectively disposed of the economic system
which I described earlier. The inequalities of income and wealth grew
to horrendous proportions reflecting the widening gap between leadership and people. Usury, the symbol of exploitation, was re-introduced
– directly, and mediated by Christian and Jewish agents, and indirectly
through various devices known as *Hiyal*. *Zakah* evasion became perva-

sive. Symbolizing the change, Al Madina became the home of the playboy poet Omar Ibn Abi Rabia – an earlier-day Paris.

The dynasties established by the Ummayads and the Abbasids were great monarchies sustained by highly developed capitalistic economies – the most developed the world had ever known before modern times. They created institutions which enriched the civilization of Islam, for example Abdal Malik Ibn Marawan arabized the language of book-keeping which had hitherto been in Latin and Persian. He also minted an Islamic currency, to replace the Byzantine dinars and Persian dirhams which had been in use. They created an advanced civilization which I shall call Islamic and not Muslim.

The withdrawal

The conscience of many a Muslim was shaped by the image of the prophetic model, and sustained by such memories as the Seal of the Prophet's dying and leaving his armour mortgaged with a Jew for a private debt, and the saying of Umar: "What I consider my due out of public funds is: two suits – one for the cold season and the other for the warm season, transport for Hajj and visit (Omra) and the expenses of my family to live moderately, neither like the richest nor poorest of Quraish", and other socially conscious memories. The conscience of those here described did not take kindly to the new socially callous society. Some resisted it. Some were outspoken in criticizing it. Al Tabari narrates how Abu Zar said to Muawya: "Why do you call the wealth of the Muslims the wealth of Allah?" (Abu Zar is here referring to the fact that Muawya called himself vicegerent of Allah and described public wealth as Allah's in order to by-pass public accountability.) Muawya replied: "May Allah have mercy upon you, Abu Zar!" Abu Zar then said to him: "Do not confuse the issue." Muawya replied: "I shall say that it belongs to the Muslims, but shall not say that it is not Allah's."

Resistance and opposition did not have the desired effect. Some sections of the Islamic community disengaged themselves from public affairs and withdrew into quietist shells, for example, the Shias and the Sufis. The *Sunnah* thinkers and jurists extended a type of *de facto* recognition to the prevailing social order but they distanced themselves from it. They refused to accept public office, disqualified oaths taken under compulsion, opposed officially ordained dogma, and preoccupied themselves with the theoretical task of formulating the law on a private enterprise basis. Abu Hanifa, Malik, Al Shafi, Ibn Hanbal and others maintained relations with the authorities which were sometimes hostile and never cordial. The most important Sunni jurist who speculated about constitutional Islamic law indicated his distrust of the authorities by willing that his book should be published only after his death. That was Abul Hasan Al Mawardi.

That multi-fronted withdrawal has sustained the spirit of the *Ummah* through times of material progress and moral degeneration. Together with the charisma imparted to the *Ummah* by the belief that it cannot, in its totality, be misled and the hope implanted in it by the Qur'an and *Sunnah* that the righteous shall inherit the earth, those temporary withdrawals constitute a vote of no confidence in the current social order, and explain the pervasive Muslim expectation of an inevitable come-back. In his heart-of-hearts every Muslim believes that the deviation must be corrected and the usurpation terminated. Such an act of return would vindicate the dearly believed-in truth of the message of the Seal of the Prophets.

The economic system of the jurists

Working on the holy texts, and being influenced by the intellectual and social environments which surrounded them, our ancestors have bequeathed us a rich corpus of ideas and regulations which is most relevant for a comprehensive understanding of the economic system of Islam. Following is a review of their ideas regarding some important economic issues – the issues of private ownership, welfare economics, and state intervention.

1 Private ownership

The general rule accepted by most Muslim jurists is that he who culti-vates land which is not previously otherwise owned, becomes its law-ful owner. But others, for example Mohamed Ibn Al-Hasan Al-Tusi, in his book *Al-Mabsut*, said that land cannot be privately owned. Effort alone entitles individuals to its use and produce. Another seri-ous difference over a related matter is that Abdel Rahman Ibn Owf, Bilal, and others demanded the division of the black soils of the river valleys among the warriors. Muaz Ibn Jabal advised Umar against that. Umar accepted his advice. Theorizing on this issue the jurists maintained:

Malik: Umar's ruling was correct, and the Quranic injunction about the five-fold division of spoils applies to movables, not to the land.

Al-Shafi: The Quranic injunction is general, and Umar's ruling cannot be justified unless the warriors have waived their rights voluntarily.

Abu Hanifa: To divide such lands is correct according to the Qur'an. Not to divide them is correct because of the consensus around Umar's ruling. The decision on the matter should therefore be left to the Imam.

Privately owned land could be exploited in one of four ways: directly by the owner, or indirectly by renting it, by water partnership, or by crop partnership.

Atta, Makhul, Mujahid, and Al-Hasan Al-Bisri rule out all indirect exploitation of land, especially renting it, as a kind of unearned income. Daud, Al-Zahiri, Al-Shibi and Ibn Sirin support the prohibition of renting but permit partnership. The Shafis and Hanafis allow land renting and variously differ over the partnerships.

Mineral wealth is divided into hidden (*Batina*) and surface (*Zahira*) minerals. The general view of the jurists is that easily accessible minerals should be publicly owned – a view supported by the fact that the Prophet refused to allocate to Abyad Ibn Hamal the surface salt-bearing land of *Marib*. Surface minerals have been counted with the three categories which the Prophet described as free for all, i.e. fire, pasture and water. Hidden minerals in publicly owned land belong to the State, but those in privately owned land drew the following opinions:

The Malikis consider them public property because their existence preceded the ownership of the land and did not enter into the terms of ownership.

The Hanblis and some Shafis say that the liquid hidden minerals in privately owned land are of public ownership, whereas the solid hidden minerals in such land constitute part of the land in which they happen to exist.

The Hanafis and some Shafis believe that all hidden wealth is part of the land in which it happens to exist and forms a part of its ownership.

2 Zakah

Differences prevailed over the collection of *Zakah* and over its distribution, for example, whether all crops are subject to *Zakah* or only some, the aggregate from which *Zakah* must be taken, whether the revenue of *Zakah* can be given to only one of the eight categories of its recipients or must be divided equally among them, and whether *Zakah* may be given directly to the beneficiaries or must be channelled only through public authorities. A more important difference of opinion is whether *Zakah* is the only liability on the private possessions of the Muslim. Some answered in the affirmative and quoted a *Hadith* for support. Others disagreed and narrated the reply of Al-Shibi who said that there were other liabilities and supported his opinion by reciting the relevant Quranic injunction: *Al Bagara verse 177*.

3 State intervention

Here opinions differed over taxation, price control, appropriation of privately owned wealth, and the enforcement of social justice.

Al-Muzni in his *Al-Mukhtasar* said that once people have paid the specific dues – i.e. *Zakah* – they should be left with complete control over their possessions. Any further taxation is unlawful. The *Hadith* of the Prophet condemns it in the following words: ''Those who collect custom dues are doomed.'' Ibn Khaldun who was both for monarchy as a basis of stability, and private enterprise as a basis of prosperity, considered more taxes a prelude to decay. Al-Gazali and Al-Shatibi permitted the imposition of further taxes when necessary, but made that conditional upon the State being a just one.

Many jurists prohibited price control on the basis of a *Hadith* that the Prophet said: ''Prices are willed by Allah and should not be meddled with by humans.'' Some Malikis and some Hanafis allowed a degree of price control under certain circumstances. Some Malikis, some Shafis, and Ibn Al-Gaiem permitted what they called equitable price control. All quoted prophetic precedents for their opinions.

This attitude goes right down the scale: should ownership be limited? Can ownership be appropriated? Some answered in the affirmative quoting the example of Umar when he took back land which was allocated to Bilal that was in excess of what he could cultivate. Another example is when Umar forced Hatib Ibn Abi Baltaa to pay in fines double the price of the camel stolen by his underpaid employees. Others replied with a blanket denial quoting the saying of the Prophet in his last pilgrimage: ''Your blood and your possessions are sacrosanct like the sanctity of this your day and this place.'' Regarding the tolerable degree of private ownership, the Quranic condemnation of the accumulation of treasures in *Tawba 34* was explained thus:

''Ibn Omar said: 'All wealth whose Zakat dues have been paid cannot be described as hidden treasures, even if it is buried in the ground.' Abu Zar said: ''All wealth which is in excess of the needs of its owner is the cursed wealth deemed hidden treasure.''

Living at a time when social injustice and tyranny prevailed, Ibn Hazm advocated State intervention to the extent of the total eradication of poverty.

This survey can go on endlessly, but I shall stop here to conclude that in the context of some of the most important economic issues the opinions of classical jurists may be divided into two schools: one advocating a large measure of private ownership, backed by a small measure of State intervention, and a limited attitude to welfare legislation – this I shall call the Individualist School. The other advocates a limited degree of private ownership, a large measure of State intervention, and obligatory social justice legislation – this I shall call the Collectivist School.

The nature of Islam

Islam is no theocracy. There are two conditions to qualify for that:

1 A representative of God on earth, or representatives, who can establish such credentials.

2 A revealed text which could be explained, interpreted, and detailed by a person or an organization.

In Islam there is no such divine vicegerency, and the only such meaning refers to the collective viceregency of man. Islam may be described as a democratic nomocracy (supremacy of law). The jurists on whose ideas the formulations were built were lay individuals working on their own initiative. All are agreed upon the two sources of policy and law: the Qur'an and *Sunnah*. But the Qur'an and *Sunnah* have themselves addressed themselves to our intuitive, rational, and empirical faculties, and urged us to employ them actively. That is why Al-Shatibi in his book *Al-Muwaragat* said: "The injunctions of the *Sharia* agree with reason because they make reason a precondition for their application, thereby exempting children and insane adults." Those noble researchers have faithfully received the holy texts and understood and explained them with the full utilization of their intuitive insights and their rational and empirical faculties. As an example of this intellectually rich response, take the question of head tax (*Jizya*). This is regulated by the Quranic injunction in *Tawba verse 29*. Reflections on the meaning of the text include:

(i) *Jizya* is from the root *Jazaa*, meaning punishment. Alternative opinion: it is from the root *Juza*, meaning "instead of" i.e. *Awad*.

(ii) Nor acknowledge the religion of truth: Al Kalbi said it means that they failed to obey the directives in their own revealed holy books about the Prophet. The alternative opinion held by the majority is that they failed to embrace Islam.

(iii) *An Yadin* explained with two views. The first refers to their ability to pay the tax. The second refers to Muslim hegemony over them.

(iv) *Wa Hum Shghirun* again offers two views. The first refers to their being subject to the Islamic order. The second refers to their being humiliated.

Those differences have been outlined by Al Mawardi in his book on politics (*Al Ahkam Al Sultanya*). The underlying difference behind them is crucial because it revolves round the issue whether the head tax *Jizya* is more of a religious or more of a political tax. If it were a punishment for not being a Muslim, then it must be exacted under all circumstances from non-Muslims. If, on the other hand, it is in lieu of participation in defence, it could be waived in appropriate circumstances. Umar considered it more of a political nature. Abu Yousuf quotes him referring to the Christians of Najran and saying that their head tax has been waived. Again, Abada Ibn Numan Al Taglibi said: "I advised Umar to win over the tribe of Taglib and prevent them from leaning towards the enemy by waiving their head tax. He complied."

At the opening sections of his book on politics, Ibn Al Gaiem quotes Ibn Agil saying:

"Al Shafi said that politics should be conducted according to the holy texts. Ibn Agil said: 'That is wrong, and to say it puts the companions of the Prophet at fault. Policy should not contradict the holy texts, but when Omar burnt Saad's palace because he used it to isolate himself from the people, and when Osman burnt the other copies of the Qur'an to unify the text, they were right according to Islamic policy although their actions were not complying with any texts.'"

In another section of his book, Ibn Al Gaiem accuses those who do not look beyond the received texts of being responsible for forcing people, under the pressure of circumstances, to by-pass Islam and seek alternative sources of policy.

With this background, i.e. an historical ideal model, an explanation of how that model was compromised, a demonstration of how Muslim jurists theorized on the texts they received, and an example of how revelation and reason interact in the Muslim mind to provide wholesome guidance – with this background we are better equipped to examine our current predicament and outline the relevance of the Islamic economic principles and regulations to the solution of our economic problems.

Our predicament

The Third World, of which we are a part, is in a desperate predicament. Its agricultural growth in the subsistence section, though considerable, has been overtaken by an average 2.6% population growth, so that Third World States' positions as food exporters have been reversed. In 1970 they imported food worth $8 bn. and the amount continued to rise yearly as their requirement for food grew by 3.6% per annum, and according to FAO it is expected to go on at that rate until 1985. Agricultural growth in the cash crop sector was quite considerable, but was rendered of negative value by the continuous tendency of the terms of trade to lean against raw materials and in favour of manufactured products. The Third World's industrial growth averaged 6.6% per annum between 1950 and 1970. From then on, with some exceptions, the inability to expand local markets and the diminishing share in international trade have restricted the development of its industrial potential. The aid balance sheet, the extent of indebtedness, the burden of debt service, the malignant urbanization, the unemployment scene, the balance of payments situation, and the brain drain – all those important aspects of the economy yield alarming figures.

The elites governing those countries have in most cases fallen prey to the ideologies of the Super-Powers. Failing to communicate with the rest of the population, those elites carried on like regimes of internal colonialism running Head of State expenditures which, on a proportionate basis, outstrip the expenses of the Court of Louis XIV of France, wielding elaborate security organizations whose real purpose is to defend the regimes against their discontented populations, and which consume, in peace-time, more than a third of public expenditure. Those elites preside over top heavy administrative establishments which consume more than 50% of revenues. They sustain a gap in payments and life styles between the highest paid and the lowest paid which could very well be described as salaried feudalism. The remedy for this situation in the eyes of capitalist economists is to protect laissez-faire at home and pursue free trade abroad. A middle-class is expected to lead development just as happened in the West. When no class is forthcoming to play that role, because it is mostly engaged in distributive trade, exports and imports, real estate speculation, and money-lending, senior army officers are encouraged to step in and spearhead the middle-class role and proceed to build society in the image of the West. In fact the economic programme of this recipe – i.e. laissez-faire at home and free trade abroad – plays into the hands of the international market. Further, in the historical circumstances of today, there is no socially neutral economic programme which could work.

The imperialistic behaviour of the advanced capitalist countries, the internal disappointment with development standards, were cashed in on by communism – offering an alternative system. This alternative had several attractions: it provided an anti-imperialist platform, a development orientated programme, and an ideology which seems to answer the questions which new social forces in the malaise of the Third World ask. Marxism is a direct product of nineteenth-century Europe, both in the negative sense of being a reaction to the failures of capitalism and the collaboration of the Church with the dominant vested interests, and in the positive sense of putting together ideas which matured in the European milieu of that time. When it was transplanted to Russia it succeeded for reasons different from the ones which Marx foretold, and with a different programme than he had expected. Lenin, and later Stalin, russified it. When it crossed the border into China, Mao had this to say about the experience: ''If a Chinese who is part of the great Chinese people, bound to his people by his very flesh and blood, talks of Marxism apart from Chinese peculiarities, this Marxism is merely an empty abstraction.'' He sinized Marxism. In the Western European context, Marxism is being rewesternized under various slogans: the new left, Eurocommunism, the historic compromise, and so on.

To the Third World, communism was exported complete with all its Western and Eastern European pedigree. Whatever the social context, a search was mounted to find the appropriate proletarian class to play the role. When for various reasons, not least among which is the fact that the workers in these countries form a small proportion of the population, and are not, anyway, the worst off section of the community, and so they do not carry out the expected historical mission, the role is given to someone else. Lower ranking officers of the armed forces are entrusted with carrying out the social revolution. The lower ranking officers of the leftist coup, and the higher ranking officers of the rightist coup, have a similar record: they have both been elitist and isolated from the masses. They have both failed to solve the problems of authority and legitimate succession in the developing world.

The position of the oil producing countries has been presented as a kind of exception to this grim scene. Their massive financial resources, the leverage they can wield, have been considered good reasons why they should be able to finance their development and shelter themselves from the adverse effects of the international forces. Before 1970 their cheap oil fuelled the economic miracles which were realized in the industrialist countries after the Second World War. In the '70s they have enforced more control over the policies of production and marketing of oil. They have also either nationalized the assets of the oil companies or participated in their ownership. Their financial resources which could be counted before in tens of billions of dollars have come to be counted from 1974 onwards in hundreds of billions of dollars. In 1974 the developed oil-consuming countries have calculated their balance of payments deficit with the oil producers to be $50 bn. By every means oil producing countries were persuaded to purchase manufactured imports to recycle their huge revenues. Robert Graham said that contractors, particularly in the military field, were quoting "one price for Iran and the Gulf, and another for the rest of our clients." Huge outlays on arms purchases followed, for example American arms sales to Iran between 1972 and 1976 reached $10 bn.

Ambitious development plans were hastily put together, but they generally suffer from two main drawbacks: first the agricultural and industrial schemes are in most cases not economically viable and rather than acting as a future insurance against oil are subsidized by the oil generated funds and cannot outlast them; second in the purchase of industrial plant, they have in most cases opted for the most sophisticated equipment which rules out any possibility of developing appropriate technology. The whole exercise simply strengthens the bonds of dependence. It would have been the rational thing to do for the oil producing countries to decide upon an oil producing policy which would gear their production to that which is necessary for a programme of the transfer of appropriate technology from the industrialized and oil consuming countries, plus making funds available for the countries' internal needs, including the finance of real, well planned, development. Further, oil is a strategic product, and the policy governing its production could have been inspired by strategic aims, for example, the need to reshape the present international economic order along lines favourable to the developing countries. The present international economic order was conceived by the developed countries in the absence of the others and is far from just. This particular line of policy was discussed but Henry Kissinger, using the considerable resources of his country, killed it stone dead. The oil producing countries having produced as much oil as they could, sold it at higher prices after 1973, acquired huge financial resources which were under various guises expatriated by, for example, investments abroad, capital flight, recycling, and so on. Because the dollar is the reserve currency used for oil transactions, the U.S. was able to sustain huge balance of payments deficits and so make the rest of the world pay for its policies. This, plus dollar devaluations, constitutes another channel of transfer of capital resources away from the oil producing owners.

The oil boom and the accompanying expenditure has led to a very high rate of inflation in the oil producing countries. In many of them, this plus a steeply unequal pattern of income distribution has upset social and political equilibria. The Overseas Development Council of the American Economic Research Institute developed a criterion to measure progress in terms of welfare, not merely GNP per head. The Council's index gives equal weight to three fundamental data: infant mortality, life expectancy, and literacy. This weighted concept they called the physical quality of life. Although the oil producing countries have a high GNP per head, their performance in terms of physical quality of life is poor. The oil boom is being allowed to fuel social tensions leading to social upheavals. So, for different reasons, the position of the oil producing countries fits in with the dismal predicament of the Third World. The patient is dying, all the same, either from being underfed or overfed!

The case of the oil producing countries could be contrasted with that of Japan where real development was effected with little or no resources. In Japan the patriotic urge to stand up to the designs of the powers, and the Spartan norms of Tokugawa culture have provided human motivation for a drive which began in 1860 and culminated in the industrial revolution of Japan. Development is a matter of human engineering and the naive Marxist notion that it will take place inevitably is disproved by the experience of the Russian Revolution itself. A political event, the Revolution, put power in the hands of a leadership which planned and effected economic development at a forced pace. Ideology, politics, ethics, and all the factors which shape human motivation are involved in the process of development. In the context of the Third World, development hinges on the emergence of a committed and powerfully motivated political leadership, which is also free from corruption and inefficiency – two causes of back-breaking waste – and which is co-cultural with the rest of the population so that the legitimacy of its authority is accepted by the bulk of the effective social forces in society, and which undertakes the following:

1. A well-planned supreme effort to increase the social surplus and to invest it efficiently to achieve a high rate of capital formation.

2. A well-integrated system of social security and welfare which will contain social tensions and buy social peace.

3. A free and independent attitude to foreign models of development, and freedom from the domination of foreign interests.

4. Above all, adherence to a creed which is intellectually coherent, and rationally defensible, to justify the identity of their society, provide extra motivation and zeal, and meet the challenge of other creeds and ideologies.

I mention that for us, at least, Islam is inevitably that creed, and that all attempts to by-pass it, as the secularists of left and right have discovered, will simply isolate the by-passers and build up a backlash. This is even more so because secular Western society is showing all the signs Ibn Khaldun ascribed to over-ripe civilizations. Far sighted authors in the West are at one in seeing the writing on the wall. Aldous Huxley said:

"Such is the world in which we find ourselves – a world which, judged by the only acceptable criterion of progress, is manifestly in regression. Technologically advance is rapid. But without progress in charity technological advance is useless . . ."

The popularity of existentialism, logical positivism, language analysis and the despair pronounced in such books as Daniel Bells's *End of Ideology*, Alvin Toffler's *Future Shock*, and Charles Reich's *The Greening of America* (which actually recommends dope as soul therapy) seems to confirm an attitude of moral and intellectual surrender. A reflection on the real beliefs of people in the West betrays a spiritual emptiness and disqualifies it as an object of emulation. Under the surface of Christian, agnostic, atheist, and other "advanced" ideologies, people's beliefs are pregnant with all types of primitive religions. The more the serious creeds and ideologies are made unfashionable and beaten with the hammer of "the end of ideology", the more people are exposed to irrational highly subjective belief. This confirms Pascal's observation: "People need to believe and to love. When they are deprived of the right objects for that, they substitute their own improvisations." So in the advanced secular societies of today you meet with the old creeds of ancestor worship in the form of father and mother fixation. You meet worship of natural forces in the form of the worship of power, success, the market . . . etc. Fetishism, ritualism, totemism, are all represented under various guises. Pet-love, gambling, drugs, alcohol, are all reflections of the search for a soul and love deficiency. The communist alternative has reached the end of its hallowed tether. Communism has provided the Soviet Union with a lever to lift itself by its own boot-straps, but there the magic ends. In the field of technology, the "decadent" West is still making the pace. The new social forces in Eastern Europe are no longer satisfied with the role of being building bricks in a soul-less edifice. One of the first books to be written in the Soviet Union after the death of Stalin is the revealing novel *Not By Bread Alone*. The slogan of communism with a human face, the historic compromise, Euro-Communism, the tumultuous reception of the Pope in Poland – all indicate one thing: a moral and spiritual thirst which the reigning ideology is incapable of quenching.

If Islam is to be our ideology, some ask, how can we cope with such sensitive issues as birth control? Birth control in the context in which we are discussing it today was never discussed before. Even the issue of deliberate economic development itself was not discussed in the Islamic classical texts. Many writers in those texts recognized the positive attitude which Islam held for enterprise. Some even reflected on which fields of economic enterprise are most beneficial, for example, trade, industry, or agriculture. None ventured far beyond that. Economic development in the deliberate sense in which we know it today is a post-industrial revolution phenomenon. Some of us treat the holy texts and the classical references as if they are a kind of encyclopaedia. This whole attitude is faulty. Family planning is permissible for the Muslims today not because this or that text can be twisted to support it. Al Shatibi in *Al Mwafagat* sought to infer the aims of *Sharia* to provide a guidance for policy. Several authors composed books to explain that in addition to providing source material for laws and regulations the holy texts of Islam supply us with general principles which are the essence of *Sharia*. Those books are:

1. *Al Furug* by Ahmed Ibn Idris Al Garafi Al Maliki (*d. 684*)

2. *Al Gawaid* by Abdel Rahman Ibn Rajab Al Hanbali (*d. 795*)

3. *Al Ashbah Wal Nazair* by Galal Aldin Al Suyuti (*d. 911*)

And so on. Examples of those general principles of *Sharia* which they deduced and explained are: harm is neither to be inflicted nor to be answered in kind; necessity waives prohibition, and urgent need is a necessity; that which is a must for the carrying out of a certain duty is itself a duty. An example of this principle is: if a certain rate of population growth is a necessity for economic development, which is, in the context of today, necessary for the preservation and protection of Muslim society, then that rate of population growth is itself a duty. With this approach we can tackle all contemporary economic issues.

Some may persist and say: We can see how Islam can respond to the issues of planning economic development and satisfying social justice, but the holy texts prohibit interest which is the life blood of modern banking and insurance. How is it possible to run a modern economy without banking and insurance? Some jurists maintain that *Al Imran 30* is the basic Quranic regulation against *Riba*. They support that by the prophetic Hadith: *Riba* involves increment on postponment. Accordingly a transaction which involves an increment but does not involve the delayed doubling of the principal, has been permitted by Usama Ibn Zaid, Ibn Al Zubair and Said Ibn Al Musaieb. This permissible transaction they called *Riba Al Fadl*. This is an unacceptable approach because the fault with *Riba* is that it involves unearned income which is a general basis of prohibition in Islam. In defence of interest, some considered it an incentive for saving. That argument was disposed of by J. M. Keynes who analyzed the motives which drive people to save and concluded that they had very little to do with the rate of interest. Some defended interest as a reward to productive capital. Islam rewards productive capital, but refuses to reward finance capital, i.e. capital which may be productive but which may, under certain circumstances, sustain a loss. To reward finance capital under all circumstances, for example, when it sustains a loss for the investor it penalizes the investor twice: the loss and the interest which he has to pay. When interest does not involve the transfer of resources from one owner to another, there is no objection to it because it then acts simply as a measure of the efficiency of capital between its various uses, i.e. an accounting device. Also a degree of interest must be introduced in an Islamic system to off-set the loss of value of currency due to inflation and devaluation. A modern Islamic banking system could perform all the functions that other banking systems are performing against fixed fees. The transactions which involve interest will be replaced by a system like the one employed in equity banking: savings in the form of deposits are channelled to the investors. The banks act as agents of the savers and as partners of the investors. The banks enter into several partnerships with the investors and exact a share in the profits. Some of the investments are bound to sustain a loss, others will be profitable. The banks will then calculate the average profits they received and reward the depositors accordingly. This system will have the additional virtue of removing the disparity between the banking system and business. In an Islamic system, besides the moral pressures on people to employ their resources and not to hoard them, the owners of resources will be economically motivated to mobilize their savings by the erosive effect of *Zakah*, which operates as a negative rate of interest to penalize idle resources. So in an Islamic banking system, the banking system will flourish in a different structural and financial setting. It will be able to make use of the rate of interest in all transactions which do not involve the transfer of resources which constitutes unearned income. Also, international banking will not change to suit Islamic purposes – as long as capitalism continues. The new Islamic system will have to deal with the international system on the basis of the seasoned Islamic principle of international policy: reciprocity.

Insurance is a very useful institution which is greatly acceptable in an Islamic economic system. It is based on the principle of interdependence and insurance against crippling loss. The Islamic reform envisaged for the modern insurance practice would involve the following: the insurance funds will be invested in divided earning shares and not interest bearing deposits.

The opinions and preferences of many thoughtful modern economists are against the institution of interest from a purely "capitalist" economic point of view. J. M. Keynes declared that the volume of savings, to all intents and purposes, depends on the volume of investment. A high rate of interest will damp down the volume of investment made by businessmen. As a result, trade, commerce, and industry as a whole will be adversely affected. Owing to this blow on the economic system the aggregate money income will shrink. As the per capita income of people shrinks, automatically the volume of savings will be reduced. He says:

"It seems that the rate of interest on money plays a peculiar part in setting a limit to the level of employment, since it sets a standard to which the marginal efficiency of a capital asset must attain if it is to be newly produced.''

He thinks that ''interest both initiates and aggravates crises.'' This bias against interest from a capitalist economic point of view is shared by others but Lord Keynes' views acquired the character of a crusade. Socialist economists are by definition opposed to interest as a source of income because they reject the private employment of capital both for production and finance. This, at least, is the theory before practice changed it to some extent. In a paragraph disparaging the tendency of interest rates to rise, Lord Keynes reaches for a position which points towards the Islamic concept of interest when he says: ''. . . so that a wise government is concerned to curb it by statute and custom and even by invoking the sanction of the moral law.'' Other creeds have prohibited usury as morally repugnant. Islam is unique in rejecting it as an economic liability contrasting it to trade, a political disease creating an envied rentier class, and as a moral abhorrence.

A message revealed 1400 years ago is today as fresh as ever and as relevant as ever to the plight of man.

Further proof of the supra-rational, supra-empirical, omniscience, omnipotence, Who revealed that message ''Such is the doing of Allah who disposes of all things in perfect order: For He is well acquainted with all that you do.''

Banking and the Islamic Standpoint

Prince Mohammed Al-Faisal Al-Saud

General outlook

As a general rule, an overall view of a subject usually helps in discerning the more specific details. An acquaintance with the main aspects provides one with an awareness of the co-ordinated relations between the various parts of the subject under study.

Bearing in mind this principle, we shall examine some of the general rules that characterize Islamic economy, and in the light of which it emerges with its independent criteria. We shall not, however, dwell at length on this broad perspective as we must not allow it to overshadow the subject with which we are dealing in this chapter. Our aim is to examine the subject in detail, anticipating that the whole will become more lucid in the perspective of the general principles.

1. The first of these principles is an axiom which is recognized by the whole free world: this axiom is undeniable. The owner of the whole universe, with its wealth and all good things, is Allah, the Creator. From an economic point of view this principle was regarded quite differently by Muslims and people of other faiths. While Islamic economy was firmly based on this principle, capitalism contradicted itself in not laying down its economic systems with this principle in mind. Capitalist societies based their economic doctrine on the concept that man was quite independent in his ownership of wealth. The relationship of the Islamic economy to that of communists is scarcely relevent, for communism denies the very existence of Allah, let alone recognizing that He is the Owner and Bestower of life.

The fact that Islamic economy is based on this principle is seen clearly in the Islamic economy's commitment in belief, acknowledgement and application of the following verses of the Qur'an:

"So seek your provision from Allah, and serve Him, and give thanks unto Him (for) unto Him ye will be brought back." (*The Spider, verse 17*)

"Blessed is He in whose hand is the Sovereignty, and He is able to do all things." (*The Sovereignty, verse 1*)

"Say O Allah! Owner of Sovereignty! Thou givest sovereignty unto whom thou wilt." (*The Family of Imran, verse 26*)

"Such is Allah, your Lord; His is the Sovereignty; and those unto whom ye pray instead of Him own not so much as the white spot on a date-stone." (*The Creator, verse 13*)

"Say (unto them): If ye possessed the treasures of the mercy of my Lord ye would surely hold them back for fear of spending, for man was ever grudging." (*The Ascension, verse 100*)

These holy verses and others like them absorb the Muslim's mind, and constitute an unvarying phenomenon in Islamic economy, dispersed in all its smallest parts and determining that wealth in all shapes, whether it be cash, goods or production elements, is owned by Allah, the Creator and Bestower of everything. We wish to stress that one of the most widely stated errors is that this stance is taken against Islamic economy from the angle of idealism or abstraction, for when Islamic economy adhered to this principle it was deeply involved in reality, for it clung to the principle followed by every free man living on this planet.

2. The second of these overall principles with which Islamic economy is characterized is that Allah has made man a surrogate to succeed Him in this ownership. Thus, man's right to ownership has come down to him by proxy from Allah. And from an abstract point of view the succeeding owner should act in compliance with the will of the real Owner. Hence arises the relationship between Islamic economy and ethics, for everything that is ethical is acceptable to the Islamic economic system, and anything unethical is thereby rejected.

Such ethical implications in Islamic economy have never been ambiguous or mysterious, but have been a clear, practical, easy, useful and applicable jurisdiction. Thus it becomes apparent that the primary basis for economy did not stop at the Muslim's inner belief, but surpassed it in the second principle. In clearer terms we may say that the practical sense of the second principle emerged from belief in the first. This represents integration and compatibility between the two bases in Islamic economy, for since the Creator is Allah the Owner, it is a divine blessing unto man that Allah has made him surrogate to succeed (Him) and has bestowed upon him the secret knowledge of handling His kingdom, and has taught him how to handle His wealth, for wealth is the backbone of life, the management of which may result in good or bad. Therefore, the Muslim economist feels that he is responsible to Allah for carrying out His commands and implementing the economic system He, the Owner of Sovereignty, has ordered, for man is but the successor of Allah. All this is manifest in the following Quranic verses:

"And when thy Lord said unto the angels: Lo! I am about to place a viceroy in the earth." (*The Cow, verse 30*)

"Believe in Allah and His messenger, and spend of that whereof He hath made you trustees." (*Iron, verse 7*)

In order that we may approach the subject of banking in Islam we must ask ourselves a question: What is the ethical or religious philosophy that determines for us the economic shape of banks in Islam?

3. To answer this question, we shall touch upon the third principle to which any economic activity approved by Islam should be committed. Emerging from this is a set of rules, the most important of which we shall sum up below:

(a) We know that the Bestower of blessings and subsistence upon His slaves is Allah, and Allah hath honoured His slaves, children of Adam, and hath given them preference over many of his creatures. He saith:

"Verily we have honoured the children of Adam. We carry them on the land and the sea, and have made provision of good things for them, and have preferred them above many of those whom we created with a marked preference." (*The Ascension, verse 70*)

On this basis Islamic economy's view of wealth adheres to this glorious reality, for wealth is a blessing in the service of man, and man here is the master of wealth, not wealth the master of man. Allah saith:

"And the cattle hath He created, whence ye have warm clothing and uses, and whereof ye eat; and wherein is beauty for you, when ye bring them home, and when ye take them out to pasture. And they bear your loads for you unto a land ye could not reach save with great trouble to yourselves. Lo! your Lord is full of Pity, Merciful. And horses and mules and asses (hath He created) that ye may ride them, and for ornament. And He createth that which ye know not, and Allah's is the direction of the way, and some (roads) go not straight. And had He willed He would have led you all right. He it is who sendeth down water from the sky, whence ye have drink, and whence are trees and which ye send your beasts to pasture. Therewith He causeth crops to grow for you, and the olive and the date-palm and grapes and all kinds of fruit. Lo! herein is indeed a portent for people who reflect. And he hath constrained the night and the day and the sun and the moon to be of service unto you, and the stars are made subservient by His command. Lo! herein indeed are portents for people who have sense. And whatsoever He hath created for you in the earth of diverse hues . . . . And if ye would count the favour of Allah ye cannot reckon it. Lo! Allah is indeed Forgiving, Merciful." (The Bee, verses 5–8)

In one verse Allah has demonstrated the subservience of all His favours under the command of man, not above him. He saith:

"And hath made of service unto you whatsoever is in the heavens and whatsoever is in the earth: it is all From Him. Lo! herein verily are portents of a people who reflect." (Crouching, verse 13)

(b) Based on this sovereignty over wealth[1] that Allah has bestowed upon man is a principle in Islamic economy that is decisive, unique and characteristic in its independent criteria. This principle is initiative and courage in manipulating, administering and giving impetus to wealth, seeking further grace of Allah. But there are strict restraints on this initiative. It is neither rash nor heedless.

The verses in support of the principle of boldness and initiative are numerous. Suffice it to mention that the first attribute of the God-fearing, after belief in the invisible and performing prayers, is good sense in spending. Allah saith:

"This is the Scripture whereof there is no doubt, a guidance unto those who ward off (evil). Who believe in the Unseen, and establish worship, and spend of that We have bestowed upon them." (The Cow, verses 2 and 3)

Spending here comprises all kinds of lawful spending including investment. As proof of this, these attributes of the God-fearing are repeated around the middle of Surah "The Cow" once more in a practical manner. Spending money is mentioned twice in two considerations in one verse. Allah saith:

"It is not righteousness that ye turn your faces to the East and the West; but righteous is he who believeth in Allah and the Last Day and the angels and the Scripture and the prophets; and giveth wealth, for love of Him, to kinsfolk and to orphans and the needy and the wayfarer and to those who ask and to set slaves free; and observeth proper worship and payeth the poor-due. And those who keep their treaty when they make one and the patient in tribulation and adversity and time of stress. Such are they who are sincere. Such are the God-fearing.'' (*The Cow, verse 177*)

This diversity in the mention of spending indicates the comprehensiveness of all kinds of useful spending. In *"The Family of Imran"* the description of the God-fearing gives a diversity of the state of the spender himself. Allah sayeth: "And vie one with another for forgiveness from your Lord, and for a paradise as wide as are the heavens and the earth, prepared for those who ward off (evil).'' (*The Family of Imran, verse 133*)

There are also verses centering on strict warnings against detaining wealth as in Allah's saying:

"And they who hoard up gold and silver and spend it not in the way of Allah, unto them give tidings (O Muhammad) of a painful doom, on the day when it will (all) be heated in the fire of hell, and their foreheads and their flanks and their backs will be branded therewith (and it will be said unto them): Here is that which ye hoarded for yourselves. Now taste of what ye used to hoard.'' (*Repentance, verses 34 and 35*)

The restraints on spending are many, among them the instruction not to give money to the foolish. Allah sayeth: "Give not unto the foolish (what is in) your (keeping of their) wealth, which Allah hath given you to maintain.'' (*Women, verse 5*)

There is also the strict forbidding of squandering wealth: Allah saith: "And squander not (thy wealth) in wantonness. Lo! the squanderers were ever brothers of the devils, and the devil was ever an ingrace to his Lord.'' (*The Ascension, verse 27*)

And Allah saith: "And pay the due thereof upon the harvest day, and be not prodigal. Lo! Allah loveth not the prodigals.'' (*The Cattle, verse 141*)

And Allah saith: "And eat and drink, but be not prodigal. Lo! He loveth not the prodigals.'' (*The Heights, verse 31*)

This set of restraints and others like them contrast the principle of boldness in spending with the principle of planning, studying and non-improvization with objective of realizing benefits from judicious spending. Thus, it is a well-studied, double-sided economic process that is enhanced by continuity, despite powerful circumstances of tribulation and adversity.

(c) Spending in this expert and judicious manner results in the return, many times over, of wealth to its spender. The faster the turnover of capital the more beneficial it is to its owner. In just the same way that Islamic economy has laid down restraints on spending it has laid down more stringent and decisive restraints on its return (or in other words, making money) to its spender. Islam, in its economy, has made unlawful anything that leads to usurpation of another's property by unjust means. "Eating people's property in vanity" is an all-embracing phrase used in the Qur'an as a comprehensive law under which comes a set of restraints that stand in the way of anyone wishing to cause harm or damage to the property of another. Allah sayeth: "And eat not up your property among yourselves in vanity, nor seek by it to gain the hearing of the judges that ye may knowingly devour a position of the property of others wrongfully." (*The Cow, verse 188*)

And Allah saith: "O ye who believe, eat not up your wealth among yourselves in vanity, except it be trade by mutual consent, and kill not one another. Lo! Allah is ever Merciful unto you." (*Women, verse 29*)

The context of these two verses indicates that the first one deals with cases of desire, intentional and deliberate, of obtaining property wrongfully, while the other verse deals with occasions where the desire for wealth is originally within lawful confines; however by resort to weakness and deception the wealth is obtained unlawfully through psychological and procedural means, with the appearance of it having been obtained lawfully. This means that restraints on making money in Islamic economy are not limited to cases persisting in unjust means, but extend to care of the hidden inner intentions when Believers deal with one another. This perception does not affect the two verses indicating a common general philosophy of compatible restraints.

In the light of these restraints that clearly caution against material violations committed intentionally or those psychological violations that lurk in the midst of the Islamic economy's provisions of specific prohibitions on the making of money, emerge the most serious restraints: making money through usury, through gambling, through deals entailing ignorance and deception[2], and all those other prohibitions described unambiguously in Islamic economy. We have chosen the former three types of making money mentioned above in their close relationship to banking for discussion in this chapter.

A balanced attitude

1. Proof of the making of usury unlawful in Islam is Allah's saying: "And that which ye give in usury in order that I may increase on (other) people's property hath no increase with Allah." (*The Romans, verse 39*).

And Allah's saying of the children of Israel: "And of their taking usury when they were forbidden it." (*Women, verse 161*).

In proof of making some parts of it actually unlawful is Allah's saying: "Devour not usury, doubling and quadrupling (the sum lent)." (*The Family of Imran, verse 130*)

2. The proof of making it partially and totally unlawful is Allah's saying: "O ye who believe! Observe your duty to Allah, and give up what remaineth from usury, if ye are (in truth) believers." (*The Cow, verse 278*) The proof of making gambling unlawful is Allah's saying: "Strong drink and gambling and idols and divining arrows are only an infamy of Satan's handiwork. Leave it aside." (*The Table Spread, verse 90*)

3. The proof of making sale by deception unlawful is what Imam Ahmad ibn 'Umar has related: "The Prophet, peace be upon him, has prohibited sale by deception."

Imam Muslim has also said much the same, quoting Abu Huraira, and Al-Bukhari has also related similarly, quoting Ibn 'Umar that the Prophet, peace be upon him, "has prohibited the sale of the pregnant she-camel." (*Fath Al-Bari, Interpretation of Al-Bukhari, Part 4, p.284*) Men used to buy slaughter camels until the she-camels gave birth to their offspring.

These rules of man's sovereignty over wealth, granted by command of Allah who has honoured man, and the subsequent rule of boldness in manipulating this blessing that is guided by a set of restraints on spending lends to the Islamic economy complete co-ordination and harmony.

This balanced attitude results in the honouring of right of ownership for all elements of humanity, without injustice, discrimination or bias. Freedom of arrangements for financial considerations resulting from this ownership are guaranteed provided no one consideration dominates another, whether this consideration be peculiar to the individual or to the community. In practice, the adherence to these strict rules of Islamic economy makes the relationship between the individual and the community one of co-operation, and integration.

The value of this becomes apparent when we compare the position of the individual in Islamic society with his counterpart under a communist regime or in a capitalist economy, where on the one hand it is easy for him to become confused and without spiritual direction, and on the other selfish and opportunist. Whereas other doctorines have resulted from human thought influenced by temporary whims and special circumstances, the jurisdiction of Islamic economy is an overflow of the Creator who cares for the interests of every single individual.

In this general outlook, we have dealt with some of the general rules of the Islamic economy as regards the real ownership of Allah, the succession of man in this ownership, thus enabling him to become master of the universe through Allah's beneficence. We have seen the subsequent necessity of boldness and wisdom in spending and making money, in accordance with those restraints that guarantee its safe movement in normal circumstances. Coupled with this we must regard the freedom of individuals and groups in safeguarding financial consideration and the requisites of ownership, without bias or prejudice. In this light we may come now to deal with the subject of banking, a matter of great importance to all countries irrespective of creed or doctrine. We shall now, however, be able to deal with the subject through an Islamic viewpoint which determines clearly its nature and function.

Banking

The word "bank" is equivalent in Arabic to *masraf* (plural *masarif*), meaning "a channel", "a place for spending". In the language of the Arabs "spending" has various meanings, among them, "weighing", "making money". *Sirafi* is one who channels in matters. So the word *masraf* means a place for spending. Hence the bank is called *masraf*.[3]

Origin of non-Islamic banks

This is a brief background to the origin of banks in general, which must be understood before we proceed to Islamic banks, and is intended to enable the reader to discern why the true Muslim does not approve of these banks.

1. Banking started with a very natural desire on the part of those who had wealth in excess of their needs to have it kept, for a fee, by people considered capable and honest enough to keep it safely.

2. Bankers and jewellers were, by virtue of their profession, the champions in this field. Of necessity they had to be honest men and regarded with trust by their fellows. Through experience they came to realize that ninety per cent of the deposits lodged with them remained in their keeping for long periods of time, and only ten per cent of them were repossessed by their owners. Gradually the idea formed that the holders could make use of this wealth, and to encourage the deposit of further sums of money the holders offered to pay annual interest rather than charge a deposit fee. This was obviously an attractive idea to the owners of wealth.

3. Some people, in particular some Jews, became so skilful in making use of the deposits at their disposal that they devised a system of drawing up a variety of legal documents and negotiable instruments for the single deposit of gold that they held within their keeping. These instruments were based on the average of the previous draft account and were lent at usurious interest.[4]

It should be noted at this point that money lenders of the time, often Christians and Jews, did not heed the sayings of Allah on the subject.

On the basis of this usurious interest banking activities have diversified until they have reached the level of the various services being conducted today.

This is a very brief account of the background that has encouraged human societies in the habit of making a secure usurious return on someone else's investment, a practice which should not be a substitute for the serious investment we shall see at the heart of Islamic banks. In the following section therefore we should recognize the difference in the aims and means of the Islamic bank.

Banks in Islam

On the basis of the previous general outlook it is easy to visualize, at least theoretically, the main features of the Islamic banks, their means and their ends. However, this theoretical view is no longer sufficient to serve our purposes as a Muslim nation, however attractive the vision may be. What is important today is to move with confidence and resolution of purpose from theory to application. The greatest spur to this is realization of the urgent need for Islamic banks, and the necessity for their establishment without delay.

Reasons for the establishment of the Islamic bank

There are many fundamental reasons that cannot be enumerated in a work such as this short article. However, it must be accepted that these reasons all convey the message that groups of Muslims with the necessary facilities should join together and work diligently and directly for the establishment of Islamic banks. Among the most important of these reasons is the religious commitment from which no individual or community can break free, for the provisions of Islam, taken as a whole, make usury unlawful and forbidden from all aspects: economically, politically and ethically. It is a danger threatening life itself.

From the economic point of view, usury does not comply, either closely or remotely, with the principles that we have described. Usury removes money from its original function as viewed by Islamic economy. Economists have attributed the malfunctioning of money to three main causes: hoarding, rates of interest, and the state's direction of expenditure to the malfunctioning of money. It is known that the first two causes are attributable to usury, for the rate of interest naturally leads to hoarding. This technical view is completely in accord with the economic wisdom of making usury unlawful in Islam.

The Islamic economy's view of the function of money is determined by an economist in the following words:

"The fair and indisputable basis for making money is that the profit be the result of work. The rate of interest is far from this basis — it (even) destroys it. With the criterion with which we began our talk about the rate of interest we may say: It is a price in return for no work and it comes through misuse. Therefore, the misuser is paid which is unreasonable and illogical. Besides, the acceptance of this matter removes money away from its original function which we have previously referred to.[5] It also induces greed for hoarding which is forbidden and destructive."[6]

One can imagine the dreadful results of usury as a social crime, even at the level of the individual. How often have usurers, as individuals dealing in loans to people, ruined families, dispersing the members, and destroyed their very supporters? If we look around we shall see the usurious network with its multiple and intricate orientations spread all over public life like veins in the body. It has cracked the social structure and corrupted the hearts and minds of countless people. Had it not been for some remnants of immunity through religious impediment in the Muslim's innermost depths that deters him from usurious banks and all dealings with them, the calamity would have been even more far-reaching.

With regard to the political aspect of usury and its relationship to Muslim's religious commitment, it would be sufficient to quote the following passage by Al Hamshari:

"However, class struggle has done away with the sanctity of religion, i.e. Christianity in Europe and exploitation and monopoly through interest have become lawful. This form of usury moved to the Arab world after the crusades which laid the Islamic world open to imperialism and occupation that sucked all the constituent factors of the Islamic nation, controlling the financial resources in the countries. No one had wealth but as a gift from imperialism whose principles and traditions dominated the educational curricula and institutes. It controlled all the public positions and no one filled these except those whom imperialists favoured. And the countries that escaped military colonialism were colonized, unawares, economically. Thus the Islamic world was forced to deal in usury despite the fact that it is forbidden by the Qur'an and the traditions."[7]

"As far as the ethical results – in the heart of the economic question – are concerned, the difference is great between the consequences resulting from partnership in which all parties endeavour, work and share the profit and the loss and the consequences resulting from interest where there is a psychological void, disinclination to positivity, selfishness, relaxation and slackness as the usurer waits for his returns without work."[8]

Usury threatens the system of life itself as usury, by its nature, is the only crime specifically excepted from the principle of speedy punishment in the world.[9] The Qur'an is quite frank on this:

"O ye who believe! Observe your duty to Allah, and give up what remaineth from usury, if ye are (in truth) believers. And if ye do not, then be warned of war (against you) from Allah and His messenger. And if ye repent, then ye have your principal (without interest). Wrong not, and ye shall not be wronged." (The Cow, verses 278 and 279)

Thus we have seen the usury network crushing humanity. Economists attribute to it the disturbance in the turn-over of capital and the development of economy which can be measured against accurate statistics. In recent times usury has concentrated real authority and practical influence in the hands of a group of people often heedless of the needs of their fellow men.

For this reason especially, besides all other reasons, there is an urgent call for the establishment of Islamic banks.

But what are the means for the establishment of Islamic banks? Praise be to Allah, the answer to this all important question does not come out of thin air. It is secured from a practical, pioneering experiment that has already achieved results. Men have realized its objectives, having exerted their energies and beliefs, thereby bringing it to its envisaged end. A man who conducted the experiment has written about the means that were used:

"The key to development in developing societies is tri-forked:

1. Presence of motive that motivates the process of reaction and cohesion between the working leadership and the client bases. And it is well known by the Islamic peoples that the most distinguished element in this connection is the spiritual element.

2. Presence of conscious, clear-sighted leadership, to shoulder the burden and set, at the same time, a good example.

3. Forming organizations and corporations of former employees able to pave the way for work and implementation provided that such organizations and corporations be clear-sighted and conscious of their objectives and ends and that they confuse not the means with the ends. The idea of Islamic banks tried under the local savings banks was but a bid to make this the key... This experiment has been capable of achieving tremendous success."[10]

Objectives, means and characteristics of the Islamic bank

There is, however, a vital question, the answer to which should be taken into consideration together with the answer to the previous question concerning the elements for the establishment of the Islamic bank. This question is: What are the objectives of the Islamic bank? What are the means with which it can attain its ends, and consequently what are its characteristics and concept?

1 Objectives
The Islamic bank aims at realizing the following:

(a) Attracting and collecting funds and mobilizing resources available in the Islamic nation together with consolidating such resources through the development of individuals' saving awareness.

(b) Directing funds to the investment activities that serve the objectives of the economic and social development in the Islamic nation.

(c) Carrying out banking activities and services in accordance with Islamic jurisprudence free from usury and exploitation, and in such a way as to solve the problem of short-term financing.[11]

2 Means

The means of realizing these objectives are summed up as follows:

(a) Provision of the three elements, which are:
pioneering scientific specialization capable of setting a good example at work; the clear-sighted client base, and personal contact is the most important element in providing this; and the organizations and working cadres of the proper standard and with the feeling of responsibility.

(b) A very careful, scientific and thorough study of the steps in order to avoid the bad effects of improvisation.

(c) Absolute objectivity in selecting the human and material elements and guarding completely against mediation that has no real justification.

(d) Strong, patient will at the beginning of any partial or total job, and dedication and sacrifice in existing effort to achieve the good end for the love of God.

(e) Complete care for maintaining friendly relations with the community on all its levels, from the humble worker to the highest. Everyone has an undeniable right, and good ethics are the best means for the realization of objectives and attaining results.

3 Characteristics

The characteristics distinguishing the Islamic bank are represented in four points:

Avoiding dealings in usury; directing efforts towards development through investment; linking economic development to social development; reviving the religious duty *Zakah*, the poor due, and its proper social and economic function.[12]

Thus, we now have a set of basic matters related to the Islamic bank which are: elements and constituent factors; objectives; means; and finally, characteristics.

With the sum total of these matters we can reach a concept of the Islamic bank, defining it as follows:

"The Islamic bank is a banking, financial organization for the collection and employment of funds within (the framework of) Islamic jurisprudence to *serve* the Islamic society of joint responsibility, achieve fair distribution and set funds along the Islamic course."[13]

This means that the Islamic bank is an entity and a receptacle in which a sound economic investment policy is combined with funds seeking lawful gains to produce channels that embody the fundamental bases of Islamic economy and convert its principles from theory to application and from vision to a tangible reality. It attracts capital that may be unused in order to save its owners the embarrassment they would feel in dealing with (certain) houses.[14]

Details of resources and the employment thereof

In order to complement the picture, we must make mention of the aspects that constitute the resources of the Islamic bank:

1. Deposits – *amanat*
2. Investment deposits
3. Specific deposits
4. Current accounts[15]

These four resources are considered the basic resources in the investment activities. There remains a reserve resource, used in special cases which are determined by the Qur'an and Islam through the religious leaders, and this is

5. The poor-due. This will be dealt with in more detail later on (*Zakah*).

Employment of resources

Employment of resources may be summed up as follows:

1. Direct investment: in the establishment of organizations carrying out a specific economic, commercial, industrial or agricultural activity (*service*)

2. Investment in partnership with others in projects in the following ways:

(a) Project capital – buying shares of other companies or participating in the capital of a specific project.

(b) Limited partnership (loan agreement) in limited deals. Part of the money or all of it is paid – (*Mudraba*)

(c) Partnership leading to ownership – (*Lease-purchase*)

(d) Operations of "resale with specification of gain" to enable individuals or bodies to procure the goods they need before the required price is available – (*Murubaha*)

3. Loans without interest in certain cases.

4. Use of the poor-due (*Zakah*) funds and allocation of them for social solidarity since the original function of the poor-due funds is to enable the poor to become rich by themselves so that they have a regular source of income, and therefore do not need to ask for further help. If the poor-due resources become abundant the funds can be used in setting up factories and other centres of employment.[16]

Consequences arising from the use of Islamic banks

The consequences arising from the effects that the Islamic bank has on society stems from its quite distinctive characteristics. The first of these characteristics is, as we have already mentioned, *avoiding dealing with interest*. This is one of the main criteria of the Islamic bank. It embraces the commitment of the bank to the Creator's forbidding of usury. It also means that the Islamic bank arises from the Islamic vision of the world and of life, which insists that an Islamic institution should work in harmony with all other institutions in society, the whole of which must adhere to the total, composite system of Islam.

When the Islamic bank rejects all dealings with usury, it is offering society the medicine it needs to cure innumerable diseases. The bad effects of the interest system have been known for generations, and many prominent economists attribute to this system all the defects that have emerged in capitalist societies. The point we wish to make here is that usury invariably opens the door to injustice and exploitation, for the creditor regains his capital, plus interest. Moreover, the weaker the debtor – for he may be in difficulty or distress – the more the creditor has to gain. Dr Naggar resumes:

"I approve of what others have mentioned in this connection, that 'usury banks find pleasure and happiness, even their lives, in distress and crises that surround people. Their expansion and growth are, to a great extent, contingent upon the ruin that befalls others'. The financial policies of states and governments have given in to the usurious interests and that such interests have so imposed stringent restrictions on the financing of states and goverments that they cannot break loose of the authority of the banks. Strangely enough, banks do not find difficulty in providing funds as with the system they follow they create money through book entries. What is even more strange is the fact that the parties to the game have succeeded in deceiving humanity and imposing their game upon it. And evident reality indicates that all the influencing tools in society – governments, parties, intellectual leaders, information media . . . are all tools in the grip of bankers and financiers.''[17]

When society is divided into classes, one of which exploits the others, then the door is open to class struggles resulting from this conflict of interests. This is the class struggle that is so often created by capitalist society and exploited by Marxism. The situation is similar under both regimes, for when Marxism succeeds in wiping out capitalist classes it puts in its place the domination of the state and capitalism of the state.

The unhappy results of the usury system are innumerable: the endless struggle among millions of people throughout the world; the disturbance in the monetary system; devaluation of currencies; ever-rising prices; worsening inflation; and the groping efforts of states and governments unable to find the remedy.

How wonderful is Allah's description in these words:

''Those who swallow usury cannot rise up save as he riseth whom the devil hath prostrated by (his) touch. That is because they say: Trade is just like usury; whereas Allah permitteth trading and forbiddeth usury.'' (*The Cow, verse 2*)

How wonderful is this characteristic so apparent in Islamic economy, removing its banks and dealings from this concept falsely called ''benefit'' (interest),[18] whereas it is, in fact, the cause of great harm.

The second characteristic is:

Directing effort towards development through investment
We have seen that the only course approved by banking practices in usury banks is the financing of projects by means of loans with interest, and we have seen the dangers resulting from this system.

The substitute for this practice which Islamic banks consider one of their most attractive features is clearly preferable: namely, directing the effort towards *real* development in investment. The means by which this is achieved are entirely different from the methods of the usury banks and are fully approved by Islamic jurisprudence:

1. Direct investment – i.e. the bank itself employs commercial funds in projects that give lawful returns.

2. Investment in partnership – i.e. the bank's participation in the capital of a productive project resulting in the bank becoming a partner in the ownership of the project, its administration and in the resulting profit or loss in the proposition agreed upon by the partners.

The difference between the Islamic and the usury system is the difference between right and wrong, or between existence and non-existence. The development of funds in investment is real development in which profit is the result of useful, serious work, whereas in usury there is no development at all since what happens is that part of the funds of the poor moves over to be added to the funds of the rich. We feel that this operation produces no real results but injustice and exploitation; and this injustice is compounded when usury banks deal in secure loans, the value of which amount to double and more of what they have in deposit, as if they were creating wealth from empty funds that are in fact the property of debtors and the needy. The greater the value of usury interest the more serious the possibility of the damage and dangers of which we have spoken.

The third characteristic is:

Linking economic development to social development
Islam is a religion of unity in which the various aspects of life are not separated one from another. Concern for the whole of society is one of the most deep-rooted principles of Islam. By the same token, the Islamic bank does not view economic development as separate from social development, for to do so would be to put greater concern on returns to the individual than to society as a whole. Thus the Islamic bank should be as much a social bank as an economic or financial bank. Out of this practice, however, many returns arise for both the individual and for society, whereas the usury bank must always remain a slave to the interest of the individual, even if this should result in the collapse of society.

The fourth characteristic is:

Reviving the divine duty of the poor-due (*Zakah*)
It is extremely important to revive this duty which Islam considers fundamental and on a par with the duties of the other testimonies,

prayers, fasting and pilgrimage. It can even be considered the linking bond between all of these fundamental duties. At the same time Islam considers it to be a fundamental duty at the heart of its economic system, and one that purifies, develops and blesses it. The name of this duty that Allah has chosen for it is strong evidence of what we state in the Arabic language, for *zakah* (the poor-due) means "growth". In the following Quranic verse, Allah addresses the Messenger, peace be upon him, saying: "Take alms of their wealth, wherewith thou mayst purify them and mayst make them grow." (*Repentance, verse 103*)

Among the operations which the Islamic bank performs is the collecting of the poor-due, ensuring that the funds are spent in legitimate channels and managing the funds in countries where the Rulers do not undertake this task.

Let us now consider the relationship between the operations of the Islamic bank and its performance in collecting the poor-due.

1. The Islamic bank is part of the community and performs its functions through continuous dealings with the Islamic community.

2. The poor-due is an important part of the economic organization of Islamic society, and also an important financial consideration to the community as a whole.

3. The function of the poor-due is very sound in its intention, for it seeks not merely to satisfy the hunger of a poor man or prevent him from suffering hardship but, more importantly, it aims to enable a man to enrich himself through his own efforts, so that he may have a steady source of income and will not need to ask for assistance again.

Therefore, if a man exercises a trade or handicraft he may be given a sum from the poor-due fund to provide the means for exercising his craft, thereby securing a sufficient income to support himself and his family.

4. One of the channels of the poor-due is to those who are indebted and unable to repay those debts. The debts may have been incurred for a variety of reasons: because of over-consumption, depression which afflicts a particular commodity, unequal competition, or indeed for reasons that may benefit the community as a whole.

5. If there are sufficient funds, these may be used to build factories, buy or reclaim land to be put under cultivation, or construct buildings to set up commercial enterprises. The poor may then be given a share in these ventures to provide them with a periodic interest to meet their needs.

The collection and operation of the poor-due is placed in an independent account called the "Alms and Social Service Account".

The operation of the poor-due, together with common social responsibilities makes insurance unnecessary in the non-Islamic sense of the term, which involves the concept of gambling against risk, and is therefore unacceptable in Islam.

Notes

1 This is a strategic perception in the Islamic economy's outlook on the sovereignty of man. There is a tactical perception in the Islamic economy's outlook as far as the function of money is concerned which will be discussed when we talk about banking.

2 Types of prohibited dealings are given in detail in all books of Islamic jurisprudence.

3 *Banking and Islam* by Al Hamshari, p. 19 (Abbreviated)

4 Ibid. pp. 23–24

5 The main function of money: It is a general means of exchange, a general means of measuring the various values of things. However, the subsidiary function of money is that it is a good means of storing wealth as well as a measure of delayed payment. (*Introduction to Economics in the Islamic System* by Dr Ahmed El Naggar, p. 129)

6 Ibid., p.150

7 *Banking and Islam* by Al Hamshari, pp.40–41

8 *Introduction to Economics in the Islamic System* by Dr Ahmed El Naggar, pp.150–51

9 There are some punishments that may be speeded up, like the emergence of sin without the intention to change, for which Allah may be about to punish all; but the only sin specified in this manner is usury.

10 *Introduction to Economy in the Islamic System* by Dr Ahmed El Naggar, pp. 197 and 198

11 From a study entitled "*Islamic banks and their impact on the development of national economy*" prepared by the International Association of Islamic Banks for the symposium *Islam and Contemporary Challenges* organized by the Jordanian Ministry of Waqfs.

12 Symposium *Islam and Contemporary Challenges*, Jordanian Ministry of Waqfs.

13 Research paper by Dr Ahmed El Naggar presented at the Scientific Seminar on the organizational studies of Islamic Banks, published by the Islamic Banks International Union, Cairo 1979

14 This embarrassment is felt by 99 per cent of the sons of the Islamic nation in Egypt and other countries.

15 Study from *Islam and Contemporary Challenges*.

16 Ibid

17 Quoting from Knupher *Over World Power*

18 *Translator's note*: The Arabic word for the two meanings is the same (*faidah*).

Islam as Culture[1]
and Civilization

Professor Isma'il Al Faruqi

1 Not relativism

Culture is the consciousness of values in the totality of their realm, implying at its lowest level an intuitive awareness of their respective identities and of the order of rank properly belonging to each of them, as well as a personal commitment to their pursuit and actualization. At its highest level, this consciousness of value implies, in addition to the foregoing, a discursive knowledge of values, of their mutual relations and order of rank, of the history of the growth processes by which consciousness has achieved the said level of awareness, as well as a self-conscious collective commitment to the pursuit and actualization of the totality of values. Consciousness of any one value does not constitute culture, the latter being a perspective of the realm of values impossible to obtain without their totality being in view. What is often called monistic axiology, whether it is the survival ethic of primitive man or those implicit in a number of "isms" by which human life or culture have been defined in modern times, is not awareness of a single value, but a reordering of the whole realm of values under the dominion of the one value recognized by that axiology as the prime, or first, determinant and *definiens* of all other values. That is why it is possible to speak of the culture of hedonism which defines and ranks all values in terms of their contributions to pleasure, or of the culture of asceticism which defines and ranks all values in terms of their contribution to the denial of the processes of life. Each is a different perspective of the total realm of values. The same is true of the culture of communism, of national socialism and democracy, as it is of group-designated cultures such as the German, Italian, French, Indian, Chinese or Japanese culture. Though unlike any one of these, Islamic culture is nonetheless a perspective on the realm of values. To analyze it as such, to lay bare the internal structure of values as Islam perceives them, is the object of this chapter.

The foregoing definition of culture does not necessarily commit us to a relativist view. In fact, the Islamic position is the very opposite of relativism. Cultural relativism holds every culture to be an autonomous whole, a hierarchical structure of values *sui generis*, which though subject to description, stands beyond critique, as it were, by definition. It denies the possibility of criticism on the grounds that the criteria are therefore themselves always culturally determined, and hence falling within the culture to be evaluated; that it is impossible for humans to rise above their own cultures and build any supracultural methodology, or system of criteria and norms in terms of which historical cultures may be criticized. A culture, relativism asserts, can hence be neither justified nor criticized, its very factuality constituting its own justification. The comparative study of religions, or of civilizations, is equally alleged to fall in most cases into the same predicament. Through and through it is, and should be, descriptive. It can only report, analyze, compare and contrast its findings in the various cultures, religions or civilizations. But it cannot criticize, judge, or evaluate its data because the criteria by which such work is possible are themselves the data in question. Cultures, religions and civilizations are said to enjoy that same autonomy which makes each its own judge. Surely, each has laid claim to universalism, to address itself to man as such, to speak of religion as such. Nonetheless, relativism asserts that all their claims were vain; because while purporting to be universal, they were in reality mere inflated provincialisms. In their investigations of men, anthropology, psychology, history, sociology and even philosophy – all these disciplines have in modern times toned down their ambition of describing man or reality or truth as such quite drastically. They reduced their claims to analyzing given configurations of humans, of their thought and behaviour, their given systems of ideas or life. None has nowadays the boldness or strength to speak about men, reality or truth *sub specie eternitatis*.

This is not the place to consider critically why the Western spirit has come to this reduction of its area of competence, or how it lost its nerve and retreated from its Christian Scholastic or rationalist Enlightenment goals. Suffice it here to emphasize two points. First, like religions and civilizations, cultures do not conceive of themselves as of one among many, not as systems whose truth and viability are only probable. "Probable truth" has no adherents committing their whole lives and energies to its pursuit, certainly no soldiers willing to lay down their lives for it. If all there is to the claims of the various cultures and religions was a mere probability, they would have never commanded the enormous energies – mental, physical, emotional – of the millions over the long centuries required for their generation, crystallization and flowering. Indeed, if their factuality indicates anything, it is that their base is firmly established on the rock of faith, on an unquestionable conviction whose object is the world *in toto*, humankind, reality as such. Second, culture, at least in its higher stages, must have developed its perspective of the valuational realm only after considering numerous options. By definition a perspective suggests the possibility of other methods of ordering, for no value may be assigned the order of rank proper to it without the possibility of relating it to its neighbouring values. But to assign an order of rank is to judge that a certain value has indeed priority over another which has different or contradictory content. Co-existence of contrary claims, of contrary obligations, of opposite norms and imperatives, which is what the relativist thesis demands, is not only not productive of culture, but it appeals only to the mediocre. No worthy mind can rest when faced with contrary claims to truth or goodness or beauty. Such claims necessarily set the mind in motion to seek a higher principle in terms of which the contradiction may be solved and the differences composed. The human mind will not give up the search without satisfaction. True, such principles may not always be conscious, explicitly stated in the given literature; but their existence is absolutely indubitable. At the very least, they must be assumed; and it is the task of the analyst and comparativist to uncover and articulate them, to place them under the light of reason and understanding.

This leads us to affirm that there is no culture which does not make a meta-cultural claim to truth, to goodness and beauty. The problem is how far meta-cultural assumptions of a given culture are truly universal, how far they correspond with reality, and whether or not they are necessary; how far the culture in question is conducive to the usufruct of nature, the doing of the good works, the felicity of all humans, the cultivation of beauty. Islamic culture certainly makes this claim, namely, that it purports to speak for all humans and for all times. Its claim is that its contents are essential to humanity as such, that its values are absolutely valid for all men because they are true, and its perspective of the valuational realm the only one which fully corresponds with the order of rank inherent in each value. This absoluteness of Islamic culture did not make it intolerant of the ethnic subcultures of its adherents, of their languages and literatures, of their folk customs and styles. But it has distinguished the culture of Islam from *'adah*, literally, the local custom, the provincial content, which Islam tolerated even to the point of regarding it juristically acceptable, but which it has always kept in the place proper to it. Such a position is one of subservience to the culture of Islam, which was assigned the status of determining the essence and core of Islamic civilization *in toto*. Only Islam acknowledged provincial culture as content of the ethos of Islam proper, and managed to maintain a universal adherence and loyalty to it amid the widest ethnic variety of the globe. Bushmen from equatorial Africa, Europeans and Chinese, Indians and Berbers, as well as the ethnic mixtures of the Near East, the world's crossroads of civilizations, all participated in Islamic culture just as they should, building their unity and hence their definition on the culture of Islam and, under its guidance, continued to keep, develop and promote their hundred ethnic sub-cultures.

The standpoint of Islamic culture, therefore, is not that of cultural relativism.

2 Islamic culture and 'urubah[2]

The above-mentioned relation of priority and subservience characterizes the relation of Islamic culture to the respective subcultures of all Muslims except *'urubah*, literally Arabness or Arab culture. To it, Islamic culture stands in a special relation. In some of its elements, Arab culture was condemned by Islam in the most emphatic terms. Other elements of it became constitutive of Islam, of its new vision, new ethos and culture. It is a principle of the phenomenon of culture, as it is, of that of revelation and religion that it take place within a matrix, a crucible which serves for it as context as well as matter. In the case of Islam, *'urubah* certainly was such a matrix. But strangely enough, the offspring (Islam) affected the matrix (*'urubah*) far more than it has been affected by it. With the emergence of Islam, *'urubah* was transformed radically, but it remained all the more inseparable from Islam.

The Qur'an is an Arabic revelation. "We have revealed it an Arabic Qur'an"; "We have made the Qur'an into an Arabic one"; "We have sent to you an Arabic Qur'an"; "We brought down the Qur'an an Arabic judgement"; "We revealed the Qur'an in the clear Arabic tongue"[3] – all these verses of the Qur'an clearly point to the fact that only the Arabic Qur'an is the Qur'an. The revelation of the Qur'an is evidently Arabic by nature, inseparable from its Arabic form, related to its form of expression in a manner which makes the form as constitutive of the revelation and as necessary for it as its very content. In accordance with this description by the Qur'an of itself, the Muslims have regarded worship – which utilizes the words of the Qur'an – as possible only in Arabic. Inasmuch as Islam is inseparable from its liturgy, from worship and prayer, it is inseparable from Arabic. Reading or reciting the Qur'an in any other language is discouraged, and to do so for the purpose of worship is prohibited. The assumption is that an English or Persian Qur'an is not the Qur'an. Only the Arabic is so. Certainly the verses of the Qur'an may be rendered into any language to assist its reader to understand its ideas. But such a reader is exhorted to learn Arabic so that he may read and recite the Qur'an in Arabic. On becoming a Muslim, or growing up as one, every person is taught some portions of the Arabic Qur'an to enable him to perform his ritual duties. A minimum of Arabization must accompany any Islamization. A measure of 'urubah is necessarily a constituent of Islam, and hence of Islamic culture.

The question should be raised: Why did Islamic culture, which addressed mankind and aimed at universality, appropriate the Arabic language to itself, declare it inseparable from itself, and thus impose upon mankind a substantial part of the sub-culture of the Arabs? Granted that revelation must have a language for its message to be revealed, why did Islam not distinguish its message from the language of revelation, the content of revelation from its form?

There are three reasons why the Qur'an's linguistic form was declared inseparable from its ideational content. The first, repeatedly advocated by the emotive theory of language, though only in the last few years since its discovery in modern times, repeats and elaborates what the Qur'an has ascribed to itself in plain, clear terms, namely, the power to move the audience, to appeal to their emotions, to stir their intuitive faculties into apprehending the meanings presented and/or acting upon the imperatives pronounced. The Qur'an called itself *Dhikr* (literally, a recitation for the purpose of remembering and minding the content recited) and repeatedly explained that "We have revealed it an Arabic Qur'an . . . that they may revere God, that they may be moved to action by its pronouncements."[4] So often has the Qur'an linked the revelation, recitation, reading and remembering of the Quranic text with the doing of the good, fulfilling the moral deeds, actualizing the ought-to-do of value, and of felicity and happiness in consequence, that the linkage of language to feeling, emotion, and to emotional intuition and influencing of the will, seems rather common-place.[5] Indeed, the emotive theory of language has never been truer than in the case of the Qur'an. This Arabic textbook, the first "best seller" before the age of printing, the most venerated of any text for the longest period of time by the greatest number of people has played on the strings of the mind and heart like no other. No book in human history has ever moved men to such heights of enthusiasm, of reverence, of contrition and tears, or pride and self-sacrifice. All this points to the fact that the Qur'an is inseparable from its Arabic form, and hence, that Islam is *ipso facto* inseparable from *'urubah*.

The second reason for this inseparability is that certain elements of *'urubah* have, by virtue of their being embedded in the Arabic language or their constituting Arab culture at the advent of Islam, passed on to Islam as internal to its matrix. Hospitality, verve and quick presence of mind, loyalty, courage, individual liberty and pride – the highest values of personal morality – have passed virtually unchanged from *'urubah* to Islam. *'Urubah's* belonging to and discipline by the tribe with all the resultant social cohesion, passed to Islam complete, but with the tribe becoming the universal *ummah* of Islam, the world brotherhood under the moral law. Eloquence, goal of all the literary arts, in prose or poetry, the distinctive excellence of all Arabs and the prime vehicle of aesthetic expression and enjoyment, remained unchangeably true of Islam as it was of *'urubah* in pre-Islamic days. Thus in the realms of personal and social morality and of aesthetic experience, significant areas are commonly constitutive of both *'urubah* and Islam.

There is yet a third reason for the inseparability of *'urubah* and Islam. Having been the matrix of revelation, *'urubah* could have abandoned, and could have been abandoned by Islam, as Christianity abandoned the matrix of Jewish culture in which it was born and Judaism and Jewish culture went their own old way after giving birth to Christianity. Islam and *'urubah* were destined for another career together. The new revelation turned its attention to the matrix and therein effected radical changes. Apart from the values already mentioned which constitute many of its constitutive elements, *'urubah* underwent a genuine rebirth. The Arabic language, the repository of the categories of consciousness and the moulder of its forms, received a radical and decisive influence from Islam. The Islamic revelation gave Arabic a new crystallization, new categories of thought, new conceptual forms, new terms, concepts and meanings. Islam gave an Arabic body to the literary sublime, and set it as the insurpassable ideal of the art of letters. Arabic grammar, syntax and construction were derived from the Qur'an and continue to govern the language fourteen centuries later. The divine status of the Qur'an as God's *ipsissima verba* sanctified the Arabic language and preserved it unchanged, thus eliminating any serious problem of hermeneutics. The Qur'an, together with the mass of pre-Islamic poetry which was collected by the first two generations of Muslims especially in order to establish and preserve the understanding of the Quranic meanings, succeeded in establishing Arabic syntax and lexicography for all times.

Moreover, the Arabic phrases of the Qur'an, its figures of speech and forms of expression of gratitude, of wonder and amazement, of fear, of hope, of love and tenderness, of anger and determination, of hardness and might have impressed all the shades of human emotions with an indelible Arabic mark. Whether Muslim, Jew, Christian or other, whether literate or illiterate, every Arabic-speaking man and woman possesses a fair capital of these linguistic forms of the Qur'an. It does not matter whether or not the person is conscious of this Quranic legacy which he carries everywhere with him. It is inseparable from his consciousness.

It was this *'urubah*, embodying the Quranic revelation and essentially affected by it that became the matrix of the whole subsequent history of Islamic thought and letters. So that it is impossible for that legacy to be reached by any Muslim anywhere except through mastery of this gateway of the Arabic language. The Qur'an made Arabic the figurization of Islamic thought. In it, it embedded its own categories of spirituality and morality, so that to Quranize a mind is to Arabize it, and to Arabize it is necessarily to Islamize it.

There is nothing more damaging to this identity of Quranization – Arabization than the introduction by the Western enemies of Islam of a meaning to *'urubah* that is foreign to it, namely, the racist or nationalist meaning differentiating the Arab Muslim from his Muslim brothers belonging to other ethnicities. This so-called Arab ethnocentrism or nationalism is a new *shu'biyyah* designed only to split the *ummah* asunder and separate Arab from Berber, Turk, Persian, Kurd, Indian, Chinese or Malay, to alienate white from black, and to set the Muslim against his co-religionists in fratricidal conflict and war. That this is the work of the enemies of Islam who first seduced the idealistic youths of Turkey in search of progress and dignity, and then turned to the Arabs to set them against the Ottoman Caliphate, is a well known fact. In both instances, Christians and Jews were the instruments of this sedition. In the Arab World, the Christians continue to be the firmest advocates of an Arab nationalism copied from the West. From Jurji Zaydan, the Taqla brothers, the Bustanis and Khuris, to Michel Aflaq and Constantine Zurayk, they have advocated a cause designed to de-Quranize and de-Islamize the Muslims. They interpret *'urubah* in ethnic terms, deliberately neglecting its de-ethnicization by the Qur'an; and they assign to it meanings borrowed from what the Europeans understand by their own nationalisms. At best, they are superficial, unable to discern that nationalism is a phenomenon peculiar to Western history and non-transferable to the Muslim World; that in the final analysis nationalism rests upon a base of cultural relativism, a thesis diametrically opposed to the universalism and egalitarianism of Islam, the other facets of divine unity and transcendence. That there is no God but Allah implies for the Muslim who affirms it that before God, all men are absolutely one in their creatureliness, whether the accident of their birth has made them black or white, Nilotic, Caucasian, Indian, Chinese or Malay.

To combat this new pestilence which Western colonialism and its stooges continue to spread in our midst, Muslims need not attack *'urubah*, but its Western or Westernized interpreters. They may not attack it *überhaupt* without damage to the Arabic Qur'an, and hence to Islam. Rather, they must needs promote the understanding of *'urubah Allah ta'ala* had ordained, namely, as Quranic cultural form. Their fight is not against those Arabs who made the Quranic apparatus of language, method, beauty and consciousness the form and content of their daily lives, but with those puppets of the West who seek to replace the Quranic and cultural meaning of *'urubah* with the ethnic meaning constitutive of a natural *Gemeinschaft*. Such ethnocentric meaning runs diametrically counter to Quranic culture, and it stands forever condemned by Islam. Indeed, *"Blut und Boden"* particularism is a lapse to pre-Islamic tribalism, to *Jahilliyyah* at its worst.

3 The view of ultimate reality

The person whose worldview is that of Islam lives as if in an enchanted world. He is convinced that reality is dual: the world of nature is not an illusion, but really exists; and it does so under the categories of space, time and causality which are all equally real. In addition to the world of nature, there is God, a Being other than nature, totally transcendent, Who is the Creator of nature, the ultimate cause of its being, and the final end of its activity and life. *Nothing is like unto Him.*[6] He is neither in space, nor in time, but outside of them. He is not caused by any other being. Universal as these categories of space, time and causality may be in nature, they are inapplicable to Him. Indeed He is their Creator. The world of nature came into being because He willed it, and it did so *ex nihilo*, at His commandment. All He needed to do was merely to command creation to be, and it was, complete just as it is.[7] Creator and creature are two distinct realities, neither of which is the other in any sense whatever. The Creator may not be confused with, diffused or infused into the creature; nor may the creature ever rise or be transfigured so as to become in any sense part of the Creator. Each is ontologically distinct, ultimately disparate from the other. God is eternal, absolutely One, and never changes.[8] Creation has come to being in time, is plural and subject to change, and will pass into nothingness just as it emerged therefrom at creation.

Everything that happens in the world does so by His command, by His action. From the movement of protons and electrons in an atom to that of the galaxies, from the growth and development of amoeba to the psychic processes of man – every event happens by His knowledge, His design, His efficiency, and does so in fulfilment of His purpose. The world in which the Muslim lives is truly an enchanted world: every object beheld is viewed as something created by God, designed by God, sustained at every moment of its existence by God. Every motion or change within or without the self is viewed and felt as something effected by God. That is why the Muslim is tirelessly repeating all day his recognition and acknowledgement, of his appreciation and admiration of the acts of God, and his gratitude to Him, *"Allahu Akbar! La Ilaha illa Allah! La hawla wa la quwwata illa billah! Al Hamdu Lillah! Subhana Allah!"*[9] are always on his lips. The cosmos around him and everything in it are not a dead realm where chance and blind causality operate, but alive with order as well as meaning.[10] The world is not a chaos, not a happenstance. It is indeed a *cosmos*, orderly and full of purpose if one has the requisite vision to see. Such vision is precisely what the faith of Islam provides.

The relevance of Allah to man is not only metaphysical, explaining the cosmos and all that happens within it. It is equally axiological, explaining the good and the beautiful. The will of God is what ought to be. From it springs every value. Indeed, it is the first principle of the metaphysic of ethics, that which makes the good good and the beautiful beautiful. Norms are norms because of it. Their moving appeal, their energizing, stirring power which leaves no human untouched, is divine power, for they are the commandments of God. It is He that guides humans to the good deed: i.e., that moves them to fulfill and obey His commandment. As value, i.e., as normatively relevant to creation, the will of God is plural, since creation itself is indeed plural, requiring a different norm for everyone of its different constituents. It is known to us as divine commandment, i.e., as ought-to-be's and ought-to-do's latent in every unit of space-time, in every situation man finds himself. In itself, i.e., in so far as it pertains to God, the divine will is one as God Himself is One. His will is embedded in the structure and essence of all creatures, in which it is fulfilled by the necessity of natural law.[11] The same is true of man's physical and psychic nature. In his moral nature, however, man is not necessarily determined by the divine will, but is free to obey or disobey its oughts. To moral man, the divine will presents only the normativeness of an imperative to which he may or may not respond affirmatively and obediently.

If, therefore, man acquiesces in the truth of God's existence, of His ultimate reality, of His absolute unity and transcendence, he would necessarily become a man *possessed*. For the reality of God impinges upon everything outside as well as inside of him, upon every object and event, not only as its cause but also as its end, its purpose and norm. Microcosm and macrocosm are effects of God's causality; their ideal ought-to-be's are contents of His commandments and will. Naturally, a man possessed by such a being as God is forever aware of His creativity, of His efficiency, of His will and of His purpose, of His judgement and ultimate disposition of all that is. The Muslim is indeed such a person, whose consciousness is dominated by this sublime idea. This is why "Allah" is always on his lips as he invokes His help and blessing, in his ears as others invoke Him and call one another to His worship and service; in front of his eyes as he beholds the minaret-dotted skyline of his town, the building façade facing him, the carpet under or the ceiling above him, or the book or utensil in his hand which he has covered with calligraphy honouring His holy, most beautiful names.

4 The view of truth

The Muslim is a person conscious of his capacity to know the truth. Islam has taught him that God has endowed him with his senses, his understanding, memory and reason; and he is conscious of them as faculties of knowledge whose reports are trustworthy.[12] Experience has shown him that when his senses err, his rational faculty corrects the error; and when his imagination soars, his reason and senses collaborate to keep his feet on the ground. His standpoint is not that of scepticism, but one of certainty and conviction arising from a free and critical application of his faculties to the data at hand.

This position of the Muslim on the question of the possibility of human knowledge makes of him a free spirit and a free seeker. He acquiesces to the truth only if he is convinced of it.

"Truth is now manifest from error, Whoever wishes to believe, let him do so. It will be to his credit. Whoever wishes not to believe, let him do so. It will be to his discredit."[13]

This proclamation by Islam tore down previous superstitions as well as the authority of priesthood. There is no church and no church magisterium to tell him what to believe, what to take as true and false. The venerated traditions of the ancestors have no value unless they are true to fact.[14] Repeatedly, Islam made its appeal to his reason; it invited him to make full use of his critical faculties.[15] It has sought to keep him free from dogmatism, superstition, from every form of irrationalism. It never asked him to acknowledge as true that which contradicts reason, that which overwhelms his cognitive faculties like an immense, incomprehensible stumbling block. Whatever he wishes to regard as true, whatever argument he wishes to accept as rational and convincing, is his own decision. However, the Qur'an declared him and his faculties responsible for the outcome.[16]

Following this breakthrough, Muslims became the greatest advocates of rationalism, of a policy of openness toward knowledge and wisdom from whatever source, by whatever carrier. They felt justified by the Qur'an's elevation of the men of knowledge to the highest rank;[17] and by its utilization of the similes of light and darkness, of sight and blindness to describe knowledge and its absence.[18] The Prophet's commendation of the scholars' ink as equal to the blood of martyrs, his commandment to seek knowledge from the cradle to the grave and to travel for its pursuit any distance however long, launched the Muslims on the world theatre as the most avid knowledge-seekers, the most fastidious students the world had known. It caused them to cherish knowledge whatever the knower's religious conviction. They honoured non-Muslims for their knowledge and wisdom, and paid them for their manuscripts with bags of gold and jewels. Caliphs and commoners alike sat at their feet to listen and to learn. The company of the men of knowledge was the object of the strongest competition among the rulers and the rich, the professionals and tradesmen, cities and villages, royal courts and inns, mosques and schools.

Behind this triumphalism in knowledge on the part of the Muslims stands the religious experience of Islam wherein God is recognized as the Truth,[19] and hence, as He with Whom the truth can never be contradictory. The will of God can be misunderstood but never permanently, because examination can only corroborate the truth. Reason can equally err, but only to be corrected by more, deeper, reasoning. This equivalence extends to revelation, giving it firm foundation in knowledge. For this reason, revelation of the Qur'an, became public, memorized and recited as well as analyzed and scrutinized by everyone. Everyone examined its meanings and diction, its syntax and grammar, the historical contexts to which each of its verses was addressed. The Qur'an's criticism of the other religions, especially Judaism and Christianity,[20] spurred the Muslims to become the first comparativists; and in its telling of previous prophets, to become the first historians of religion. All this happened not in the exclusive ivory tower of the academician, but in the market places everywhere. Islam gave its adherent a full "liberal arts" education, and made him an expert in religion, not merely as a system of beliefs and rituals, but as a science, the queen of the humanities' disciplines.

The principle of *tawhid*, or the unization of God, the recognition of Him as one, absolute and transcendent, is also at the centre of the Muslim's curiosity regarding nature. Islam taught its adherent that God created nature and implanted therein its laws and ends.[21] It commanded him to discover these in order to enable him to enjoy nature as God has entitled him to do. For nature is all subservient to man. Therefore, the sciences of nature became the Muslim's second preoccupation. Everybody who could, did participate, whether in the search or in contemplating and putting to use the secrets of nature which enquiry disclosed and established. Everything in creation was the object of this scientific quest: the realms of nature (astronomy, geometry, mathematics, the health disciplines, zoology and botany, chemistry, physics and geography; the realms of the self (psychology, philosophy, religion, personal ethics); and, finally, the realm of society (law and jurisprudence, politics and economics, sociology and history).

When some Muslims, over-excited by Islam's affirmation of reason and knowledge, raised reason above revelation and sought to give it dominion over all knowledge, the majority's answer was not one of total repudiation of the claim, but the elaboration of a critical epistemology wherein reason and revelation being equivalent, no contradiction or disparity between them could be ultimate.[22] The net result of this critical stance was to push even higher the Muslim's quest for the meaning of revelation and of empirical nature. The more he researched, the more variation, difference or discrepancy he discovered, and hence, the more research he had to do to fill in the gaps. All this amounted to making the Muslim a person for whom the truth is God, and the quest of the truth in all things, an act of worship. His Muslim peers paid respect and admiration to him in proportion to his piety which is tantamount to wisdom and reasonableness.[23]

5 The view of man

Man, Islam teaches, is God's creature and His vicegerent on earth. To the angels' question, Why would you place on earth a creature capable of evil? God answered that He had indeed a purpose unknown to the angels who cannot but obey God.[24] This divine purpose or truth, rhetorically offered to mountains, earth and heaven but to be refused, was accepted by man because it was his *raison d' être*.[25] It consists in fulfilling the moral part of the divine will, a part whose fulfilment requires that the subject be free to fulfill as well as to violate it. For only if his deeds are free in this sense do they constitute fulfilment of the moral. Where the deed is unconscious, the fulfilment may be utilitarian but not moral; where it is coerced, it is immoral despite its utilitarian value. The moral part of the divine will is the higher, i.e., the more desirable and imperative. For its sake the other parts, namely the elemental values of utility and instrumentality which include the very existence of creation itself, were created. The axiological hierarchy is not complete without the moral which serves as its end and capstone.

Being alone capable of moral action, man is indeed God's *chef d'oeuvre*.[26] Higher than the angels,[27] he is the only being through whose action the highest part of the divine will may be actualized and become history.[28] Evidently, he is a cosmic being whose significance is very great, precisely on account of this possibility. Naturally, in creating him for this purpose. God has equipped him with all the faculties and prerequisites necessary for this function and destiny. He has given him eyes with which to see, tongue and lips with which to speak and communicate; ears with which to hear, arms and limbs with which to act, to move and to effect change.[29] He has given him understanding and reason with which to discover and grasp the secrets (laws) of nature,[30] a memory and reading, writing and eloquence[31] with which to accumulate and multiply experiences and wisdom.[32] He placed him on an earth where things are always malleable, i.e., capable of undergoing man's action, and of transformation in causal consequence of such action.[33] To top it all, God has directly disclosed His will to man through revelation. He "taught" it to Adam.[34] Subsequently, He revealed it to His prophets – the known (Abraham, Moses, Jesus, etc.) and to many others about whom little or nothing is known (Lippit Ishtar, Sargon, Hammurabi, etc.).[35] To all these, God revealed His will in prescriptive form, ready for fulfilment through human obedience. Many a time the revelation was tampered with to serve the desires and passions of men, necessitating a repetition of the divine favour. Finally, in the prophethood of Muhammad, He caused the revelation to be forever incorruptible and to be preserved forever with its words and letters,[36] the linguistic apparatus of grammar, syntax, lexicography and *balaghah*, as well as the categories of understanding embedded in the language and inseparable therefrom, so that henceforth, no hermeneutical difficulty would stand in the way of anyone's achieving an understanding of the revelation identical to that of those who heard it fresh from the mouth of the Prophet fourteen centuries ago. The only condition is for that person to learn the Arabic language.

The revelation is a statement of all the values of life. It contains the hierarchy of values and the principles of their identification, of their relation or hierarchization, and of their deontological relevance to humans. The first principles of religion, of personal and social ethics, of metaphysics and knowledge, of human history and destiny, were revealed in the Qur'an and thus are to stand and be understood in their verbatim form forever. Some constitutive prescriptions of personal, societal and international ethics were also revealed in permanent form, and are hence to be observed perpetually as their verbatim form indicates. In other fields, the revelation was silent, or no prescriptive form was given, thus giving man the freedom to figurize in conformity with changing times and conditions.

With such preparation for his cosmic task, man has no excuse for violating the divine imperatives. His theatre – the world –, and he – its central player –, are jointly established precisely for the end of fulfilling the divine purpose.[37] Indeed, God had pre-emptively implanted in man the love of the good, of the values which are the constituents of the divine will. Man is thus predisposed by nature toward such fulfilment. And, to complete the picture, God has equipped man with a unique faculty, the *sensus numinis*, with which all humans may acknowledge God as God, and recognize His commandments as the norms or ought-to-bes of all that is.[38] To know as well as to obey the divine commandment is therefore second nature to man; to misinterpret, flout or violate it, is unnatural though possible. It is committed only where human ulterior motive or passion has corrupted the natural mechanism.

Certainly this creature of God called man is innocent. Islam lays out the drama of human destiny on earth after man's birth, not before. No matter who his parents and ancestors were, his uncles and ancestors, his brothers or sisters, his neighbours or society, man is born innocent. Islam repudiates every notion of original sin, or hereditary guilt, or vicarious responsibility, of tribal or national involvement of the person in past events before his birth. Every man is born with a clean slate; his autonomy and individuality as a person being absolute. "No soul will bear but its own burden," Allah affirmed in His holy Book.[39] Islam defines man's responsibility exclusively in terms of his own personal deeds entered into consciously and voluntarily. Rather than vitiated by original sin, man has been favoured with too many favours, too many preparations designed to make his task easy, his progress towards the ultimate goal possible as well as momentous. Nothing could be farther from the truth than the claim that he is "fallen", "sinful", necessarily suffering from an evil predicament from which there is no escape but with external help. That he is liable to make mistakes of perception and judgement, to incline to egotistic satisfaction and self-centredness, to prefer the lesser value over the greater, the nearer or selfish advantage over the farther or altruistic, indeed to aggress and commit injustice – are platitudes, obviously true of most humans. But none is necessary; none is so embedded in human nature as to make its avoidance impossible. Indeed, granted their reality, they are precisely the stuff which man is to combat and surmount in his moral struggle. Had they been logically necessary, morality itself would lose its meaning and all its injunctions would fall to the ground. Indeed, to claim that man is "fallen" as the doctrine of original sin proclaims, is to impute to God the incapacity of creating a creature capable of fulfilling His own will, or the mediocrity of winning a battle against a strawman of His own creation.[40]

In equal measure, nothing could be farther from the truth than the claim that human salvation is a *fait accompli*, accomplished once and for all by the divine events of incarnation-crucifixion-resurrection, as saviourist Christianity proclaims. Ontological saviourism is bound to a theory of man in which humans lost their pristine natural felicity and regained it through the divine salvific event professed by Christian dogma. The saved person is alleged to be ontologically different from the non-saved. A lost and found *imago dei* is supposed to distinguish the Christian ontologically from the rest of mankind. He is only one step removed from the thesis of racism which assigns value to men on the basis of ontology, of their being what they are, not of their doing what they do. That is why saviourist Christianity regards morality as flowing *out of* faith not *into* faith, and regards man's vocation on earth as consisting primarily, if not entirely, of thanksgiving for what had already taken place, and of proclamation of the news of salvation which had taken place. The whole career of man on earth is robbed of its achievement-meaning because the ideal has already been achieved and all that needs to be done has already been done.[41]

Wherever it is taken ontologically, such a view of salvation as a *fait accompli* destroys morality and religion. The only reasonable view of Jesus' accomplishment is that he was a prophet of God, sent by Him to convey a divine message, to disclose an option, a road, for felicity which man has yet to resolve and undertake. This view departs from traditional Christianity which holds the advent of Jesus to have been an event which happened to God, i.e., a divine self-disclosure in the phenomenon of Jesus Christ. Rather, it asserts that that revelation was no more than a divine lesson conveyed, thus reducing the role of Jesus from that of an incarnated divinity to that of a human prophet, teaching a message from His Lord and Master. This line of logical thinking repudiates the dogma of Catholic Christianity with its "scandalons" of incarnation, trinity, and redemption through crucifixion and resurrection. These two views are contraries; they cannot be held together. To hold them both at the same time, despite their contradictory nature, appeals only to minds habituated to flouting the laws of thought.

This is all diametrically opposed by Islam which sees man's career, as it were, still before him, laid out for every individual after his birth, not before. Man's worth, and hence his overall merit and salvation, Islam views as functions of his own personal deeds. "Nothing," the Qur'an asserts, "will be charged to any soul except what that soul itself has wrought."[42] Thanksgiving for our creation and planting on earth, for all the perfections, all the gifts and providing and, above all, for the revelation of the law – the true path to felicity – is certainly incumbent upon the Muslim. His deep-felt gratitude to God is expressed a hundred and one times a day in the ubiquitous refrain *"Al hamdu lillah!"* But his felicity or "salvation" depends not on what has been done, but what he yet may, can, should, and will do.

This is why *'ibadah* or worship in Islam is not a "celebration", a "Eucharist". It includes but is never exhausted by, the ritual acts of *salat, zakah, siyam* and *hajj* (ritual prayer, wealth-sharing, fasting and pilgrimage). Beyond these minima, *'ibadah* is "service" in the sense of tilling the soil, bringing up and educating children, organizing and mobilizing mankind to the end of making creation and history a voluntary concretization of moral values constitutive of the divine will. Man's career on earth is service to God, service in His manor (the earth) as the ancient Mesopotamians used to say. It is the reconstruction of the planet earth,[43] the making of culture and civilization, bringing about children as well as their happiness and prosperity. Islam sees ethical value not as indifferent or opposed to the processes of life on earth, but as their very affirmation and promotion under the moral law.

6 The view of nature

Hindu cosmology regards nature as an unfortunate event that happened to Brahman, the Absolute.[44] Creation (i.e., every individual creature) is an objectification of it (the Absolute) that should not have taken place because it is a degradation of its perfection as absolute. Everything in nature is hence regarded as aberration, as something encaged in its creaturely form, pining for release and return to its origin in and as Brahman. While it continues as a creature in the world, it is subject to the Law of Karma through which it is upgraded, or further degraded, according to whether it acknowledges and complies with this first cosmological principle, namely, that it is merely an ontological mishap of the Absolute.[45] Christian cosmology regards nature as the creation of God which was once perfect, but which was corrupted in the "fall" and hence became evil.[46] The evil of creation, ontological, essential and pervasive, is the reason for God's salvific drama, of His own self-incarnation in Jesus, of His crucifixion and death. After the drama, Christianity holds, restoration has and has not come to creation, theoretically. Practically, the Christian mind continued to hold creation as fallen, and nature as evil. The great enmity to matter which characterized gnosticism passed on to Christianity and reinforced its contempt and antagonism for nature and "the world" so avidly pursued on every level by Christianity's first enemies – the Romans. Nature, with its material potentialities and propensities, was the realm of Satan. On the material level, its momentum is the pull away from "the other world" to "the flesh", to "sin". On the social level, it is the temptation to politics, to will power and self-assertion, to "Caesar." Programmatism – the will to order the movement of history towards transformation of nature – is by Christian definition vain.[47] For a millennium or more, "nature" was contrasted with "grace" as its opposite. Both were treated as mutually exclusive; pursuit of the one was necessarily violation of the other. Under the impact of Islamic thought first, and later of the Renaissance, of scholasticism and the Enlightenment, Christians opened themselves to life- and world-affirmation. World denial and condemnation, however, was never eradicated but only muted. In more recent times, with the triumph of romanticism and secularism following the French Revolution, "naturalism" came to occupy and sometimes dominate the Christian's attitude to nature and the world.

In Islam, nature is creation and gift. As creation it is teleological, perfect and orderly; as gift it is an innocent good placed at the disposal of man. Its purpose is to enable man to do the good and achieve felicity. This treble judgement of orderliness, purposefulness and goodness characterizes and sums up the Islamic view of nature.

The order of nature

God has created everything in nature perfect.[48] He has fashioned each creature and given it an essence, a structure which determines its life and from which it never deviates.[49] He has built into it a propensity that never fails to move it in the direction of self-fulfilment.[50] He has placed every creature within the general nexus of nature so that its birth, its whole life and its death, all happen according to patterns which are themselves constituents of the divine will.[51] To every creature He has ordained a career to which its existence is forever subject.[52] He has adequately provided for it the measure it needs to fulfil its destiny. There is no gap in nature. No object or event in nature is an accident. Everything that is or happens does so because of predictable causes and with predictable consequences. These may or may never be known, but they exist and their real relation to the real thing or event is real. That is why nature is a real cosmos, not a chaos where events never take place with cause, or sometimes with, and sometimes without, cause. As the Qur'an put it so eloquently:

"Look and look into nature! Will you see any discrepancy? Look again and again! Your searching eye will return to you convinced that there is none, humbled by its failure to find what it set itself out to discover."[53]

That nature is orderly means that it is causal; i.e., that natural events happen as consequences of causes, and that they in turn act as causes producing further consequences. Cosmic order is indeed causal regularity. But is it necessity? The Greek and the majority of Muslim and Western philosophers thought it was. They conceived of the causal sequence as necessary, constraining all, including God Who, they thought, was incapable but of following the causal sequence.[54] This they did regardless of whether they were realists – assuming causality to pertain ontologically to real things; or idealists – holding that it is merely a category of human perception of things. In either case, they deemed it impossible to have nature under any other terms. Beyond their epistemological concern stood an existential, metaphysical concern that, should the case be otherwise, scientific knowledge as well as ordinary life would be impossible.

As the modern empiricist tradition of thought has demonstrated, the scientific exploration of nature may well continue without such assumption.[55] It is true that the researching scientist working in his laboratory assumes causality to be necessary in all cases. But his assumption is regulative rather than constitutive. He has no categorical proof that effects do in fact come from their causes. All he knows is that past instances of a certain effect did follow upon their causes. Assuming that a cause is to be discovered for the effect, he makes it his duty and objective to establish such cause and its relation to its effect. His assumption is therefore regulative in the sense that it calls for and sustains the search, and is impervious to the ultimate factuality or otherwise of the cause-effect relationship. Ultimate factuality is not proven by science which is happy to operate with probability instead. Modern science has repudiated the dogmatism of nineteenth-century scientists and theoreticians who believed in a causality that is as ontological as it is absolute. In this century, science has come of age, is far more sober and modest in its claim. George Santayana has called the scientist's assumption of the law of causality "animal faith", a habit of mind to which man grows conditioned with experience.[56]

The same immodesty has characterized a few Muslim philosopher-scientists; but these were put in their place as early as the eleventh century AC by the great al Ghazali.[57] His argument anticipated David Hume's by nearly a millennium, and restored to Muslim thought the sanity taught by Islam.[58]

Islam teaches that nature is indeed orderly, but that its orderliness is God-given and God-sustained. There is good reason why God made nature orderly. Since God has laid down on us the obligation to act morally, and moral action implies intervention into the causal processes of nature and the deflection of their flow to pre-conceived ends, it would be impossible on the part of man to fulfil this moral purpose of God without the provision of effects and their assumption as targets of action – which only an orderly cosmos can make possible. Both an orderly nature and the scientific knowledge of it are necessary for morality. Had nature not been orderly, that is, were it a realm where causes do not produce effects and effects do not follow upon their causes, this world would be a "ship for fools" where morality is not possible. Such creation would be a cruel and senseless act on the part of a malevolent deity. God, however, is most beneficent, just and merciful. He created us and charged us with a mission – fulfilment of His commandments – that we may succeed.[59] Our success in our mission is actualization of value, of moral value which is nothing but the will of God Himself. That is why God placed us in a theatre – malleable nature – where moral action is possible, i.e., where prevision of effects and production of their causes are possible.[60] For this not to be the case is to put the divine will in contradiction with itself, or to charge it with malevolence and cynicism.

How then did the illusion arise that the world is causal, but necessarily so; orderly, but blind? Causal regularity does indeed seem to be the inexorable law of nature. A thousand years ago, al Ghazali suggested a solution which is still valid today. Nearly all the causal sequences of nature, he argued, do not prove one necessary cause. All they do prove is that in the normal course of events, E, the "effect", does follow after C, the "cause". A thousand and one such followings prove only the fact of following, not causation by the cause. As he put it, "following after" proves neither "following from" nor "following by". It only proves itself, namely, "following after".[61] We simply assume that causes will produce their effects. In reality, we have grown accustomed to expect the effect when the cause is present, an expectation whose basis is trust, an attitude, not certain knowledge. Such trusts rest on our faith that the beneficent deity will make causes produce their effects; that He will make them do so at every point of space-time because He is beneficent and rational, willing our existence, growth and prosperity, and commanding us to act morally. Therefore, our consciousness of morality, and hence, its first principle, namely, God, is the only cause of causality, the order of nature being only the effect of His will. Obviously, God, the transcendent Creator, is not bound by it. Obviously, He can, if He desired, alter, suspend or annul it altogether. On the other hand, if God were not omnipotent, if He did not stand outside of space, time and causality and was not their very Creator, He would not be God.

The teleology of nature

The order of nature is not merely the material order of causes and effects, the order which space and time and other such theoretical categories make evident to our understanding. Nature is equally a realm of ends where everything fulfills a purpose and thereby contributes to the prosperity and balance of all. From the inanimate little pebble in the valley, the smallest plankton on the surface of the ocean, the microbial flagellate in the intestine of the woodroach, to the galaxies and their suns, the giant redwoods and whales and elephants – everything in existence, by its genesis and growth, its life and death, fulfils a purpose assigned to it by God, which is necessary for other beings. All creatures are interdependent, and the whole of creation runs because of the perfect harmony which exists between its parts. "To everything," God says in the Qur'an, "We have given a measure proper to it."[62] This is the ecological balance which contemporary pollution of nature has brought to the consciousness of modern man with alarming threat. The Muslim has been aware of it for centuries, and has seen himself as standing within it. For he is as much a part of it as any other creature.

That each element of creation feeds on another and is fed upon by a third is certainly a nexus of ends, perhaps the most obvious among the higher creatures. The dominion of the same nexus over the unseen world of algae, microbes and enzymes is harder to observe, to establish and to imagine in all its reaches. But it is no less real. Still more difficult to discover than the feeding patterns of vegetal and animal life are the chains of interdependence in the very activities of all creatures, activities other than feeding whether or not connected with it, in the continuous action and reaction of the elements on one another whether in the earth, in the waters, in the air and among the bodies of outer space. Our knowledge of the intricacies of nature's ecology is still at an infant stage. The sciences of nature have revealed enough of it for our imagination to construct the system as a whole.

As a teleological system, the world presents us with a sublime spectacle. The size and comprehensiveness of the macrocosm, the delicate minutiae of the microcosm, as well as the infinitely complex and perfect nature of the mechanisms of the balance, are overwhelming and fascinating. The mind is literally "humbled", as the Qur'an says, before it; but it is the humbling of love and admiration, of appreciation and value-apprehension. For the world as the purposeful creation of the Almighty is beautiful, indeed sublime, precisely on account of its teleology. The exclamation of the poet, "How wonderful is the rose! In it is visible the Face of God!" has no sense other than this, that the rose serves the purposes of man and insects by its fragrance and visible beauty, purposes which have been endowed to it by God and which it renders to perfection, reflecting, to those with the eye to see, the glorious efficacy and sublime workmanship of the purposive Designer and Creator – God.

Nature as divine manor

So much for the metaphysical arm of Islamic doctrine. The other arm is the ethical. Islam teaches that nature was created as a theatre for man, a "field" in which to grow and prosper, to enjoy God's bounty and in doing so to prove oneself ethically worthy. Firstly, nature is not man's property but God's.[63] Man was granted his tenure therein by God and to the end prescribed by Him. Like a good land-tenant, man ought to take care of his Master's property. The right of usufruct which man certainly holds does not entitle him to destroy nature, or to so exploit it as to upset and ruin its ecological balance. The right of usufruct which is all he possesses is an individual right which God renews with every individual at his birth. It is neither vicarious nor hereditary, and hence, does not entitle man to pre-empt the future of others' enjoyment of it. As steward of the earth – indeed of creation – man is supposed at death to hand over his trust to God in a better state than when he received it.

Second, the order of nature is subject to man, who can bring to it such changes as he wills. Nature has been created malleable, capable of receiving man's intervention into its processes, of suffering deflection of its causal nexus by his deeds. No realm or area of nature is out-of-bounds. The firmament with its suns, moons and stars, the earth and the seas with all that they contain are his to explore and to use, for utility, for pleasure and comfort or for contemplation. All creation is *for* man and awaits his usufruct of it. Its disposal is utterly at his discretion. His judgement is the only efficacious instrument of intervention, the only arbiter. But nothing relieves him of responsibility for the whole of creation.

Third, in his usufruct and enjoyment of nature, man is enjoined to act morally. Theft and cheating, coercion and monopoly, hoarding and exploitation, egotism and insensitivity to the needs of others, are unworthy of him as God's vicegerent and strictly forbidden.[64] Islam also frowns upon extravagance and forbids wasteful and ostentatious consumption.[65] Islamic culture is incompatible with any of these. Not poverty or want, but contentment is what the refined Muslim ought to have and show, expressing his satisfaction with what God has provided.[66]

Fourth, Islam demands of man to search for and understand the patterns of God in nature, not merely those which constitute the natural sciences, but equally those which constitute nature's general order and beauty. The fact that nature is God's handiwork, His plan and design, the actualization of His will casts upon it a halo of dignity. It must not be abused or raped or exploited, though it is subject to the usufruct of men. Sensitivity to nature and tender care given to it as garden or forest, river or mountain, is attunement with the divine purpose.

7 The view of society and history

In Islam, society is neither an evil nor a happenstance, nor an inevitable growth of nature in satisfaction of basic material needs. These are respectively the views of Christianity, Indian religions and utilitarian-ism. The Islamic view of society differs from those of the first two which deprecate the social aspect of life by assigning all ethical value to the subjective-personal aspect exclusively. The Islamic view differs from the third, where society is said to have evolved out of the need for exchange of economic goods, for collective services such as defence, transportation, etc. It affirms society as the realm for actualization of the highest ethical values; and it regards societal action as such, as embodiment of a higher order of moral existence. The Islamic view is also different from those theories which regard the social order as the creation of heroes, kings and princes, an outgrowth of their courts and entourage, or as an accidental outgrowth of the family, clan, tribe or village, which came to exist naturally and without pre-planning; but once it developed, it provided such advantages as made it worthy and/or necessary in the eyes of its beneficiaries.

Islam views society as a divinely ordained institution, a pattern of God, as necessary for man's fulfilment of the purpose of his creation as nature.[67] First, society is necessary for knowledge. Without consultation, criticism and validation by other humans, all claims to the truth are suspect. All knowledge must be tested against evidence, and would be more trustworthy the larger and more varied the evidence, the other views, against which it is rubbed.[68] The principle of *shura* (consultation, dialogue and argument) is declared by the Qur'an the method of felicity and is buttressed by the prescription of collective pursuit of knowledge.[69] Jurisprudence added the principle of consensus (*ijma'*) as a practical check upon the creative flight of the individual, as well as a confirmation of the creative breakthrough achieved by the individual.[70] Every person is entitled to reinterpret, re-understand, re-crystallize the truth; but it is his duty to convince his peers of the validity of his findings. The right to creativity (*ijtihad* in its general sense) belongs to all; the duty to follow it up with *shura* until consensus is reached, makes exercise of that right responsible and beneficial.[71]

Second, society is necessary for morality. Ethical values require the existence of others, interaction with them, and conditions under which there are needs to which the moral subject responds if ethical action is to take place. It is impossible for love, charity, justice and sacrifice, for example, to be realized unless there are other humans to be loved, to be charitable and just to, to assist and rescue through sacrifice. It is necessary for such others to be in interaction with oneself, for it is hard to imagine how one can act ethically all alone, or toward an "other" that is not real, that exists hypothetically on the other side of the moon.[72] The necessity of society for morality stems, in addition, from another consideration which separates the Islamic ethic radically from that of Christianity, of Buddhism, or of Upanishadic Hinduism. That is the fact that all these religions profess an ethic of intention, whereas Islamic morality is essentially an ethic of action. The former built their personalist ethic on a subjective foundation. They defined the moral good in terms of determinants of the subject's state of consciousness and will alone, declaring effects and consequences in space-time irrelevant to the moral value of the ethical deed. Islam built its societist ethic on an actional basis; and defined the moral good in terms of both the subjective determinants as well as the spatio-temporal consequences. The Islamic ethic does not deny the ethical value of the good intention; but it regards that value incomplete and inadequate to constitute morality. The Qur'an's emphasis on action can hardly be overemphasized. Interference in the processes of space and time, and the successful diversion of these processes toward the actualization of ethical values which the consciousness has set up as goals and objectives, is demanded by Islam. In consequence of this prescription, the Muslims have respected but avoided the ascetic withdrawal and monkery of Christianity[73] and the Indian religions, and plunged themselves into the rough and tumble of the market place, of tribe, village and city, of war, peace and international order.

Third, society is necessary for history. Judaism and Christianity grew and developed in history in situations of weakness and persecution, over protracted durations of centuries. This weakness in their formative period so impressed itself upon the minds of Jews and Christians that it determined the very nature of their faiths. It is primarily responsible for making Judaism and Christianity essentially religions of messianism and redemption; i.e., religions offering a hope for better things – whether eschatological or realized in internalist subjectivity, or both at once – in face of the desperate hopelessness of the real present. The state of exile, of homes and country shattered, of men and women a-whoring after other gods and tyrannizing over one another, of a decaying Roman imperium bent on the pursuit of power, and a corrupt society caring for little more than *panem et circences* – all these facts repulsed the conscience and turned men away from the world. It was a violent reaction to an extreme situation. World-denial, mistrust of the human self, condemnation of nature within as flesh, of nature without as sin and mammon, of the process of history as doomed never to realize the absolute, were the result of this pessimism. The "Kingdom of God" was understood as alternative to this kindgom, the former as absolutely good and the latter as absolutely evil. Man looked forward to it as bringing cessation to the misery of the present. The Day of Judgement was interpreted as the cataclysmic passage from one to the other. Life and history under this scheme could have little value besides that of bridge, or transient passage, to the other side.

Islam, on the other hand, also suffered persecution in Mecca; but it migrated to Medina where it relieved itself of Meccan oppression and developed itself outside of its influence. Moreover, only eight years passed since that emigration, when Islam – fully grown and all its institutions fully developed – returned to Mecca to conquer it and move ever forward in the world. Islam was not determined by its wordly success; but its worldly success helped free it from determination by Meccan persecution. Its theory of society and of history flow from its theory of man and of creation which equally flow from its conception of the nature of God.

Islam conceives of God's purpose of creation as the realization of His will, the highest part of which is the moral. It conceives of the morally imperative as fulfilment of all the potentialities of creation – the natural and the ethical – by human free choice, decision and action. The morally imperative is indeed possible of realization; otherwise human existence would be the tragic game of a trickster-god, not the purposive creation of the benevolent, beneficent God Islam recognizes. Therefore, history and its processes are the theatre for the morally imperative. Involvement in them is the meaning of normativeness; actualization in history of the ought-to-be of value is the objective of human existence on earth.

That is why Islam does not countenance any separation of religion and state. The state is society's political arm which, like society itself, is meant to bring about the realization of the absolute in history. Between the state proper, society with its other organs and institutions, and man as person, there is only a division of labour, a distinction as to function. All are subject to the same purpose and goal. The transitiveness of man's actions demands a public law to regulate it. It cannot be satisfied with the verdict of conscience. That is why Islam had to develop the *sharia*, a public law governing the personal as well as the societal fields of action. That is why Islam must be relevant to the economic, social, political and international realms, as surely as it is relevant to the subjective realm where conscience alone rules supreme.

This is why the Muslims could not allow history to be directed by chance, or by Caesar, as evil principle. That is why they hurled themselves on its stage from the very beginning, as it were, seizing history by the horns and directing it towards realization of the purposes of morality. That is why 'Umar ibn al Khattab recognized in the emigration of the Prophet from Mecca to Medina the axial moment from which Islamic history was to be reckoned. It was indeed the very beginning and launching of that history.

To live as a member of the society Islam seeks to create is to do so in an open brotherhood where every member is equal – except in righteous achievement. In this field, Islam invites all humans to compete and prove their moral worth. The arena is open to all mankind. Within it, all of them are equal until they have distinguished themselves from one another in deeds. Their lives are subject to no arbitrary authority, the ultimate and supreme criterion being the law of God. The nature of political authority is executive, the caliph or chief of state, his ministers and all their employees are workers hired to implement the divine law. Both the executives (as subjects) and the citizens (as objects of law-implementation) shared under the authority of the jurists in interpretation of the law. It is the jurists who spend their lives in its study, analysis and elaboration that know it best. They are the ones to determine the questions of spirit versus letter of the law, and to extrapolate the law to items and cases not envisaged by it originally. Even when they are appointed by the Executive as judges, their loyalty is to the law. Their dispensation of justice is absolutely free, available to any citizen who wishes to have recourse to them without cost. "Free justice" constitutes no threat to the judiciary in the Islamic state because the appellant who loses his case must compensate the defendant for wasting his time, and could in case of charges involving the defendant's integrity, be fined and punished. On the other hand, the least citizen, if offended by the greatest ruler, can obtain justice without cost or hindrance. The citizen of the Islamic state, therefore, is confident that his right will not be violated or usurped, however mighty the violator may be. As Abu Bakr al Siddiq (RAA) said in his inaugural address: "The weak among you will be mighty in my eye until I obtain for him his right from the mighty; and the mighty among you will be weak in my eye until I have obtained from him the right of the weak."

The cement which holds Islamic society together which God called "*Al 'urwah al wuthqa*" is mutual love and affection. Every citizen is a "pilgrim" on that road of achievement through obedience to God and fulfilment of His law. The pilgrim-to-pilgrim relationship is one of reciprocal affection, of mutual protection and support, of education and persuasion. Since the moral act must be the deliberate decision of the doer and the result of the free exercise of his faculties of decision and arms of action, if it is to be moral at all, all that the Muslim can do for his fellow citizen is to educate, convince and persuade. He may not coerce; for coercion destroys the ethical character of the deed. Should the neighbour's welfare require coercive action, the action is devoid of morality though it may be necessary from a utilitarian view. This consideration makes of the Islamic state a college on a very grand scale, a college for ethical endeavour and felicity where every person is at once a student and a teacher. To be a citizen of the Islamic state is hence to go through life as a perpetual pupil and perpetual leader.

8 The view of beauty

Certainly no culture has ever put as high a premium on the aesthetic experience as Islam has done. Unlike those cultures which regard beauty as a luxury, an intrinsic value to be apprehended for its own sake, the culture of Islam regards beauty as the value on which hangs the whole validity of Islam itself. To the question, "What is the ultimate proof that the Qur'an, the revelation which supports and embodies Islam, is indeed a revelation from God and not a human and hence relative achievement?", the answer throughout the ages has been – the sublime beauty of the Qur'an. There is nothing higher than the Qur'an in authority except God Himself, its Source and Author. In fact, the Qur'an is God's presence on earth *in percipi*, i.e., inasmuch as the divine presence can become the object of human knowledge. The Qur'an is the expression of God's knowledge and wisdom, of His guidance and beneficence, of His will and commandment. The argument for its truthfulness and genuineness is the argument for its divine provenance. And the final base on which that very argument rests is its sublime character, the kind of *fascinosum* beauty proper to divinity. The aesthetic experience must therefore be extremely important and extraordinarily powerful for it to constitute *the* base for divine revelation and authority.

Compared with Islam on this matter, all the religions of mankind fall on the other side, and Islam remains absolutely without parallel. In most of them, the aesthetic phenomenon has no bearing at all upon the constitution or formation of the religion. It came centuries after the religion had been complete and established. If a religion had anything to say about the ruling aesthetic at the time of its formation, it was to condemn it as integral to the old religion it combated or came to replace. A case in point is that of Christianity. Once Hellenized and established as a religion, it hurled devastating attacks against the aesthetic life of classical antiquity. The fury of the Christian attack upon Rome and Athens stemmed from indignation at the Roman's aesthetic enjoyment of nature, of sex, of sport and adventure, of luxury, of grandeur in architectural beauty and urban planning, of the spectacular in parade and arena. Centuries later, Christianity began to develop a taste for icons – its first aesthetic experience, promoted largely by the iconoclast controversy in the eighth century. Through the transvaluation of the Renaissance, Christianity began to adopt the very aesthetic of Greco-Roman naturalism which it combated a millennium earlier. Throughout Christian history, the aesthetic element remained an instrument, useful as an illustration of Christian meaning, but nonetheless dispensible. Even a Caesar Borgia, who patronized the arts more than any other Christian, would never agree to assign to the aesthetic a constitutive place or function in Christianity. Because of that history, Christian thought has so far defined Christianness in beauty as being the creation of a Christian, as being used by a Christian, or as belonging historically to Christians, or serving to illustrate a Christian representation. In no case has Christian thought advanced beyond these positions to give beauty a constitutive role in the religion itself.

The case of India is simpler because art has consistently remained a tool of religious consciousness, often extravagant and varied in kind (music, sculpture, dancing, architecture, poetry), but nonetheless accidental and superfluous. The essential nature of Indian artistic creativity is figurative illustration of religious truth. It has remained Byzantine, iconic, giving less to aesthetic intuition than to discursive understanding. It conveyed its message primarily through plastic figures and movements whose role was that of logical symbols. This was especially true where the figures were alive and mobile, as in temple dancing. Indian art has not moved beyond this position. The idealization of nature, and the representation of a sublime supernatural reality in nature – the forte of European Renaissance art – was not and continues not to be the concern of Indian religious consciousness.

Artistic production among the Indians may well have been regarded as religiously meritorious; and it is certain that at times the activity itself was regarded as an act of worship. The religious audience was grateful to the artist who succeeded in expressing religious truth through aesthetic works. All this notwithstanding, the category of beauty remains a dispensible addition, not a *sine qua non* to the whole religious edifice. To the question, Why has Brahman become objectified in time and space? the Indian mind provides no answer. This is not due to any inconsequence at all, but to the fact that in the Indian perspective the objectification of the Absolute is an aberration, an aesthetic *untergang*. The revelation of this objectification (i.e., the realization of the truth that all is Brahman) cannot be aesthetically pleasing, *a fortiori*. Hence, all aesthetic experience is to be lifted out of creation and concentrated on the Absolute. Thus, beholding the Absolute through the mystical exercise becomes the highest aesthetic experience. Creation, on the other hand, is left empty, sometimes capable of reflecting a broken form of Brahman, and on that account nearly always morose and tragic even in its most joyful moment. Therefore the most beautiful object can only fulfill the role of illustration, and must forever remain a despicable need in those who are incapable of dispensing with it. Where a different function is readily acknowledged to the aesthetic category – namely, that of justifying, validating and/or constituting religion – the aesthetic experience stands on a totally different level.

The case of Judaism is simpler still, because it has remained a religion without art. Nothing visual or aural qualifies as Jewish art though some surely exists which may have been used or produced by Jews. In its early manifestation, Judaism borrowed its culture, and hence all its visual and aural arts, from the Canaanites, and since the Emancipation in Europe, the Jews have cultivated the arts of Europe without relating them to Judaism at all. That in the main Judaism separated itself from all aesthetic pursuits in deference to the transcendence of the divine Being, to the end of avoiding His confusion with "graven images" is certainly praiseworthy. But it cannot have any more than the negative value of a preventive.

Islam has made its validity and divine origin rest in final analysis on the authenticity of the Qur'an as the eternal work of the divine Author. And it has, through its thinkers and exegetes, declared sublime beauty the proof of divine authorship. They called this quality of the Qur'an *i'jaz*; and they analyzed it into active effect and intrinsic condition, defining the former as the power of the text to defeat and surpass all competition, and the latter as eloquence of its literary style.[74] The Qur'an itself did indeed challenge its audience to imitate it, even to produce one short *sura* like its own.[75] The enemies of Islam rose to the challenge where success would not only defeat Islam cheaply and easily, but would equally save them their lives, their properties, their state and hegemony over Arabia, their religion, culture and tradition, all of which were at stake in their war with the Prophet Muhammad and his followers. Thus they mobilized their own geniuses for the task; but they were the first to judge their products defective when compared with the Qur'an. The Qur'an itself predicted their failure; and when they failed, it ridiculed its enemies and rubbed their noses in the dust.[76]

The second element of *i'jaz*, namely, the intrinsic character of the text, its eloquence or literary style, was defined as the composition, flow of its verses, the literary excellence (or *balaghah*) of its prose, the perfect propriety of its diction and its fitness to the meanings intended, a fitness so strong that words and meanings, form and content, have become utterly inseparable from each other. The literary discipline further elaborated that the literary art is very much like that of the jeweller. The "idea", they explained, is the "metal". Obviously, no jeweller wastes his art on base metal, only precious metals like gold and silver are relevant here. But a noble idea, barely stated, is a piece of bullion, precious to be sure, but no more than unattractive metal. When the noble metal is worked up by the jeweller and made into jewelry, then and only then its beauty, or moving appeal, shines forth and begins to affect human consciousness. The same is true of the noble idea. When embodied in the rendering proper to it, the idea comes to life and begins to act as it should, to move humans to say yes to it, to admire, to love, to enjoy and contemplate its beauty, and to act in accordance with the oughts radiating out of it like sunrays.

The Qur'an has achieved even more. Jewelry is not made only of metal, beautifully worked and rendered, but also of precious gems which have an intrinsic beauty of their own. When precious gems are encrusted into the jewelry that fits them, both the beauty of the gem and that of the jewelry are multiplied by their reciprocal enhancement of each other. The result is a work of art of superior value. Likewise, the Qur'an is equally composed of the noblest and greatest ideas which act as precious gems. Indeed, it is all precious gems of the greatest beauty. These have been encrusted in the finest crafted jewelry producing a work of sublime beauty, of an aesthetic quality so great that only God can be its author. That is what the literary composer achieves by rendering the ideas in words. The divine Author, knowing all ideas and all words, has poured the noblest ideas into the most fitting words in the most fitting way, and produced a text so eloquent as to be sublime, absolutely without match or parallel. The *i'jaz* of the Qur'an is universal. It is addressed to all humans in all ages, and anyone is capable of recognizing and appreciating it as divine, if one's innate capacity to sense beauty, one's susceptibility to be moved by the sublime, is activated through adequate learning and experience.

The *i'jaz* of the Qur'an is a cultural phenomenon of tremendous importance. The Arabic-speaker, as well as others who know enough Arabic to experience it, have undergone a radical transformation of their aesthetic consciousness. The Qur'an has become the ultimate norm of beauty, of the linguistic and literary disciplines, the ultimate judge of thought, of all expression in words. Where the mother-tongue is not Arabic, the Qur'an's vocabulary, phrases, style and rendering have become the standard elements of *balaghah*, or literary eloquence, in the vernacular languages of Muslims. In the process, the languages themselves developed into something new, and quite Islamic. Thus Turanian became Ottoman Turkish, Pahlavi Persian became Persian, Bantu became Swahili, Sanskrit became Urdu, the primitive, *alsi* languages of the Malay basin became Malay, etc. Along with their transformation, the Muslim languages themselves began to build literary traditions of their own, achieving heights hitherto unparalleled in their history as a result of their enrichment by the Islamic experience, the centre of which was the Qur'an. Everything literary carried the Qur'an's brand and exemplified its literary style and modalities. Indeed, borrowing the Qur'an's very words and phrases and encrusting them appropriately into the metal of the author's prose or poetry became the supreme sign of literary craftsmanship. The poetry of these new languages which Islam developed among its non-Arab adherents followed in every respect the styles, modalities and categories of Arabic poetry.

The Qur'an, as perfect and unique embodiment of the literary sublime, has affected the aesthetic consciousness itself of all Muslims. The literary effect of the Qur'an spilled into the visual, first affecting the art of calligraphy, and through it, the arts of decoration, whether in the illuminated page, bookbinding, bookstand decoration, prayer rugs, mosque pulpits, walls and lamps, or of the house and its utensils and the garden with its horticulture and aquaculture. The same spilled over into the aural, first affecting the art of Quranic recitation or chant, the *adhan* or call to prayer, and then into all forms of vocal and instrumental music. The life of the Muslim, whether Arabic speaking or otherwise, thus became totally infused with aesthetic values stemming from the Qur'an.

At the centre and core of these aesthetic values stands God Himself, the Absolute, the Transcendent, the One and only God. His transcendence precludes any visual or sensory intuition of Him, a truth which the Mosaic commandment against graven images had honoured. But it does not preclude any sensory representation conducive to an intuition of the truth itself that God is unrepresentable, unintuitable by means of the senses. This unrepresentability visual art represents as infinity. Infinity-art is the opposite of development-art. In the latter, the threads of movement (motives and actions in drama; colours, physiognomies and positions in painting and sculpture; light, dimension and mass in architecture; melody and rhythm in music; etc.) lead progressively to a culmination which is the concluding terminus of the work of art. Absolutely nothing can be added to or extended beyond that point without destruction of the unity of the work. *Per contra*, "infinity-art" always has numerous centres, each of which has its own climax, inviting a repetition of the aesthetic experience of these centres *ad infinitum*. Infinity is never given to sense, but it is intuited immediately in what is given to sense if the latter suggests it through a momentum which the work of art generates. That is why the Islamic work of art, having said no to naturalism and empiricism by stylization, the apex of which is the abstraction or formalism of the geometrical figure, proceeds by the movement of its own internal rhythm, a centrifugal momentum for extension *ad infinitum* through repetition of its constitutive units. The imagination is moved, indeed pressed, to produce the design, or repeat the rhythm, to infinity; and its realization that it cannot ever do so is the very moment at which the intuition of infinity is gained. Thus the consciousness is moved to awareness of the infinite, the absolute, which is certainly not-creation, not-nature or natural, but transcendent. That is the nature, function and purpose of the arabesque, the ubiquitous art form of all Muslims. Every arabesque, on whatever carrier or medium, is an aesthetic affirmation of the truth that there is no God but God, that God is not His creation, that

He is transcendent Creator, the one and only Absolute.

The idea of God possesses the imagination of the Muslim as God Himself possesses his actual life. For him, God, the Sublime, is the first and last object of aesthetic contemplation. Whether in his recitation of the Qur'an, the word of God, or his daily speech if it is refined and cultured enough to act as carrier for the divine words, or the Quranic modality, or in the household objects of his daily use, in his house architecture and decoration, his consciousness perceives the infinity and unrepresentability of God. His culture consists precisely in his ability to order all the departments of his consciousness and life around the axis of God. His thoughts, deeds and contemplative moments are all focussed on God. From Him they derive their energy as well as their goals, their method and style. Islam means submission to God; but submission means the constant preoccupation with the contemplation of God as God and the fulfilment of His will out of devotion to Him. As God has taught His Prophet: "Say, all my service, all my devotion, all my life and death are to God alone, the Lord of the worlds."[77]

Notes

1 "Culture" is sometimes translated as *thaqafah*, which means the act of becoming more intelligent or knowledgeable. It is more proper to translate it as *adab*, which in the classical tradition means *husn* (beauty, goodness) of word, attitude and deed, as the Prophet has said of himself: ("My God has given me my culture. He has made it a good culture.")

2 For a fuller analysis of the relation of Islam to *'urubah*, see this author's *On Arabism: 'Urubah and Religion*, The Hague: Djambatan, 1962.

3 Qur'an 12:2, 20:113; 43:3; 42:7; 46:12; 13:39; 26:195; 39:38; 41:3.

4 Qur'an 20:113.

5 Consider in this regard the verses which use the root word *dhikr*, and its derivatives. Also, the verses in which the subjunctive *la'alla* and its conjugations are followed by the terms *yazzakka, yattaqun, yarji'un, yatadarra'un, yatafaqqahun, yahtadun, ya'lamun, yantahun, yashkurun, yarshudun, yatadhakkarun, yatafakkarun, yahdhirun, yunsarun, ta'qilun, turhamun, tuflihun*, etc.

6 Qur'an 42:11.

7 Qur'an 36:78−83; 6:73; 2:116−117.

8 Qur'an 6:100−103; 21:21−24; 28:88; 59:1, 22−24; 112:1−4.

9 Allah is greater! There is no God but Allah! There is neither power nor force except Allah's!.

10 Qur'an 57:1; 59:1; 61:1; 24:41; 17:44.

11 Qur'an 30:30; 17:77.

12 Qur'an 32:8; 90:8–10.

13 Qur'an 2:256.

14 Qur'an 5:107; 10:78; 31:21; 43:22–24.

15 As witness a countless number of verses in the Qur'an summoning the reader to think, to consider, to weigh, to contrast, to reason, etc.

16 Qur'an 17:36.

17 Qur'an 35:28; 39:9.

18 Qur'an 6:50; 13:17; 35:19; 40:58; 13:17.

19 Qur'an 10:32; 20:114; 23:117; 22:6; 31:30; 24:25.

20 The criticisms occur in many places in the Qur'an Cf., any topical index of the Qur'an, e.g., Jules LaBeaume, *Le Koran Analysé*, tr. by Muhammad Fuad 'Abd al Baqi, Cairo: 'Isa al Babi al Halabi, 1374/1955, Chapters IV: *"Banu Isra'il"*, V: *"Al Tawrah"* (The Torah), and VI: *"Al Nasara"* (The Christians), pp. 55–117.

21 Qur'an 77:23; 41:10; 25:2; 65:3; 54:49.

22 This was the substance of the confrontation of the Mu'tazilah under the caliph al Ma'mun who appointed their leader, Ibn Abi Du'ad, as Chief Justice. Ahmad ibn Hanbal, leader of the opposition, was jailed because of his rejection of the Mu'tazilah position. Details of the confrontation and arguments may be read in any work on the history of Muslim philosophy.

23 Qur'an 35:28; 29:43; 20:114; 39:9

24 Qur'an 2:30

25 Qur'an 33:72

26 Qur'an 15:29; 38:72

27 Ibid

28 Qur'an 51:56; 75:36

29 Qur'an 9:90

30 Qur'an 2:31

31 Qur'an 96:4–5; 55:4

32 Qur'an 2:151

33 Qur'an 55:10; 67:15.

34 Qur'an 2:38–39.

35 This was the subject of Muslim erudition in the classical age entitled *Tarikh al Rusul*, or *Tarikh al Anbiya'*. But their interest, however, waned when they declined. In modern times, Muhammad Jawad 'Ali of Iraq, Muhammad 'Izzat Darwazah and this author have addressed themselves to the subject with new vigour and perspective. See this author's "Towards a Historiography of Pre-Hijrah Islam", *Islamic Studies*, Vol. I, No. 2, 1962, pp.65–87 and *Historical Atlas of the Religions of the World*, New York: The Macmillan Co., 1976, Part I "The Ancient Near East", pp.3–13; 29–34.

36 Qur'an 15:9.

37 Qur'an 21:16; 44:38.

38 Qur'an 30:30. Both the Qur'an and the Hadith acknowledged true religion to be something innate, natural and universally possessed by all humans at birth.

39 Qur'an 53:30–31; 38:42

40 Further analysis of the Christian position on original sin, called by this author "peccatism", can be read in his *Christian Ethics: A Systematic and Historical Analysis of Its Dominant Ideas*, Montreal: McGill University Press, 1962, Chapter VI, pp.193–222.

41 Al Faruqi, *Christian Ethics . . .* , Chap. VI, pp. 223–236.

42 Qur'an 52:21; 74:38.

43 Qur'an 11:61.

44 P. T. Raju, *The Great Asian Religions*, New York: The Macmillan Co., pp.5–6.

45 *Ibid.*, p. 6. See also Al Faruqi, *Historical Atlas . . .* , pp. 77–78.

46 John Wesley, *Wesley's Standard Sermons*, ed. by E. H. Sugden, Nashville: Methodist Publishing House, Vol. II, Sermon 38, pp. 222–223. The same position is of course true of all great Christian thinkers, St Paul to Paul Tillich.

47 Karl Barth, *Church Dogmatics* II, Part 2, p.558.

48 Qur'an 75:38; 87:2.

49 Qur'an 25:2; 80:19.

50 Qur'an 54:49.

51 Qur'an 65:3.

52 Qur'an 65:3.

53 Qur'an 67:4.

54 Abu Hamid al Ghazali, *Tahafut al Falasifah,* tr. by Sabih Kamali, Lahore: Pakistan Philosophical Congress, 1963, pp.63ff.

55 C. I. Lewis, *Analysis of Knowledge and Valuation*, La Salle (Ill): Open Court Publishing Co., 1946, pp.316ff.

56 George Santayana, *Scepticism and Animal Faith*, New York: Charles Scribner's Sons, 1950.

57 Abu Hamid al Ghazali, *op. cit.*, Preface, p.11.

58 Ibid., pp.96ff.

59 Qur'an 11:7; 67:2; 18:7.

60 Qur'an 67:15.

61 Al Ghazali

62 Qur'an 65:3.

63 Qur'an 3:26.

64 Qur'an 5:38; 104:1–4; 4:37; 92:8.

65 Qur'an 17:26–30.

66 Qur'an 2:268.

67 Qur'an 3:102–105.

68 Qur'an 49:6.

69 Qur'an 42:38; 9:122.

70 I. R. al Faruqi, "Al Ijtihad wa al Ijma' Katarafay al Dinamikiyyah fi al Islam", *Al Muslim al Mu'asir*, Vol. 9, 1397/1977, pp.5–18.

71 Ibid.

72 This is the substance of the story of Hayy ibn Yaqzan, the hero of the famous story known by his name, versions of which were written by many Muslim philosophers including Ibn Sina and Ibn Tufayl. The story is that of a solitary foundling on a tropical island, nursed and cared for by a gazelle. As he grows, his mental powers develop and he arrives at the truth of Islam naturally, without the help of either revelation or other humans. Having reached the truth, however, he is compelled to leave his island in search of the *ummah* or community of Islam. In his *Risalah Tadbir al Mutawahhid*, Ibn Bajjah advised that the Muslim ought to leave society for solitary self-discipline and learning, to the end of returning to society as an accomplished societal leader and servant.

73 Qur'an 57:27.

74 The Arabic library possesses a large amount of literature on *i'jaz al Qur'an*, a subject to which almost all great Islamic minds addressed themselves. Classical are the treatises of 'Abd al Qahir al Jurjani (author of *Dala'il al I'jaz* and *Al Risalah al Shafi'iyyah fi I'jaz al Qur'an*), Jalal al Din al Suyuti, Abu Bakr Muhammad al Baqillani, Ibn Abi al Isba', Abu Sulayman Hamad al Khattabi, Abu al Hasan 'Ali al Rummani, Al Qadi Abu al Hasan 'Abd al Jabbar, Al Qadi 'Iyad, Mustafa Sadiq al Rafi'i, 'Abd al Karim al Khatib, etc.

75 Qur'an 11:13; 10:38.

76 Qur'an 2:23.

77 Qur'an 6:163.

Islam and Modern Science

Dr Seyyed Hossein Nasr

So many diverse works have been written, mostly by Muslims but also non-Muslims, about science and its relation to Islam, that it has become necessary to clear the ground and define once again exactly what we mean by science before delving into its implications for Islam. The term "science" as used in the English language obviously cannot be translated into an Arabic or Persian term bearing the same meaning. In fact the English word "science" is not even synonymous with the French *science* and is even more removed in the scope of its meaning from the German *wissenschaft*. One cannot therefore translate the English word "science" into Arabic as *al-'ilm* (or the Persian *danish*) and then proceed to discuss the relation between Islam and *'ilm* as has so often been the case in the kind of modernistic Muslim apologetic writings which would go to any extreme to placate modernism and would pay any price to show that Islam is "modern" after all and that in contrast to Christianity it is not at all in conflict with "science".

In this study at least we use the term science to mean not organized knowledge or *scientia* or *al-'ilm* as such, but that particular type of "knowledge" – or what some of its critics have called "learned ignorance" – which developed in a unilaterally quantitative fashion from the seventeenth century onward upon the foundation of the traditional sciences, but in a direction and with a purpose very different from the traditional sciences, whether these be Graeco-Alexandrian, Islamic or mediaeval Christian. By science in this essay we mean modern science, that is that type of knowledge which was developed by such men as Galileo and Newton with certain assumptions made concerning the nature of the spatio-temporal complex, matter, movement, etc.; the independence of the physical domain of reality from all higher orders of reality, and scientific knowledge from all higher orders of knowledge.[1]

The type of science which threatens the hold of Islam upon its adherents is neither *al-'ilm* in its general traditional sense, nor the traditional sciences such as mathematics and physics which were cultivated in Islamic civilization. Rather, it is science as it is currently understood in the English language, the science which claims a monopoly of knowledge of the natural domain independent of any higher form of knowledge. Therefore, it is essential to turn to this type of science and its implications for Islam if we are to understand the problems which Islam faces in the modern world, in a world moulded to a large extent by this science and by modern technology, which is its application. But this problem can only be studied in depth by first preparing the background by analyzing the Islamic attitude towards knowledge and the development of the traditional sciences in Islam. This type of analysis, although necessary, does not, of course, replace the study of modern science itself and its implications, but should provide the necessary matrix for an understanding of the problems posed by the encounter between Islam and modern science.

Many modern Muslim apologists have insisted that Islam has always been in harmony with science and has in fact aided its advancement. What they really have in mind, however, is *al-'ilm* in general or at best the traditional sciences rather than modern science. Without doubt Islam has always held knowledge in the highest esteem and has seen knowledge as the primary means of reaching God. The *shahadah, La ilaha illa'allah*, is after all a statement concerning the *knowledge* of the Divinity and the world as a manifestation of the One. Knowledge, ranging from its highest meaning as contained in the Sufi understanding of the term *al-ma'rifah* to the simplest interpretation of knowledge as it concerns man's daily life, has certainly dominated Islamic civilization[2] and made the pursuit of knowledge central to the religious life of the community. Even the name of the man of religion in Islam is *al-'alim*, literally "He who knows".

In the confrontation of Islam with the modern world it is not Islam's respect for knowledge in general that is in question, but the kind or kinds of knowledge which can be, and those which cannot be in conformity with the Islamic perspective. An examination of the foundations of the Islamic revelation, namely the Qur'an and *Hadith*, immediately reveals the kind of knowledge which is central to the Islamic perspective. This knowledge is that of Unity (*al-tawhid*) which includes knowledge of the Divine Essence, Names and Qualities (*al-Dhat, al-asma'* and *al-sifat*) as well as of the Divine Effects (*athar*) and Acts (*af 'al*) embracing God's creation. But this traditional knowledge of God's creation is seen in the light of God's wisdom and the reliance of creation upon the Creator; it is not based on the notion of creation as an ontologically independent order of reality. It is a knowledge which is sacred even if it concerns the world of physical reality, a knowledge which is a science of nature in the profoundest sense without being in any way an embryonic modern science.

It is important to realise that Islam extensively developed forms of organized and systematic knowledge which would be called "science" even according to the most rigorous modern definitions of the term. After making the sciences of the Graeco-Alexandrian, Persian and Indian worlds its own, Islam produced one of the most remarkable scientific traditions of any normal, pre-modern civilization.[3] The astronomical writings of an al-Farghani or Nasir al-Din al-Tusi, the geodetical and geographical works of an al-Biruni, the medical and pharmacological texts of an al-Razi or Ibn Sina, the optical studies of an Ibn al-Haytham or the mathematical studies of a Ghiyath al-Din Jamshid Kashani remain by any standard among the major achievements of the history of science, not only the history of science among the Islamic peoples but the history of science in general.

The sciences developed by Muslims, however, were never a challenge to Islam in the same way as modern science has been. Young Muslim students in traditional *madrasahs* did not cease to perform their prayers upon reading the algebra of Khayyam or the alchemical treatises of Jabir ibn Hayyan as so many present day students lose their religious mooring upon studying modern mathematics or chemistry. Lavoisier is not simply a linear continuation of either the Islamic Jabir nor the Latin Geber although chemistry made use of the "material residues" of traditional alchemy. Something of great importance separates modern science from its traditional antecedents, a "something" which lies at the heart of the profound problems inherent in the confrontation between Islam and modern science today. Until this "something" or the factors which separate modern science from the traditional sciences are understood, there is no hope for a solution to the challenge which modern science poses to the world view of Islam. No amount of denying that the problem exists and of proclaiming in loud slogans the "scientific" character of Islam will prevent the spread of this kind of science – based on the forgetting of God – from corroding the foundations of the citadel of the Islamic faith.

One of the fundamental features of modern science, like modern philosophy, is its profane character, that is, its divorce of knowledge from the sacred. Whether a scientist be a mystic, theist, deist, agnostic or atheist as an individual, he must divorce "his science" and his mental activity while he is functioning as a scientist from the sacred concept of knowledge. One *can* study nature with reverence as a scientist, but one can also be an outstanding scientist without an awareness of the Divine. The sacred character of knowledge is thus not innate to modern science *qua* modern science. The findings of modern science have themselves a metaphysical and symbolic significance because they correspond to an aspect of reality, and all that shares in the real must be symbolic of a higher order of reality than itself, the only exception to this principle being the One and Absolute Reality. But the symbolic and metaphysical significance of modern science cannot be taken into consideration by modern science itself unless there be an essential and fundamental change in modern science, which would be tantamount to making modern science something other than what it is now. If it were to undergo such a change, modern science would no longer be science as it is understood today.

Obviously the profane conception of knowledge, which is the marrow of the bone of the modern scientific world view, cannot but pose a challenge for the Islamic conception of knowledge, which sees knowledge as immersed in the ocean of the sacred and as the chief means of access to the Divine. Whatever devout Muslim scientists may believe as individuals, they cannot prevent their activity as modern scientists from emptying the Islamic intellectual universe of its content unless this science is shorn away from its secular and humanistic matrix where it has been placed since the Renaissance, and unless it is integrated into a higher level of knowledge. Modern science remains profoundly anthropocentric in its total reliance upon human reason as the supreme instrument for the attainment of knowledge, and in its emphasis on the human senses as the final criterion for the distinction between truth and error. A truly Islamic science, however, cannot but derive ultimately from the intellect (*nous* or *intellectus*) which is Divine and not human reason (*ratio*). It is a profoundly non-anthropomorphic science, based not on man as the ultimate judge and criterion of things, but on God; or from another point of view on man not as a fallen being, but in his theomorphic aspect, as the vicegerent of God on earth (*khalifatallah fi'l-ard*). The intellect which enables man to gain knowledge is rooted in man's primordial nature (*al-fitrah*). Its seat is the heart (*al-qalb*) rather than the head, and reason is no more than its reflection upon the mental plane.[4] This intellect which is ultimately of Divine Nature is the source of true knowledge and all science must ultimately refer to it and be confirmed in its light in order to be worthy of being considered as legitimate knowledge in the perspective of Islam. Even the knowledge of the anatomy of a gnat is legitimate if it does not remain limited to the perceptions of human reason but becomes illuminated by the light of the intellect (al-'aql).

This "independence" of reason from the intellect in modern philosophy and of scientific knowledge from higher orders of knowledge is closely related to the loss of the vision of hierarchy in both the realm of existence and of knowledge in the modern world. In Islam, as in every traditional civilization, one can observe a hierarchy of knowledge corresponding to the nature of reality itself. The knowledge of higher orders of reality stands obviously on a higher plane than the knowledge of lower orders as the classical Islamic treatises on the classification of the sciences reveal so readily. Moreover, there are different hierarchical modes of knowledge of the same order of reality. The botanical knowledge of a tree is like a step in a ladder whose highest rung is knowledge of the tree as the tree of paradise, and a most powerful symbol of the states of being. Modern science, however, does not accept the legitimacy of knowledge of an order higher than itself nor does it consider the possibility of the legitimacy of other modes of knowledge of the world of nature, to which it claims exclusive rights. The reason that Muslims could study the optics of Ibn al-Haytham without becoming impervious to the teachings of Suhrawardi concerning the nature of light[5] was among other things due to the awareness of the hierarchy of knowledge and the fact that the physics of that time did not envisage itself as a closed world independent and divorced from metaphysics any more than it could conceive of physical light as being totally independent of the light which shines upon the Heavens and the earth. Islam can never accept a science which seeks to explain the world as if it were an independent order of reality and which explains the effect without having recourse to the Ultimate Cause, the centre which is everywhere and nowhere.

Not only does modern science remain oblivious to higher orders of being, but it is also aware of the origin and the end, the *alpha* and *omega* which relate this world to the Divine Who is at once the *alpha, al-awwal*, and the *omega, al-akhir*. The cosmogonic process cannot be envisaged by a science which generalizes the physical laws of here and now for all times past and future; nor can such a science understand the Apocatastasis by which all things are absorbed into the centre from which all multiplicity has issued.[6] Islam sees the life of the Universe as determined by a beginning which is related to the act of creation, the *fiat lux* or the *kun* of the Holy Qur'an, and an end (*al-ma'ad*) which is of an eschatological nature and which cannot be arrived at by the simple extrapolation of the physical events and forces observable in the world today. The modern world does not possess a proper cosmology which would be able to situate the world between two moments which belong to God, between the birth of the world from its angelic prototype and the sudden rending asunder of the veil of material existence by direct Divine intervention. How can Islam remain undisturbed by modern science when the latter speaks of eons past and future as if the Universe were *sui generis* and functioned as a closed system independent of the Divine Will or at best related to the Divine only through a far away act of creation whose effect upon the subsequent history of the cosmos remains inconsequential.

The Holy Qur'an speaks in the most vivid language possible of the eschatological events marking the end of the present world cycle as well as of the renewal of creation (*al-khalq al-jadid*) to which reference is made especially in *Surah al-Qaf* (*al-Qaf* being itself the symbol of the cosmos). But in the same way that the events described in what is known as the Last Judgement take place in a "space" above and beyond the space known to modern science, the rhythms and cycle of time, both cosmic and historical, remain unknown to this type of science. The various sciences dealing with long periods of time, such as geology, palaeontology, physics and astronomy all base themselves upon the well-known theory of uniformitarianism according to which laws of nature abide in a uniform fashion through processes which take place in linear time. Modern science remains singularly neglectful of cosmic cycles, of the *adwar* and *akwar* of Islamic cosmology[7] or the *yugas*, *kalpas* and *manvantaras* of Hinduism.[8] It has no awareness of the qualitative nature of the unfolding of cosmic cycles and the gradual modification of each world as it moves away from its Divine Origin.[9] The whole Islamic conception of prophetic cycles as well as the qualitative conditions governing each period of history is based on the qualitative conception of time, although the cosmological implications of this doctrine have been developed in certain schools more than in others. Islam cannot therefore remain indifferent to a science based on reducing time to a merely quantitative factor, and processes taking place in time to events following uniform laws discovered by man's observation and study and the generalization by rational man of a particular moment in the history of the cosmos in which he happens to be living.

Perhaps no aspect of modern science is more opposed to the teachings of Islam than that pseudo-dogma known as biological evolution, based as it is on the idea of the greater coming into being out of the lesser. In order to remove the hand of God from His creation and destroy the sense of wonder and mystery in nature, a theory has been postulated according to which given enough time life somehow evolves from the lifeless, man from the animals and, to complete this deception which is an insult to intelligence, superman from common mortals.

Somehow the world moves towards an *omega* point without there having been an *alpha* as if God is not *both* the First and the Last and as if Christ did not say, "*I am the alpha and the omega*". Despite both scientific and metaphysical arguments offered over the years against the Darwinian and other theories of evolution[10], those whose world-view would flounder if such theories were disproved refuse to consider even the scientific evidence provided against their claims. But even worse than the dogmatic stature that this theory of evolution has gained in biological circles, is its withering effect upon other domains of knowledge, including theology itself. In Islam, although the grace of God has prevented as yet a figure such as Teilhard de Chardin from appearing, there are many modernized Muslims, especially from the Indo-Pakistani sub-continent, who even write of the evolution of Islam and of the *Sharia* and take evolution as a scientifically proven fact rather than a hypothesis.

Actually the teachings of Islam are quite clear on this point. Man has always been man and the first man (*adam*) was also the first prophet Adam. Recall the well-known saying attributed to both 'Ali ibn Abi Talib and Ja'far al-Sadiq – upon both of whom be peace – according to which someone asked what was there before Adam, and the master answered "Adam". Again the question was asked, "What was there before this Adam?", and the answer came: "Adam". The Imam added that if this question were to be repeated until the end of time the answer would be Adam. Man is like the centre of a circle; the centre is always the centre and cannot be partly central and evolve gradually into centrality. The very intelligence of man, which can know objectively and distinguish between the absolute and the relative, is proof of the centrality of man and the fact that he could never have been anything less. The writings of the few Western anthropologists and philosophers who have rediscovered the traditional concept of man – in opposition to official Western science based on the theory of evolution – confirms the Islamic conception which, being based on the nature of man as he *is*, can never be negated through any process of becoming.[11]

Islamic sources have also always been aware of the fact that simpler life forms have preceded man on earth; that animals came before man, and plants before animals. But they never interpreted these successive crystallizations of the dream of the World Soul as stages in a biological evolution which negates the ever-present act of the Spirit upon the world of material forms. The uncritical teaching of theories of biological evolution to Muslim children – and also adults – as if these theories were scientific facts is, therefore, pernicious and dangerous beyond reckoning. It makes a farce of the Islamic conception of man, of the spiritual relation and harmony between beings, and of God's continuous presence and intervention in His creation. The uncritical acceptance of the theory of evolution, as usually taught, destroys belief in higher states of being and in the immutability of Islam itself, leading to an erosion of faith and claims to "reform" God's religion, claims which cannot but result in monstrous deformations.[12]

Another important point to consider, which is in fact the fruit of the same mentality that has given birth to the theory of evolution, is the reductionism which would reduce biology to chemistry, and life – not to speak of intelligence – to no more than a somewhat more complicated play of the same forces which are to be found in physics. Although certain notable contemporary physicists have rebelled against this idea, the main movement of modern science has been to reduce the higher to the lower. In Islam one of God's Names is the Alive (*al-Hayy*) and it is by virtue of the theophany (*tajalli*) of this Name that certain forms have been endowed with life in a manifest manner, although from another point of view one could assert that all things possess a degree or form of life of their own, even those which are called inanimate. Be that as it may, Islam cannot accept the reductionism of modern science which would reduce metaphysics to psychology, psychology to biology, biology to chemistry and chemistry to physics, thereby bringing all elements of reality down to the lowest level of manifestation which is the physical domain. In order to remain true to itself, Islam must re-assert its own teachings according to which life, like intelligence, comes from God and is bestowed upon certain physical forms that "Invisible Treasury" (*khaza'in al-ghayb*) that invisible or non-manifested world which is so blatantly neglected by modern science.

Putting aside specific teachings of modern science which challenge the Islamic world view, there is a general characteristic of modern science, and in fact modern thought in general, which does not accord with the Islamic conception of knowledge. In traditional Islamic teachings, all forms of knowledge are related to each other and to Quranic revelation like so many branches of a tree:

> "Seest thou not how Allah coineth a similitude: A goodly saying, as a goodly tree, its root set firm, its branches reaching into heaven, giving its fruit at every season by permission of its God? Allah coineth the similitudes for mankind in order that they may reflect." (*Sura 13 – Abraham verses 24–25*).

This verse, dealing above all with the cosmic tree refers as much to states of being as to degrees of knowledge.[13] There is only one principal knowledge, the supreme knowledge of Unity. All other knowledge must either be in some way related to that knowledge or be no better than ignorance parading under the guise of knowledge.[14] Islam has never held a place for "learned ignorance" in its citadel nor accepted those intelligent forms of being unintelligent which comprise most of modern philosophy. What is positive in modern science cannot be refuted by Islam because it is a knowledge corresponding to an aspect of reality. But what is completely unacceptable from the Islamic point of view is the positivism and relativism to which modern science lends itself because of its divorce from other forms of knowledge and despite the valiant effort of certain outstanding scientists.

Moreover, the compartmentalization which characterizes modern science is alien to Islam, which could never allow a branch of the tree of knowledge to grow to such an extent as to destroy the harmony and even the life of the tree. How can Islam allow knowledge of the particular to develop at the expense of knowledge of the Universal, to allow science in its modern sense to develop at the expense of wisdom, of *hikmah* or *sapientia* as was to happen in the West? St Bonaventure also believed that *scientia* should be subordinated to *sapientia*, but the later development of science at the expense of wisdom in the West was such that after several centuries science has become the most common of words, while wisdom remains for many an airy abstraction; for scientists are to be found everywhere but even in the direst of circumstances one must take a lamp in hand and like Diogenes look in the most hidden corners in order to find a wise man. Surely the lesson of the effect of the development of science at the expense of wisdom in the West cannot go unheeded by Muslims. All serious Muslim thinkers who are concerned with the integrity of the Islamic intellectual tradition must take into consideration both the separation of science from wisdom and the compartmentalization of various disciplines within science. If this fragmentation is not compensated for by a unitary knowledge that can integrate and synthesize, it cannot but lead to the death of the civilization which has allowed such sciences to develop whatever may be their relative success in the particular domain with which they are concerned. It must be remembered that a house divided within itself cannot stand; least of all if this house happens to be Islam, which is based on a doctrine of Unity (al-tawhid).

This compartmentalization within science, and its separation from *sapientia* as a result of the loss of the vision of the hierarchy of knowledge, he aslo had a result of the gravest consequence. Science has become divorced from morality despite the moral concern that can be observed in many scientists, who in fact suffer most from the painful situation in which their "neutral" scientific endeavour is often put to the service of immoral ends over which they have no control. This is one of the most powerful challenges of modern science to Islam. In Islamic society there was never such a thing as knowledge for its own sake. Science was cultivated either for a greater knowledge of God and His creation – which helped perfect the human soul – or for practical needs of mankind in such domains as medicine and agriculture. In both cases the needs of man were concerned, but not simply the earthly animal who happens to possess the power of reason. Rather, man was seen as an immortal being with both an intellect and a soul as well as a body and as much in need of spiritual and intellectual nourishment as of the wheat and barley he produces in his fields.

Moreover, both morality and science were based on the same principles in Islam. The foundation of morality is the *Sharia* which has its roots in the Holy Qur'an and *Hadith*. The principles of all knowledge in Islam are also to be found in the Holy Qur'an and are elucidated by the *Hadith*. There is therefore no conflict possible between them in a traditional setting. But Muslims have begun to combat infantile mortality, leading to a population explosion with unforetold ecological consequences, and to build atomic power plants the exact effects of whose refuse is unknown even in those countries which are much better prepared from the point of view of nuclear technology to deal with these matters. Of course these problems, and many others, are already being avidly debated in the West. But surely these debates will not cease simply because Muslim as well as Christian, Jewish or agnostic scientists have now become engaged in the activities of modern science. Rather, the debate must of necessity become more intensified because of the strongly defined morality based on revelation which dominates Islamic society. Islam can certainly provide answers, but only under the condition that it does not take the modern scientific enterprise and the technology based upon it as an inevitable necessity and surrender before it in practice while defending Islamic values merely through rhetoric.

Something must also be said about the relation of science to beauty. There are, of course, mathematicians and theoretical physicists, as well as men and women in other fields of science, for whom the beauty, symmetry or harmony of a particular equation, theorem or hypothesis is almost more essential than its being true.[15] But there is also no doubt that the application of modern science in the form of technology is usually accompanied by that monstrous ugliness which the modern urban environment – dominated by the machine – displays so clearly. It seems that the missing dimension of modern science from a metaphysical point of view is laid bare for all to see in the form of the ugliness which characterizes most of its applications on the physical level.

Islam is a religion based on intelligence of which beauty is considered as an essential aspect of reality: God is *al-rahmah*, Mercy, and Mercy is one of the "Names of Beauty" (*al-asma' al-jamaliyyah*) of God. In fact *al-rahmah* is itself the beauty through which all things are created and through whose attraction all things return to the One. All authentic manifestations of Islam are combined with a sense of beauty, including its science and technology. One of the challenges of modern science and technology to Islam, therefore, is – despite certain notable exceptions – their neglect of beauty as an aspect of the Truth as it was understood so well by Plato and Pythagoras. In the modern world beauty is a luxury, whereas in traditional Islam it is as essential for man as the air he breathes and the water and food which sustain his life.

All the problems mentioned here, and many more which cannot be elaborated save in a more extensive study, could be solved by Islam if modern science were to be taken out of its humanistic, rationalistic and agnostic context and placed within the world-view of Islamic metaphysics and integrated into the hierarchy of knowledge provided by that *hikmah* or *sophia* which Islam has been able to preserve within its bosom to this day despite all the vicissitudes of time. But this could only be done by an Islamic world which would remain faithful to its own intellectual and spiritual roots and not be in subservience to the various mental fashions and "isms" which have issued from the West since the Renaissance. Whether such an integration can be accomplished and the process toward world-wide suicide averted is known only to God. As for the Muslims who have been destined to live in this day and age, their duty remains to come to know and then assert the truth and fight against the errors, which comprise the modern world, to the best of their ability, leaving the outcome in the hands of God. Surely truth will finally triumph; pseudo-knowledge, in whatever form it might manifest itself, cannot take the place of that Truth which has always been and will always be. Moreover, in an age when the sun is momentarily eclipsed, the duty of those who know becomes even greater than before, for they are distinguished by God and held responsible because of the very knowledge He has bestowed upon them. As the Holy Qur'an asserts:

"Are those who know equal with those who know not?" (*Sura 39 Al-Zummar*)

Notes

1 So much has been written over the past years concerning the foundations and assumptions of modern science that one hardly needs to recall the evident truth that modern science is not *the* science of nature but *a* science based upon a particular manner of looking at things. See, for example, F. Brunner, *Science et réalité*, Paris 1955; S. H. Nasr, *Man and Nature*, London, 1977, chapter one; F. Schumacher, *A Guide for the Perplexed*, London, 1978; and Th. Roszak, *Where the Wasteland Ends*, New York, 1973.

2 See F. Rosenthal, *Knowledge Triumphant*, Leiden, 1974, where the role and function of knowledge in Islam and various Islamic intellectual disciplines is thoroughly analyzed. Although the perspective of this work is not Islamic, it contains a vast amount of valuable information concerning the meaning of knowledge in Islam drawn often from a wide range of sources, some of which have not been studied previously.

3 On the history of Islamic science and the achievements of Muslim scientists as well as the relationship of the Islamic sciences to Islamic civilization see S. H. Nasr, *An Introduction to Islamic Cosmological Doctrines*, London, 1978; Nasr, *Science and Civiliza-*

tion in Islam, Cambridge (U.S.A.), 1968; and Nasr, *Islamic Science – An Illustrated Study*, London, 1976.

4 On the Islamic conception of man which underlines the Islamic conception of science see F. Schuon, *Understanding Islam*, trans. D. M. Matheson, London, 1963 chapter 1; F. Schuon, *L'Oeil du coeur*, Paris, 1977; and S. H. Nasr, *Ideals and Realities of Islam*, London, 1975, chapter one.

5 On the contrary, the illuminationist (*ishraqi*) doctrines of Suhrawardi helped revive the science of optics and the leading commentator of Suhrawardi, Qutb al-Din Shirazi, was also an outstanding physicist in the field of optics.

6 This doctrine has been expounded majestically in many of the writings of F. Schuon such as *The Language of the Self*, trans. M. Pallis, Madras, 1959; and his *L'Esotérisme comme principe et comme voie*, Paris, 1978, part one.

7 See Nasr, *An Introduction to Islamic Cosmological Doctrines*, part one.

8 These doctrines, which have been particularly developed in the Puranas, have been dealt with in the numerous writings of A. K. Coomaraswamy, H. Zimmer and M. Eliade. See especially the latter's *The Myth of the Eternal Return*, trans. W. R. Trask, New York, 1959. See also Zimmer's, *The King and the Corpse; Tales of the Soul's Conquest of Evil*, ed. J. Campbell, New York, 1960; and Zimmer, *Philosophies of India*, ed. J. Campbell, New York, 1956.

9 This has been dealt with in a remarkable fashion by R. Guénon in his *The Reign of Quantity and the Signs of the Times*, trans. Lord Northbourne, Baltimore, 1973

10 See for example D. Dewar, *The Transformist Illusion*, Murfreesboro, 1957; and L. Bounour, *Déterminisme et finalité, double loi de la vie*, Paris, 1957. F. Schuon comes to the heart of the refutation of the theory of evolution, basing himself on the primacy of consciousness, when he writes, "Our thought recalls to us and proves to us that in the beginning was the Spirit and that nothing is more absurd than to claim to derive intelligence from matter. For the evolutionary leap from matter to intelligence is the most arbitrary, the most inconceivable and the most foolish hypothesis possible, in comparison with which 'simple faith' seems like a mathematical equation. The key to the psychological enigma of evolutionism lies in the fact that reason, once separated from Intellection and from Revelation (which replaces Intellection), is joined to a Luciferianism which, by its nature, tends to reverse the normal relationships between things and, in consequence, to exclude God, who is the real cause of the world . . .". "Consequences flowing from the mystery of subjectivity", *Studies in Comparative Religion*, Autumn, 1977, p.197.

11 We have in mind especially such men as G. Durand and J. Servier. See Durand, *On the disfiguration of the image of man in the West*, trans. J. A. Pratt, Ipswich, 1977; Durand, *Science de l'homme et tradition: le nouvel esprit anthropologique*, Paris, 1975 and Servier, *L'Homme et l'invisible*, Paris, 1964. Criticizing the modern Western conception of man in the discipline currently called anthropology, G. Durand writes: "Autrement dit, sur ces plans de développements essentiels en Occident: médecine, psychologie et sociologie, la Science de l'Homme se trouve toujours réduite à la science de causes, de conditionnements, d'infrastructures qui échappent à l'anthropologie. Finalement, c'est la machine – et le progrés technologique triomphant – qui sert de

modèle et de réference à la Science de l'Homme en Occident''. G. Durand, *"Science de l'homme et islam spirituel"*, in S. H. Nasr (ed.), *Mélanges offerts à Henry Corbin*, Tehran, 1977, p.43.

12 On this question see Nasr, *Islam and the Plight of Modern Man*, London, 1975, chapter ten.

13 This verse can be interpreted in the sense of both an upright and an inverted tree each of which possesses its own symbolism. Concerning the symbolism of the inverted tree as it is to be found in various traditions, see A. K. Coomaraswamy, *"The Inverted Tree"*, R. Lipey (ed.) *Coomaraswamy – 1: Selected Papers, Traditional Art and Symbolism*, Princeton, 1977, pp.376–404; and R. Guénon, *Les états multiples de l'être*, Paris, 1947.

14 We have dealt extensively with this doctrine in our prolegomena to *An Introduction to Islamic Cosmological Doctrines*, and also the introduction to *Science and Civilization in Islam*.

15 I remember when I was a student of physics and mathematics at M.I.T., some of the foremost scientists and mathematicians of the day who taught us would invariably speak of the beauty of a particular mathematical theorem or solution; one can hardly deny the attraction of abstract beauty and even elegance for the type of mind drawn to mathematics.

Islam and Aesthetic Expression

Dr Lois Lamya' Al Faruqi

Introduction

The chapters of this book are attempts to articulate the Islamic message of *tawhid for* the benefit of our contemporaries in this fifteenth century of Islamic presence. They, like the Islamic legacy of the past fourteen centuries, deal with a wide range of topics and exemplify the demand for cultural unity made by Islam. The arts are no less determined by that religious ideology than other aspects of civilization; and therefore this chapter on aesthetic expression is seen as further clarifying the wide significance of *tawhid*, and providing one more tessera in the total mosaic of Islamic life and culture.

In a broad sense, these presentations are lessons in *da'wah*, for they speak not only to the contemporary Muslim, but to contemporary man as such. These writers address the questions of modern man and present Islamic solutions for his problems. The aspirations with which they deal are meant to inspire not only members of the Islamic community, but also humanity as a whole. It is only by exemplification of Islamic ideals and their effect on the complete spectrum of activities, institutions and ideas that *da'wah* can be truly effective in contemporary society. There is little power in a religious doctrine which separates itself from other aspects of life and which fails to address itself to the social, economic, political and intellectual problems of the age. The Friday (or Saturday or Sunday) ritual which does not transform life on Monday and Tuesday as well, offers no viable appeal to humanity.

Islam and Islam's message of *tawhid* are particularly fitted to fulfilling the task of providing a source of inspiration and hope for modern man. This is due in part to the very content of that message called *tawhid*; in part, it is due to Islam's definition of the role that the message of *tawhid* should play in society and civilization. If we examine the application of these two aspects of Islam's contribution (i.e., the content of the message of *tawhid* and the role of that message in life) to the field of art or aesthetic expression, we find the same penetration, integration and interrelationship of the ideology with the various arts that are found in all other fields. Every Islamic contribution to civilization might, in fact, be thought of as a "translation" into political action, economic and social institutions, legal code, etc. of the message of *tawhid*. The art products of the Muslim peoples are also a symbolic translation – in this case, into the media of colour and shape, silk and wool, bricks and stone, notes and rhythms, poetry and prose – of that message.

Let us now consider briefly the main premises of that doctrine and try to determine its significance as a message for the arts.

1 Islam's contribution: tawhid, the message and its influence on the arts

The message of tawhid

Tawhid is a monotheistic doctrine which posits two clearly separate realms of existence. One of these is synonymous with Allah, *subhanahu wa ta'ala*, the Creator, the Transcendent, that timeless, spaceless, indescribably unknowable infinity. The second realm is the created, natural world in which man operates as vicegerent of the Transcendent. In this world, man benefits from and enjoys the bounties of creation, at the same time as he is called upon to organize and discipline life in that sphere in conformance with Allah's will and commands. The two realms are utterly distinct, the only connections between them being the revelation or guidance bequeathed on man at chosen stages of history by a merciful God. The role of one is then Creator; the other is His creation.

Allah is not therefore the anthropomorphic or naturalistic god who can be described or symbolized by reference to anything in the natural realm. In fact, the whole thrust of *tawhid* draws attention toward the transcendent realm and its purifying influence on life in this natural world. It seeks to emphasize the oneness, the uniqueness, of Allah *subhanahu wa ta'ala*, and to direct man's attention and allegiance to Him. The effect of this doctrine was so pervasive and so captivating of the Muslim mind and heart that even when the Muslims sought to add beauty to their lives, *tawhid* had a determining effect on that embellishment which humanity finds so important in life.

Translation of the message of tawhid in art
Content: abstract quality Perhaps the most obvious effect of *tawhid* on aesthetic expression is the abstract quality which is found in every type of Islamic art. Since the Muslim is possessed of the idea of Allah's utter transcendence, the beautiful is anything that reminds him of that transcendent realm, anything which reinforces the commitment to serve Allah and fulfill His commands. No naturalistic image of man or beast, as symbol from the natural world, can adequately provide such aesthetic stimulus. Early on in Islamic history, it became obvious that the message of *tawhid* demanded creation of a new vocabulary of artistic achievement.

Shunning the figurative art of earlier peoples, which drew attention to creation rather than to Creator, the Muslim artist, before the end of the first Hijrah century, had already shown the direction in which his genius was to draw him, for example, in the Qubbah al Sakhrah of Jerusalem. This magnificent early architectural creation, with its calligraphy, geometric and floral arabesques rather than naturalistic scenes or portraits, already revealed the Muslim propensity for non-figural design which was to dominate Islamic art down through the centuries. It is but one example of the artistic breakthrough provided by Islam – not only in architecture and architectural decoration, but also in calligraphy, in textiles, in ceramics and woodwork, in metal design, in literature and music. In none of these arts produced under the influence of the Islamic ideology is it possible to mistake this propensity for abstraction. It is this demand inherent in the representation of *tawhid* in art that brought calligraphy to the forefront of Islamic artistic production and skill. It was this demand which stimulated the creation of beautiful geometric and vegetal patterns and caused the Muslim artists of every geographic area and century to excel in the creation of a never-ending stream of abstract designs.

Stylization The Qubbah al Sakhrah was also an important exemplification of a second characteristic of the expression of *tawhid* in the arts: the importance of stylization. Certainly, abstraction was the ultimate goal; and therefore, whenever motifs from the natural world were used, they were treated in special ways which de-emphasized their naturalistic qualities. Only thus could they redirect the spectator's thoughts toward the Transcendent. This transformation of the naturalistic is called stylization, and it is found in every art medium utilized in the Islamic World. Human and animal figures are, as one would expect, rare. When they are used as motifs (for example, in book illustration), they show little attempt on the artist's part to present the illusion of three-dimensional, real-life naturalism. Bodies are encased in voluminous garments which disguise any impression of real flesh and bones beneath. Depth and perspective are ignored or rejected as criteria. Facial features and expression are simplified and stereotyped rather than asked to reveal characteral or emotional validity.[1] Animals are often depicted as fantastic creatures which have no counterpart in the real world. Plant forms too were stylized to create the elaborate vegetal arabesques that are so much a part of Islamic art in all regions of the Muslim World. Even letters of the Arabic alphabet were pressed and expanded, shortened and elongated, squeezed and moulded to conform with other motifs and decorative space, or to simulate non-calligraphic forms (e.g., plaited Kufi, or floriated Kufi scripts). Poetry and music were involved with the nameless beloved or the ambiguous theme rather than with the telling of tales or the depiction of character and mood. Islamic literature and music certainly aroused emotion in the listener, but in its best examples, it avoided depicting examples or instances of specific moods or emotions. Islamic art is not an act to concentrate on the mundane, the individual, the particular. It is an art which draws the viewer, the user, the listener away from these features of the world of creation, and toward the world of the Creator, toward the sublime.

Dematerialization of structure After abstract quality and stylization, a third important effect which the message of *tawhid* can be seen to have had on the arts is that which could be called "dematerialization of structure"[2]. This feature arose as a response to the same motivation which determined the abstract and stylization characteristics of Islamic art: i.e., the demand for an art which would direct the attention of the beholder away from himself and his worldly environment toward contemplation of the Transcendent. We have seen that this orientation greatly influenced the kind of motifs and subject matter used by the Muslim artist, as well as the stylized way in which they were used. The characteristic of dematerialization can be seen as doing to structure what stylization does to figures and motifs from the natural world – that is, removing them as far as possible from the realm of naturalism and thus making them suitable carriers of the divine message.

The Muslim architect's goal is not to make the beholder feel or sense such structural features of his building as how the dome is supported, the gravity and weight of a mighty façade the layout of the overall plan of a complex structure. Instead, he unites his building so closely with those that surround it that the precise shape and plan of the building is disguised, its naturalness thereby de-emphasized. The dome is so lightened by honeycomb-like decorations that it seems ethereal, suspended weightless in air, rather than the heavy mass of brick or stone that it actually is. Each segment of the palace or *madrasah* forms a unit centralized around a court, a pool, or a fountain. It gives little visual hint of the other units of the complex.

Transubstantiation of materials Even materials are denaturalized and their normal natures disguised. This process will be designated as ''transubstantiation'', for it is a use of materials in such a way as to reduce the perceived natural quality of that material, that is, to transform the visual impression of its very substance. Many Western artists, especially in recent decades, have striven to accentuate the luxury of the wood in their carved pieces of art, to emphasize the impression of the natural stone out of which they produced a building, even to leave the holes and lines of concrete forms exposed on the finished building to accentuate the impression, the naturalness, of raw concrete. This aesthetic expression of nature is far from the goal of the Muslim artist. Instead, the latter has striven to present an art object so transformed by the arabesque patterns which cover its surfaces that the material is transubstantiated in the process. Marble and stone are so intricately carved that they appear to be lace. The stones, brick and even rubble used to build a solid wall are transubstantiated with a facing or ornamental brick patterning, an airy covering of stucco latticework, or a bright, sparkling ceramic veneer. The heaviness of the wall is alleviated and the naturalness of the base materials is disguised as the façade, through this transubstantiation, takes on an unearthly beauty to provide a reminder to the viewer of the message of *tawhid*.

Islamic literature and the sound arts are no less abstract. The Islamic literary or musical genius has concentrated on those forms of poetry and prose, of vocal or instrumental organization of sound patterns, which are non-narrative, while his counterpart in the visual arts concentrated on the non-figural. Instead of dramatic portraits and epic accounts, we find in early Islamic literature a great popularity for the ode with its stereotyped content detailing in poem after poem the scene of the deserted tribal camp, the beauties of the beloved, or the prowess of the noble man of the desert. Even when the Muslim author wrote about heroes, kings and rulers, these were denied their real-life natural-ness. The revelation of historical deeds and events was not the concern of the story teller who recited or sang his tales. Neither did he attempt to reveal the personal character, nor the deeper psychological motivations behind the characters' deeds. These personages of the Islamic poem, prose story or song could never be confused with true-to-life men and women. Neither was the writer's or reciter's primary concern one of conveying knowledge. Instead, whether as poet or orator, as chanter-singer or instrumentalist, he showed a penchant for the subtle, the perceptive, the succinct, the brilliant aperçu.

Structural characteristics: The Islamic view of God and reality has influenced the organization of those non-natural or denaturalized motifs, just as much as it has influenced their choice. Two formal characteristics of Islamic artistic creations reveal their aesthetic conformance with the Islamic message: (1) their non-developmental nature; and (2) their conjunct or disjunct arabesque structure.

Non-developmental form in Islamic art When we say that an Islamic work of art is non-developmental, we are maintaining that its constituent parts are not evolved, one after the other, in a seemingly inexorable and unbreakable chain which leads to a climactic moment and a decisive conclusion. Islamic painting, for instance, has no one focal point to which all minor elements of the picture point and subordinate themselves. The architectural floor plan of an Islamic palace such as Alhambra in Spain or the Fatihpur Sikri in India reveals this same lack of progress toward one focal point of attention or activity. Nor is the artistic literary composition any different. Each episode of *One Thousand and One Nights* is a gem, complete in itself. It stands on its own, without necessary support from and without essentially supporting the other tales with which it is surrounded. Only a thin thread, the situation of the story teller Shahrazad and her caliphal lord, hold the stories together. An example from the works of poetry would be equally revelatory of this non-developmental nature of Islamic art.

The Qur'an, the archetype of Islamic literary excellence, also gains its reputation from its flashes of brilliant presentation rather than from its logically evolving presentation of materials. For this reason, it is possible to start reading at any place in the Qur'an, or, for that matter, in any other truly Islamic literary creation. One need not read the chapters (*suras*) in unvarying order. Each unit in the series is an independent item, without the irrevocable, individuated position in the whole which we would find in the verses of a poem of Longfellow or Keats or the chapters of a Dickens novel. The beauty of the creation lies not in its logically progressive thought, but in the sparks of genius which flash before us for a moment in each successive partition.

Since one section of the literary work is no more conclusive than another, even the ends of these works produce no impression of finality. Instead, they reveal an attempt to aesthetically express the infinity emphasized so strongly in the Islamic view of the transcendent realm. They try to impart to the viewer an intuition of that which is beyond sense, beyond knowledge. The scene of a picture seems to extend beyond its limits in its endeavour to express this open-ended inconclusiveness. Even rigid borders cannot always contain the limb of a tree, the tail of a horse, a protruding dome or minaret. These elements in the picture often break through its borders in their effort to give a hint of a transcendence never completely explainable or expressible. The façade of a building with its crenellated outward-moving top is another instance of this Islamic aesthetic treatment related to non-developmental structure.

Lack of development in the arts of Muslim culture is further emphasized by the use of repetition and symmetry. There is essentially little qualitative difference between these two means for providing unity in non-developmental art. They both involve an obvious organization of multiple repetitive items. Quantitatively, however, symmetry is confined to repetitive pairs which are also distinguishable as being opposed in some aspect of their composition or arrangement. Repetition, on the other hand, is not confined to pairs. It may involve as few as two or an unlimited number of repeated items without the necessity for any kind of opposition. In an Islamic art work, whether it be drawn from architecture, painting, literature, or any other field, each part or element is combined by repetition or symmetry with other like or similar elements. There is no attempt to rob a unit of its separate existence. There is no attempt to make it grow organically out of that which went before and in turn give birth to a new whole of inseparable parts. Repetition and symmetry check such integration and evolution and help establish that feeling of never-ending pattern demanded by the culture's aesthetic conscience.

The arabesque in Islamic art The structural characteristics of Islamic art are not confined to a negative rejection of development. Also involved is the elaboration of a new structural entity: the arabesque. Called *tawriq* (foliation) in Arabic, the arabesque is usually described as a complicated organization of geometric figures, calligraphy and/or stylized elements from the plant and, less often, animal world.[3] Most definitions in encyclopaedias or dictionaries do not get beyond these facts to determine for the reader what is the essence of this aesthetic contribution of Islamic culture. Putting their attention on the elements used instead of on the structure to which those elements conform seems to be the basic and common mistake. Actually the artist imbued with the Islamic world view will find himself capable of using a great variety of motifs from the world around him to express himself. He needs only to de-naturalize them to make them fit his purpose. His singularity then is revealed not so much in *what* motifs he chooses, but in the way he *alters* those motifs and, even more crucially, in the way he *joins* them in his design. It is here that the essential character of the arabesque lies. The definition of arabesque is primarily a matter of art structures.

Arabesques can be separated into two types: the conjunct and the disjunct or, borrowing equivalent words from the Arabic, the *muttasil* (from *wasala*, "to connect") and the *munfasil* (from *fasala*, "to divide in sections"). A conjunct or *muttasil* arabesque resembles a continuum. The abstract or denaturalized motifs used are not combined like the parts of a living organism or in a manner resembling their organization in nature. Instead, they occur in an unlimited, never-ending succession which expresses artistically those religious and philosophical ideas which are implanted in the typical artist who grows under the influence of Islamic culture. It is conjunct because of the cohesiveness of the various elements or motifs of which it is made up. It goes steadily, relentlessly onward, leaf after leaf on a seemingly endless vine, room after room of a palace or *madrasah* (school) complex, line after line of a poem, musical segment after segment of a *taqasim*. One gets the impression that even if the artist's or architect's or poet's inspiration fails, the vine portrayal, the building, the poem, the *taqasim* could ideally continue forever. The artist thus establishes the impression of "infinite pattern",[4] an aesthetic expression of the Islamic notion of *tawhid*. By making only part of this pattern visible, by cutting his arabesque before its completion, the artist further emphasizes this impression of infinity as he provides to the perceptive viewer a microcosmic intuition of the macrocosm found and fully known only in the Transcendent.

The second kind of arabesque, the disjunct or *munfasil*, is equally suited for directing attention toward the transcendent world. It comprises a combination of motifs in such a manner as to present a series of self-contained units, each complete in itself. At the same time, it is loosely interwoven with those other units around it in such a way as to produce a larger pattern of which each small unit is but a single element. This type of arabesque can be seen in the well-defined units of a garden or geometric rug, in the diverse, bordered panels of stucco or tile decoration on a single façade, in the room-groupings around a series of open courts which are typical of architectural design in the Muslim World, or in the self-sufficient episodes of Hariri's *Maqamat* (Assemblies). Firdawsi's *Shah-Namah* (Book of Kings), or Rumi's *Mathnawi*.[5] These units and their repetition conform with the culture's rejection of development as a mode of organization. With their countless visual, aural and thought centres – any of which may provide a starting or ending point for the spectator – they aesthetically give expression to that infiniteness, that limitlessness, which characterizes the Islamic view of transcendence.

Some arabesques, rather than being simply conjunct or disjunct, are a combination of these two forms. This occurs when the artist, be he poet or painter, sculptor or writer, architect or musician, uses the well defined series of units to produce his overall arabesque pattern; and yet within some or all of those autonomous units he employs a continuum type of arabesque. For example, a façade may be made up of a disjunct series of autonomous bordered panels, each of which contains a unique internal continuum, i.e., a conjunct arabesque of stylized leaves and flowers, geometric figures or decorative writing. Even a work of art which can be considered figural, such as a miniature painting, might disclose a multitude of disjunct units or centres which draw the eye's attention with kinaesthetic insistence from place to place, at the same time as it reveals smaller conjunct arabesques within those units. Various rooms or groupings of figures may provide the disjunct arabesque units or centres for attention in the overall arrangement of the painting. A rug on the floor, a decorative wall screen, a patterned ceremonial tent within any of those units may be the locus of the intricacies of a continuum arabesque.

The arabesque of the visual, literary or musical arts, whether conjunct or disjunct, is distinguished by two other characteristics: (1) small, intricate movement; and (2) a periodic "launch" at the end of an arabesque section. Arabesques move the eye, the ear, the mind with a proliferation of minute details. The tiny flowers traced with his single- or double-haired brush by the miniaturist, the intricate geometric designs of a carved table, the complicated floral patterns of a carved stucco facade, the melodic intricacies of a *taqasim* performance, all achieve their aesthetic results with small and intricate patterns. These miniscule movements catch the trained viewer or listener at any one of their many centres or points of aesthetic departure and draw it persistently to new areas. Up or down, in or out, to right or to left, or perhaps in several directions at once, the eye, the ear, the mind is caught up in the aesthetic movement. As each arabesque pattern is grasped and understood, the spectator feels a launch of his spirit with this success, and he moves to the next arabesque pattern. This launch or *dafqah* (outpouring), as it is called in poetic terminology, comes at the end of each section or pattern of the arabesque. The term *dafqah* has never to my knowledge been associated with the non-literary arts, but its fittingness warrants its being adopted to help explain the arabesque of any medium.

Movement seems to increase as the spectator is caught up in the aesthetic activity and he encounters the many bifurcations in the unfolding of the arabesques. This increased momentum is produced in part by technical means. The artist can increase the proximity, the complexity, the interrelation, as well as the actual numbers of his arabesque components. Equally, the movement is increased within the spectator himself. He grasps, with eye or ear or touch or mind, the first pattern. Then he makes the jump to another similar or a larger, more inclusive pattern. Each time he progresses to a new point in the visual, architectural, literary or musical arabesque, he grasps with greater certainty the special character, the unique quality of that design and is therefore enabled to progress in his investigation with ever-increasing speed. This movement continues from figure to figure, from panel to panel, from verse to verse, from musical phrase to musical phrase, until the edge of the plate, the border of the carpet, the sky above the façade, the end of the poem, or the last note of a sound performance catapults his imagination off in yet another *dafqah* of aesthetic resolution. Just as the world of Islam created name after name to describe the one and only God,[6] so the artist painted or carved or wrote or sang one pattern, then another, and still another. He was stopped at the extremities of his work of art by external limitations, and not because he had finished his expression of infinity or could, for that matter, ever exhaustively describe Allah.

The Qur'an as core for the arts: a hierarchy of the arts: It is possible to recognize another effect on the arts which seems to result from the message of *tawhid*. This is the corollary of those effects on content and structural characteristics discussed above. It involves determination of the kinds of art which are appreciated and cultivated by the Muslim peoples. Of course the greatest work of art of Islamic civilization is the Holy Qur'an. This literary exemplar revealed to the Prophet Muhammad was the new aesthetic ingredient that produced the "chemical reaction" in the artistic ingredients of Hellenistic, Byzantine and Semitic cultures and resulted in what we define today as Islamic art. It is to the Qur'an that Muslims owe their greatest debt for their art, as well as for every other aspect of their lives. Not only did it supply the substratum for Islam the religion, it was also the artistic determinant for future artistic production. In this single piece of literature, the so-called "first work of art in Islam".[7] the Muslim found all the artistic principles he was to demand of his art objects, regardless of medium. Abstract content, non-developmental form, and the arabesque – they were all present in the Holy Book.

Some Western authorities have claimed that the Muslim Arab of the seventh century had nothing to contribute to the development of Islamic art.[8] On the contrary, the new art obtained from those first Muslims and from the Qur'an itself, its spirit, its principles, its method, its purpose and the means of achieving that purpose. Islamic art took motifs and new materials for its efforts from whatever sources were available in the cultures of the peoples with which Muslims came in contact. But it clothed them in its own special garments and moulded them to conform with its unique categories of consciousness and underlying spirit.

These garments, these categories of consciousness, this underlying spirit were already available to the Islamic soul in the Qur'an. This literary exemplar has continued to inspire and mould artistic creation in every field of the visual and aural arts to this day. It has been the timeless, absolute ideal of all literary production, an unreachable ideal because of its *i'jaz* quality or inimitability.[9] This influence even guaranteed the literary arts a special place in Islamic aesthetic expression. There is no art form that is held in such esteem by the Muslim peoples as is literature.

The Qur'an provided no less an example and model for aesthetic as well as religious effect in the art of sound. One could say that the chanted Qur'an has been so important an example of the aural art of the Muslims that it has tended to make other forms of organized pitches and durations, i.e., music, unimportant by contrast. These forms, whether vocal or instrumental in execution, were strongly influenced by the well-guarded and unchanging Quranic chant. They took their abstract quality, their improvisatory nature, their structure and form, even the comparable use of pitches and durations, from that model. Islamic society was ever wary of the influence on Quranic chant of the native musical traditions of the various regions of the Muslim World. It guarded this strictly, with periodic literary and religious reformations, at the same time as it unconsciously promoted the influence spreading out in the other direction – that is, from the Quranic chant to the various kinds of music used in the Muslim World. This type of influence was so prevalent, in fact, that today we might consider much of the sound art of the Muslim peoples as variants, to a greater or lesser degree, of the Quranic aural model. If we were to put this idea in a diagram, we would draw concentric circles radiating out from a central core, the Quranic chant, each successive circle representing a genre or type of performance which is influenced by *tartil al Qur'an*. Those near the centre of the diagram are of course closely allied to their model, those farther removed showing less, but still significant conformance to the core.[10] While the conformity to the Quranic model is found more consistently in the Muslim nations of the Near East, even communities of Muslims as far removed as those of the southern Philippines (Mindanao) recite the Qur'an in a manner strikingly consistent with that of Muslims in other parts of the world. They even perform certain genres of secular music which reveal strong associations with that cantillated model.

The Qur'an was also influential in determining the importance of calligraphy in the arts of Islam. In all the arts, the aesthetic expression of *tawhid* was better suited to certain types of expression than others. For example, given the importance of the Qur'an as revelation sent by God and as the greatest work of art in Islam, its reproduction and copying, and therefore the art of calligraphy, soon became the most important visual art of the Muslim peoples. Though writing was of little importance for the pre-Islamic Arabs, the need for it soon developed in the first century of the Hijrah. There was a tremendous desire to know the contents of the Holy Qur'an. Copies of it were requested by all the new Muslim communities, where the Qur'an was used as a guide for the thinking and behaviour of the converts to the new faith. The script was perfected, with the addition of dotting and diacritical marks (*harakat*) to insure accuracy of the reading. No mistake in reading the word of God could, of course, be tolerated. Soon after this perfection of the letters was completed, the elaboration of various scripts began. Angular and rounded scripts of various kinds were developed, followed by further elaborations which plasticized the letters, making them malleable to any desired vertical and horizontal expansion or compression, at the same time as their legibility was faithfully retained. Artistic calligraphy has been used as beautiful embellishment not only for copies of the Qur'an, but as an important element in the artistic production of other books; in architecture; in textiles; in carved art works made of wood, stone or plaster; and even in metal, ceramic and glass objects for everyday as well as religious use. Most frequently used for such renderings are Quranic passages; next, *Hadith*s; next, poetry, proverbs and common sayings.

Architecture has been perhaps the next most important form of visual art practised by the Muslims. Given the human role as vicegerent of Allah on earth, Muslims through the centuries have felt anxious to support that responsibility by endowing buildings for the public use, especially those used as mosques and schools. Hospitals, rest stations along the pilgrimage routes, wells and fountains were also seen as worthy projects for the wealthy patron. These projects often produced magnificent examples of Islamic art, as is evidenced throughout the Muslim World.

After architecture, a wide number of other important types of art expression should be mentioned which were also promoted by the Islamic ideology. They include items (e.g., textiles, rugs, ceramics, wood carving, metalwork, etc.) needed for every occupation of life. They are so numerous, however, that it is impossible to treat all of them here or even to determine the hierarchy of their importance. One might ask – but are all these items examples of Islamic art, when they are known to be used for non-religious or a-religious activities? The answer to this question is "yes"; for, regardless of what use is made of them, art products from the Muslim World show the same characteristics of content and structure. They are all influenced, even determined, by *tawhid*. In Islamic culture, there is no need to differentiate between the religious and the secular, as would be suitable in the arts of Western Europe. On the whole, those examples of Islamic art used for a religious function differ little, if at all, from those which are utilized in the salon, in the courtyard, or even in the kitchen. This certainly stems from another premise of *tawhid*, with which we will soon deal under a discussion of the role which that message plays in Islamic society and civilization.

Certain art forms that have been particularly important in other cultures have made little impact on us as Muslims. This too we see as an effect the message of *tawhid* has had on all of us. For example, sculpture in the round, figural painting, and dance are three art forms which, despite their importance in other cultures, have played a subordinate role in Muslim civilization. Whether one investigates these arts from the stance of quantity or quality of production, or from the standpoint of audience appreciation and participation, their subordinate position is obvious to any but the most casual observer. This stems from the fact that these three kinds of art are less successful in directing our attention to the transcendent realm rather than to this world or its objects, activities and living creatures. The creation of life-like statues of men or animals could never successfully fulfill that aesthetic goal. When such statues have been created at rare moments of Islamic history, they represent examples of the effect of an alien culture on the Muslim peoples.[11] Such examples have often been violently opposed by Muslims who consciously or unconsciously felt the incongruence of these objects with the rest of their life and thought.

Despite the great importance which the Western audience gives to the miniature art of the Islamic World,[12] these items carry a much lower importance and interest for the Muslim populace than calligraphic design or the abstract ornament of metalwork or wood carving. Now, even more than in the past, the miniature paintings of the Muslim World have a tremendous monetary value on the art market. A list of sales from Sotheby's could give ample evidence of this fact. But this value, even when supported and encouraged by Muslim buyers anxious to secure a hedge against inflation, should not be seen as a contradiction of the influence of *tawhid*. Rather, it is the effect of economic pressures, or perhaps a desire to appear cultured in an alien environment, not of aesthetic demands and preferences.

Though dance is also documentable as an art form in Islamic culture in certain religious as well as non-religious situations, it too has played a strikingly minor role in the culture as a whole. The neglect and suspicion with which Muslims have regarded this art form – one that is so important, for example, in Hindu India, in sub-Saharan Africa, in Western Europe and America – can best be explained by reference to the *tawhid*-inspired orientation toward transcendence. Without doubt, movements of the human body lend themselves, perhaps more than any of the other arts, to the depiction of moods and actions emphasizing this world. It is only with great difficulty that they can be constrained to convey an intuition of transcendence. This is the most important reason for the lack of concern, the uneasiness or even, at times or in some circles of Muslim society, the complete rejection of dance as an art form.[13]

2 Islam's contribution: determination of the role of tawhid in culture

Now let us consider Islam's definition of the role the message of *tawhid* should play in society and civilization. This has been an equally affective factor in the art world of Islam. Islam considers any division of civilization into that which is religious and that which is secular, into that which is to be regulated and determined by *tawhid*, and that which is not, as detrimental to the whole of society. The loss of effective influence which the former (the religious) can have on the latter (the secular) in any matter, whether big or small, is one of the basic arguments of Islam and the Muslims for the total integration of their lives with their new-found or inherited religious commitment. In addition to the *Shahadah*, prayer, fasting, *zakah* and pilgrimage, Islam teaches that political and legal theory, economic order, science and arts, social relationships – even dress and manner of greeting – should be affected by *tawhid*. Islam is the ideology which attempts to create a unity of all aspects of the adherent's life, thus ensuring the stability of the person, a person who is thus whole and free of the psychic tensions which plague our contemporary society. It seeks, by combating the notion of a religious-secular dichotomy, to free mankind from the disaster of living in a world which practises morality at home and "dog-eat-dog" activity in the market place, which invites a commitment to ethical behaviour between individuals while it condones an international tolerance, or even commitment to, actions governed by expediency. Even such schizophrenic contradictions in contemporary society are now being evidenced as only a stage on the way to more serious troubles. There is a new tendency revealed in conversations with our contemporaries, a tendency to escape these contradictions, not by returning to an Islamic doctrine of unity of intent and purpose in all aspects of life, but by creation of a new frame of mind in which there is an absence of all standards which are not determined by expediency and individualistic benefit.

It is time therefore to re-enunciate the contribution which Islam brought fourteen centuries ago. That contribution is not only the message of *tawhid per se*; it is also the Islamic notion of the place of that message, its interrelation with the other aspects of life and civilization, which make it that hope for humanity which this book, published on the occasion of the beginning of the fifteenth Hijrah century, proclaims as its message to mankind.

The negative gain

We have all heard the doctrine expounded by various thinkers and writers that art should be cultivated without ulterior ideological motive, that art is intrinsically a value and is therefore to be pursued and encouraged regardless of its nature or content. Their doctrine is encapsulated in the following expression: art for art's sake. A corollary of this view is that any exterior influence on that art is bound to be detrimental. In fact, the adherents of such a doctrine argue that a connection between ideology and art is bound to result in fascism or communism, in the taking over of the arts by forces which would use it as a propaganda tool to subjugate their peoples. True art, they argue, would be stifled and suffer inevitable suffocation under such a system.

Therefore, art for many contemporaries is not ideally a "translation" of an ideological message, as we have seen it to be in Islamic culture. It is argued that art must be the sole determinant of its own worth and suitability. No one, according to the advocates of this idea, should judge a work of art as good or bad, except for the sake of identifying one's own appreciation or rejection of it. They maintain that it might be considered excellent by one person while another judges it ugly and/or ineffectual. Art, under such a doctrine, becomes a law unto itself, a system in which no criteria can be arrived at by the majority of the people for the judging of the worth of any work of art. This is completely unacceptable to the Muslim. Backed by the Islamic notion of the role which *tawhid* is to play in all aspects of life, the Muslim would argue that art, just like any other aspect of civilization, must reflect the dominant spiritual ideas governing his life. It must conform to the doctrine of *tawhid* and remind one of the one God. It should provide an influence for good within the individual and the community. Therefore, all or any art can never be condoned and supported by the thinking Muslim.

But why should Islam demand such a role for the works of its artists, whether they be calligraphers or painters, sculptors or architects, weavers or metal workers, poets or musicians? In the answer to this question lies another contribution of Islam to the arts which is no less important than the contribution of Islam to the content and structure of art. It is probably more important today than it has ever been, since the arts of the contemporary world intrude on our lives through such a plethora of media: the radio, television, the movies, advertising, to name only the most insistent and persistent of these media. These force themselves on our lives even without our seeking them out, or sometimes even without our being aware of their insistent presence. While contemporary man of both East and West has often rebelled against that in art which he found repugnant or unfitting, there is little left to the inhabitant of our world today which is considered as properly and rightfully purgable from the arts. Even the notion of purging is condemned as an indulgence in or subservience to a fascist brain washing. Any idea, any motif, any figure, any musical combination of tones is permissible and admissible under this system. Any objection is labelled reactionary or restrictive of the artist's or the spectator's individual freedom, of their right to expression and enjoyment.

The results of such a doctrine are not difficult to predict. In fact, many features of the substantiation of the prediction are already evident in contemporary society. Since no external determinants are allowed, by definition, commercialism and sensationalism soon creep in, in ever-increasing quantities. Instead of reinforcing the ideology of the people involved, as they are meant to do, the arts are undermining the culture of our contemporaries, are even gnawing at the very moral and spiritual body of modern man. There is little sign that alleviation of this disease is to come from within Western ideology and society, despite its roots in quite a different tradition regarding the role of the arts which underpins Western culture.[14]

It falls to Islam and the Muslims therefore to teach contemporary man about the dangers inherent in the doctrine of art for art's sake. It is naïve to think that art is a free agent, acting purely and exclusively for the production of "beauty" divorced from any ideological message. On the contrary, art is always the expression of some meaning inherent in the culture or the period. What is considered beautiful is in fact determined by that message. To shut one's eyes to this fact is to invite disaster, for it opens the flood-gates to dominance by any mean and despicable force or idea, which can operate completely uncontrolled and undirected in such a situation. How much better that art express the most noble ideas of the people and their age than give way to the banal and the opportunist, the commercial and the exploitative.

The positive gain

Unity of cultural environment: By adhering to the idea that *tawhid* should play a major determining role in the arts, we are not only liberated from the oppression of the negative forces mentioned above, but we achieve other positive benefits as well. First of all, we can thank Islam's definition of the role of *tawhid* in the arts for ensuring the unity of our cultural environment. How incongruous it is to enter the home of a contempory Muslim of the *effendi* class and find oneself surrounded by the artworks and decorations of an alien culture and religion. How is it possible to adhere to a religion which describes itself as a complete way of life and have no concern for the art that surrounds us and influences us in our daily life? We must ask ourselves what effect on our souls does the separation of ideology and the means of joy, relaxation, beautification and entertainment have? We leave the leisure hours of our children and adults to be dominated by whatever the television, the movies or the radio can offer. And, more often than not, what these media offer contributes not merely neutral influences, but has actually negative effects on the personalities and the ideas of the viewers or listeners. No one needs to be reminded of the damaging effects of the exploitation of violence and sex which are standard ingredients of entertainment; every newspaper and magazine carries articles on this problem. These facts alone should be convincing. In addition, Islam teaches us that preaching *tawhid* on Friday will have meagre results if we live and play non-*tawhid* for the rest of the week. The Islamic arts can serve a valuable function if they are encouraged to flourish as an avenue for refreshment and entertainment as they have done in the past.

Reinforcement of ideology

A second positive result of the definition of the role *tawhid* should play in its relationship to the arts is that art, under this framework, becomes important not just for its refreshment and enjoyment, but also for its role in strengthening the ideology. Art under the Islamic system becomes a reinforcement and emphasizer of the message of *tawhid*.

But how can a painting, a building, or a performance of music reinforce a religious truth? When art is based on the same premises and ideas as the religious precepts of a people, art can open the door to depths of meanings, to intuitions, which are difficult to achieve through discursive explanation. Anyone who has heard a verbal explanation of the idea of universal brotherhood which Islam teaches, and experienced as well the feeling of universal brotherhood as he stands shoulder to shoulder with his Muslim brothers in prayer, can testify to the immediacy and depth of understanding which the sensory experience can provide to the discursive message.[15] The effect of finely done art work, whether appreciated by the eye or the ear, can provide the same heightened translation of the discursive lesson to the sensitive spectator. A Muslim will not fail to be moved as he or she reads a passage describing some episode in the Prophet's life. Yet compare the depth of feeling and understanding which a beautifully chanted poem about the Prophet can evoke in the same Muslim believer. As another example, let us consider that often repeated message of the Holy Qur'an to take heed of the marvels of creation. The perfectly co-ordinated functioning of the sun and the moon,[16] of night and day,[17] of the rain and the seasons,[18] of the animal species[19] – all of these reveal Allah's expert and masterful hand in creation.

> Is there (not) in these
> An adjuration (or evidence)
> For those who understand?[20]

They are surely "Signs for those who believe."[21]

Suppose we were to couple such discursive statements with contemplation of an intricate arabesque in which interlocking patterns of beautiful and varied shapes cause our eyes to move in fascination from one coloured motif to the next in never-ending succession. We would find in that arabesque a beautiful reminder of Allah's mastery in creation. To recall this perfection, which is present in the tiniest crystal and largest galaxy of stars, produces a powerful effect on the Muslim believer. It draws him irresistably to a contemplation of Allah's transcendence and produces a feeling of wonder and awe for His unlimited perfection and ability. We could not help but deepen our understanding of Allah's message by the contemplation of Islamic art if we understand these arabesque patterns, whether in two- or three-dimensional forms, as subtle metaphoric or symbolic representations of these deepest teachings of our faith.

Summary

Tawhid, the monotheistic message of Islam, has important contributions to make to our contemporary society in its influence on the arts as well as in its influence on other aspects of civilization. Some of these contributions in the realm of art pertain to the content and structural characteristics of Islamic art. *Tawhid* determines four basic content characteristics in the various arts: abstract quality, stylization, dematerialization of structure, and transubstantiation of materials. Structural characteristics derived from *tawhid* pertain to two aspects of the art of the Muslims: non-developmental form and arabesque structure. The Qur'an is seen as the exemplar and core of other artistic products, thus establishing a hierarchy of the Islamic arts. Islam also made a contribution to the arts through its determination of the role its ideology, *tawhid*, shall play in culture. This brought the negative gain of saving us from the doctrine of art for art's sake or the determination of artistic tendencies by banal or destructive elements in the society. The positive gains to be realized from the Islamic determination of the role of *tawhid* on the arts are the contributions to the unity of our cultural environment and the reinforcement and deepening of our commitment to the Islamic ideology.

Notes

1 "As a rule the actors in these pictures look out upon the scene with unconcerned, emotionless faces, whether they be kings or attendants, soldiers or peasants. Warriors in the frenzy of battle deal blows and receive mortal wounds with apparent unconcern; a head just about to fly from the shoulders at the vigorous blow of a stalwart foe seems to regard the unwonted separation with entire indifference, and a knight from whose body the blood is pouring with an abundance that bears evidence more to the possession of plenty of crimson paint than to any knowledge possessed by the painter as to what happens in such circumstances, stolidly refrains from exhibiting any outward sign of the agony that must accompany such a painful experience. Even moments of ecstatic delight leave the actors in the scene with unimpassioned faces, as though they did not know that they were attaining the zenith of delight in the sphere of human experience." Thomas W. Arnold, *Painting in Islam* New York: Dover Publications, Inc. 1965, p.134.

2 Another possible expression for this characteristic is "camouflage of forms." Richard Ettinghausen, "The Character of Islamic Art", *The Arab Heritage*, ed. Nabih Amin Faris Princeton: Princeton University Press, 1944, p.260.

3 Ernst Kühnel, "Arabesque," *The Encyclopaedia of Islam*, new edition, Leiden and London: E. J. Brill and Luzac and Co., Vol. I, pp.558–561.

4 Ernst Grube, *The World of Islam* New York: McGraw-Hill Book Co., 1966, p.11.

5 In contrasting Jalal al Din Rumi's *Mathnawi* with Dante's *Divine Comedy*, the late Marshall G. S. Hodgson likened Dante's work to "a mountain, with a fixed structure. On the lower slopes you take each path in its turn as it leads you higher; as you go on, more and more of the overall shape of the mountain becomes clear to you. Finally at the top you see the whole displayed in order. Dante's last line contains the whole poem in nucleo. Rumi's poem on the other hand is fluid; it is like a river. As you float down a river, sooner or later everything is displayed to you – rapids and still ponds, towns and farmhouses and parks; at the end you slip into the all-absorbing ocean. But, to change the thought a bit, if you stand in a spot in the river, sooner or later the whole of it will appear to you also – every stick that floats in it, every drop of its water will pass by your feet. Similarly, at every spot in Rumi's poem the whole is present by implication... A Western reader may feel the anecdotes to be interminably expanded by extra verbiage and the poem as a whole to be shapeless. He must rather dip into the waters and feel all their varied ripples as they flow by." Marshall G. S. Hodgson, *Introduction to Islamic Civilization* Chicago: The University of Chicago Press, 1958, Vol. II, pp.296–297.

6 Qur'an 59:22–24.

7 Isma'il R. Al Faruqi, "Islam and Art", *Studia Islamica*, Vol. XXXVII, p. 95.

8 K. A. C. Creswell, the famous historian of Islamic architecture, writes: "Now the men who formed these armies [the first Arab armies of Islam] were mainly Bedawin, but even those who came from permanent settlements, such as Mekka and Madina, knew nothing of art or architecture." K. A. C. Creswell, *A Short Account of Early Muslim Architecture* Harmondshire, England: Penguin Books, 1958, p.6. Oleg Grabar has told us that from its Arabian past, "... the new Muslim art could draw almost nothing." Oleg Grabar, "Islamic Art and Byzantium". *Dumbarton Oaks Papers*, Vol. XVIII [1964], p.79.

9 Early non-Muslim poets attempted to match its excellence but finally accepted the futility of their efforts. See Qur'an 2:23–24, 11:13–14; also Abu Bakr Muhammad ibn al Tayyib al Baqillani, *I'jaz al Qur'an* Cairo: Dar al Ma'arif, 1963, pp.16 ff.; Jalal al Din al Suyuti, *Al Itqan fi 'Ulum al Qur'an* Cairo: Matba'ah Hijazi, 1941, Vol. I, pp.197–199.

10 Such a diagram was created for a presentation by this author for a Princeton University Symposium on *The Status of Music in Muslim Nations*. The presentation and its diagram is published in Asian Music, Vol XII, no. 1 (1981), pp. 56–84 under the title "The Status of Music in Muslim Nations: Evidence from the Arab World."

11 The statues of Muhammad 'Ali, Sulayman Pasha and Mustapha Kamil in Cairo are a case in point.

12 For example, an elaborate exhibit of Persian miniature art is now on display in the National Gallery of Art, Washington, D.C. A similar exhibition was held at the Metropolitan Museum of Art (New York City) in 1973.

13 This, however, did not prevent *tawhid* from having its permeating effect even on this peripheral artistic medium, as has been outlined in an article by the present author, "Dance as an Expression of Islamic Culture", *Dance Research Journal*, Vol. X, No. 2 Spring-Summer, 1978, pp.6–13.

14 See, for example, Friedrich Schiller, *On the Aesthetic Education of Man*, tr. Reginald Snell New Haven: Yale University Press, 1954.

15 Note the use of the word "sensory", meaning "a translation transmitted through one of the senses". I do not mean "sensuous" or "sensual", words which carry the idea of voluptuous indulgence of the appetites.

16 Qur'an 10:5

17 Qur'an 10:6; 17:12

18 Qur'an 41:39; 45:5

19 Qur'an 45:4

20 Qur'an 89:5

21 Qur'an 45:3

Islam and the Secular Thrust of Western Imperialism

Altaf Gauhar

An attempt will be made in this paper to define imperialism, to discuss its brief history and then to formulate the issues confronting the Muslim nations which have emerged from colonial domination in the last forty years. It shall be argued that the main thrust of secular imperialism was cultural in character, though it served powerful commercial interests and fulfilled the strategic and military requirements of expansionist and competitive colonial powers. The main target of Western secular imperialism was the Islamic faith and culture everywhere including Europe, the Middle East, South Asia and Africa. Culture represents beliefs, values, attitudes and manners of a society and these precisely were the areas where the greatest erosion was caused by western imperialism. The destruction of Muslim cultural identity was the principal aim of Western imperialism in the 18th and 19th centuries. I shall identify those Western cultural influences which continue to dominate and govern our life alienating us from our own tradition, making us strangers to our own culture, compelling us to adopt alien manners and institutions. It is my hope that my views will be of some help in drawing up a realistic programme for the future.

The word "imperialism" and the concept which it came to represent was not defined until the beginning of the present century. The word was still a newcomer in 1900.[1] The Latin word *imperium* signified supreme political authority and the *imperator* enjoyed not only military powers but also authority in matters of state. Dante used the words *monarchia* and *imperium* to signify hegemony. In modern usage, the word is "most readily applied to the movement by which certain Western European nations gained political control over practically the whole of Africa and parts of Asia in the late nineteenth century".[2] Early in the 16th century, Henry VIII declared that "this realm of England is an Empire." Edmund Burke spoke of Empire as "the aggregate of many states under one common head". But till the end of the 18th century dependencies overseas were not treated as part of the British Empire. A fundamental change in the British attitude toward the Empire becomes noticeable in the second half of the 19th century. This was the time when Rudyard Kipling wrote *A song of the English*.

"For the Lord our God Most High,
He hath made the deep as dry,
He hath smote for us a pathway to
The ends of all the Earth"

Imperialism developed a new dimension under the influence of Professor John Seeley.[3] He advanced the view that there was nothing unnatural in treating the State as capable of "indefinite growth and expansion" and suggested that the colonies should be regarded as "a simple extension of the mother-state".[4] He had no doubt that science would soon abolish distance thus making the concept of political unity over vast areas "a robust reality". Along with Seeley, appeared another powerful strand of thought which has been described as "the vision of the special mission of the British to bring freedom and civilization to the world."[5] Underlying this was the assumption that "race was a fundamental determinant of all history and culture" which had given rise to certain key beliefs:

"(a) non-Western culture is far inferior to that of the West; (b) non-Western people are racially different from Europeans, and this difference is hereditary; (c) therefore, the cultural inferiority is also hereditary."[6]

In a letter to the Under-Secretary of State for the Colonies on Jan. 6, 1847, Shuttleworth said:

"Christian civilization alone was capable of developing all the faculties in a child and, therefore, the object of education for the coloured races should be to inculcate the principles and promote the influences of Christianity, by such instruction as can be given in elementary schools." Along with this efforts should be made "to diffuse a grammatical knowledge of the English language, as the most important agent of civilization for the coloured populations of the Colonies."

The vision of a special mission was thus converted into a responsibility of the imperial powers to transform the cultural life of the people over whom they had been able to establish military and political control.

The threads of missionary endeavour can be seen in the literature of the time which reflected a strong "desire to propagate the Glorious Gospel to the heathens and savages falling under our sway."[7] George Popham, an English writer, addressed a letter to James I in which he spoke approvingly of colonies "since they seem to redound to the Glory of God." The commission for Raleigh's voyage was authorized "to advance the conversion of savages".[8] It was the spiritual salvation of heathens which became the principal purpose of occupation and annexation of overseas territories. "It shall fall out in proofe that the savages shall hereby have just cause to blesse the houre when this enterprise was undertaken." Every imperial agency was inspired by the thought of turning the savages "from their blind superstition to the religion of light".[9] In the early 17th century 76 ministers submitted a petition to Parliament in which they complained that not enough was being done for the propagation of the gospel in the colonies and too much attention was paid "to possesse the land of those infidels or of gaine by commerce."[10] William Howitt accused the government in *Colonies and Christianity* in 1838 of indifference to the cultural purpose of the imperial mission. He condemned British merchants as "rapacious and unprincipled monsters" and was deeply shocked "that the divine and beneficent religion of Christ should thus have been libelled by base pretenders." Albert R. Carman in the *Ethics of Imperialism*, published in 1905, complained that Christian ethics had been destroyed by imperialism in pursuit of commercial gains.

No serious thinker would maintain that Western Imperialism was a purely economic phenomenon. In *Africa and the Victorians; the official mind of Imperialism*, (1961), Robinson and Gallagher rejected the traditional explanations of imperialism. They refused to accept that the "scramble for Africa" was caused by economic compulsions.

"As an explanation of European rule in tropical Africa, the theory of economic imperialism puts the trade before the flag, the Capital before the Conquest, the cart before the horse."

In a chapter in volume XI of the *New Cambridge Modern History*, they suggested:

"Imbroglios with Egyptian proto-nationalists and thence with Islamic revivals across the whole of the Sudan drew the powers into an expansion of their own in East and West Africa . . . . The last quarter of the century has often been called the 'Age of Imperialism'. Yet much of this imperialism was no more than an involuntary reaction of Europe to the various proto-nationalism of Islam . . . . ."

There is a great deal of historical evidence to show that Europe's reaction to any possibility of reassertion of Islamic Culture, was voluntary, calculated and deliberate. The strong cultural purpose of imperialism is seen clearly in the Charters, Statutes and proclamations issued by the British Government in the 17th century. The Charter of the East India Company granted in 1600 gave the Company

"the exclusive right for 15 years of trading to and from the East Indies, that is to say the continents of Asia and Africa from the Cape of Good Hope to the Straits of Magellan, with the exception of such places as were in the possession of any friendly Christian Prince, without his consent."[11]

The exception speaks for itself. When a new Charter was granted in 1661 the Company was recognized "as a state within a state as it could send out ships of war and soldiers and wage war with non-Christian peoples and otherwise act in a sovereign capacity".[12]

When the British introduced their own laws in the Indian subcontinent they claimed that the Qur'an and the body of customary law developed under the Muslims was entirely personal in character and could not be regarded as a territorial law in the European and modern sense. They then decided that the provisions of the Muslim system "were so different from the usages of the West" that it was impossible to enforce them.[13] By the end of the 18th century the whole legal system developed by the Muslims was virtually discarded.

There were strong protests against the introduction of British customs and laws even in Western political and academic circles. Merivale wrote in 1841:

"the history of the European settlements in America, Africa, and Australia presents everywhere the same general feature – a wide and sweeping destruction of native races by the uncontrolled violence of individuals if not of colonial authorities."[14]

In an official document entitled *Observations upon the administration of justice occasioned by some late proceedings at Dacca* it was said,

"instead of framing a new Code of Law for this new Institution, the English Laws are introduced in their full extent, and with all their consequences; without any restriction or modification whatever to accommodate them to the climate and manners of Asia; without any regard to religious institutions or local habits, or to the influence of other laws handed down from the remotest antiquity, and fixed in the hearts of the people; without any latitude allowed to the magistrate to relax, compress, or change their application, according to the exigency of the circumstances, upon a more attentive observation of them. But

all are transplanted entire into the opposite quarter of the globe, to be administered by Judges educated under them and wholly unacquainted with the religion, character or manners of the people over whom they were to preside.''[15]

But these protests made no difference, the imperial cultural mission
had developed into a powerful driving force. Joseph Chamberlain
declared in 1897:

"We have to carry civilisation, British justice, British Law, religion and
Christianity to millions and millions of people who until our advent had lived
in ignorance, in bitter conflict and whose territories have fallen to us to
develop.''

In a speech at the Royal Colonial Institute in 1897 he explained why
the British must destroy all the established cultural and political
institutions in the colonies:

"You cannot have omelettes without breaking eggs. You cannot destroy the
practice of barbarism, of slavery, of superstition ...... without the use of
force.''[16]

In a recent series of lectures, Professor D. A. Low[17] has explained
how imperialism in the 19th century received support from three
schools called respectively evangelical, liberal and utilitarian. Indian
society in the eyes of these three schools was marked by a "general
corruption of manners and sunk in misery''. The principal evangelical
figure was Charles Grant who had served the Company for forty years,
first in India and then in London. In 1792 he said in a pamphlet that
the Indians were "a race of men lamentably degenerate and base.''
His solution was the introduction of Christian missionaries to India:

"the pre-eminent excellence of the morality which the Gospel teaches and the
superior efficacy of its divine system taken in all its parts, in ameliorating the
condition of human society, cannot be denied by those who are unwilling to
admit to higher claims; and on this ground alone the dissemination of it must
be beneficial to mankind.''

His associate, Wilberforce, said in the House of Commons in 1813:

"Are we so little aware of the vast superiority even of European laws and
institutions, and far more of British institutions, over those of Asia, as not to
be prepared to predict with confidence, that the Indian community which
should have exchanged its dark and bloody superstitions for the genial influence of Christian light and truth, would have experienced such an increase of
civil order and security of social pleasures and domestic comforts (the 'good

life' that is) as to be desirous of preserving the blessings it should have acquired.''

The evangelicals were joined by the liberals who believed that Western education should be introduced in India to ''silently undermine . . . . . the fabric of error''. The utilitarians argued in favour of the extension of British culture in the interest of Indian Society. The great debate about imperialism, Professor Low has suggested, ended with the adoption of the settled view when efficiency became the keynote of imperial policy and politics was reduced to administration. Toward the end Imperialism was marked by a development fever when it concentrated on programmes of rural uplift and adult education. According to Professor Low, Christianity and the British Empire spread with arms linked. An Anglican establishment existed within the Government of India from 1813 onward and Christian missionaries received strong moral support from Government officials, while they were provided with finances in a variety of ways. Hold Mackenzie recorded a note for the Education Committee in India on 17th July 1823 in which he said:

''The education indeed of the great body of the people can never, I think, be expected to extend beyond what is necessary for the business of life; and it is only therefore through religious exercises, which form a great part of the business of life that the labourer will turn his thoughts on things above the common drudgery, by which he earns his subsistence. Hence it is under the Christian scheme alone that I should expect to find the labouring classes really educated: and their station in the scale of instructed and humanized beings will, I imagine, be pretty closely proportioned to their piety.''

I shall sum up by giving some facts and figures to show the rapid expansion of Western imperialism. The British Empire increased by nearly 5,000,000 square miles and by 88,000,000 people in the last 30 years of the 19th century. By 1900, it covered one fifth of the globe and governed 400,000,000 subjects. The French Empire expanded from 700,000 to over 6,000,000 square miles and from 5,000,000 people to 52,000,000 people. Germany, which had no Empire, acquired 1,000,000 square miles and a colonial population of 14,000,000 people by 1900. During the ten years between 1841 and 1851 Britain got New Zealand, the Gold Coast, Laebuan, Natal, the Punjab, Sind and Hong Kong. In 1870 only one tenth of the African continent was under European control. By 1900 only one tenth remained independent.

I suggest that a majority of the people who were affected by imperial expansion and cultural domination were the Muslims and it is the Muslim culture which has been the main victim of Western culture. There were three categories of colonies. The first comprised areas either newly discovered or thinly populated and included America, Canada, Australia and New Zealand. The native population was swiftly driven into slavery or wiped out and European emigrants in large numbers occupied those areas to develop them for their own benefit. Direct British domination over these areas did not last for very long because there was no cultural conflict and disputes over commercial interests were quickly resolved, though in some cases they were attended by violence. No theory of racial superiority or hereditary deficiency was pressed into service to defer the grant of independence to these territories, nor was any question of education or lack of political experience raised to perpetuate metropolitan control. In the second category came areas which were considered climatically suitable for the settlement of European population and these included Algiers, South Africa and Rhodesia. The Algerians had to fight a prolonged war to win their independence. During the era of cultural domination all Algerian traditions and institutions were replaced by French culture, language and customs. The Algerians are today making strenuous and successful efforts to recover the links with their own history and tradition.

The struggle in South Africa continues and while it is agreed in conferences that there should be black majority rule, nothing is likely to happen unless the European minority settled there can be adequately compensated for loss of prospects of continued economic exploitation. The battle for political and cultural freedom in Africa will not be won by words in Geneva but by blood on African soil.

In the third category fell those areas which the Europeans did not consider suitable for settlement and these represented the major part of the colonial empire. It was in these areas that the population was treated as ''lamentably depraved'' and their institutions and cultural traditions were destroyed without hesitation. I mentioned the introduction of British laws in the Indian sub-continent; more relevant to my thesis is the introduction of the British system of education and the English language which had a devastating effect on the cultural life of the people.

Educationists are familiar with Macaulay's minute of February 2, 1835. This minute is a mirror of the imperial mind and reveals how prejudice and ignorance were enshrined in official policy – a policy to which the British adhered until the end of their stay in the subcontinent. A certain amount of money was provided in the Charter of 1813 for "the revival and promotion of literature and the encouragement of learned natives of India". The question under discussion, when Macaulay came into the picture, was whether the British Government should continue to provide financial assistance to what were called native educational institutions. Macaulay was incensed by the suggestion that the Government was bound by the Statute to encourage education according to the Indian tradition and in the languages of India. He asserted:

"that the dialects commonly spoken among the natives of this part of India contain neither literary nor scientific information and are moreover so poor and rude that until they are enriched from some other quarter, it will not be easy to translate any valuable work into them."

Macaulay had no knowledge of Arabic, but he asserted that no-one "could deny that a single shelf of a good European library was worth the whole native literature of India and Arabia". He concluded that the question was "to educate a people who cannot at present be educated by means of their mother-tongue". He did not want the Government to abandon its posture of neutrality in religious matters, but he would not countenance "the study of a literature admitted to be of small intrinsic value only because that literature inculcates the most serious errors on the most important subjects", meaning subjects held sacred by the people of India. He could not see why the British should teach a language and literature which was "fruitful of monstrous superstitions". He said, "we are to teach false history, false astronomy, false medicine, because we find them in company with a false religion". It was this minute of Macaulay's which was approved by the Governor-General, Lord Bentinck who said, "I give my entire concurrence to the sentiments expressed in this minute." In April 1835 the minute was turned into the Governor-General's Resolution which provided that the "great object of the British Government ought to be the promotion of European literature and science among the natives of India; and that all the funds provided for the purpose of education would be best employed on English education alone".

What was Macaulay's object? He stated it clearly in his minute:

"We must at present do our best to form a class who may be interpreters between us and the millions whom we govern; a class of persons Indian in blood and colour but English in taste, in opinions, in morals and intellect. To that class we may leave it to refine the vernacular dialects of the country, to enrich those dialects with terms of science borrowed from the Western nomenclature and to render them by degrees fit vehicles for conveying knowledge to the great mass of the population.''

In a speech in the House of Commons two years earlier Macaulay had said;

''it may be that the public mind of India may expand under our system till it has outgrown that system; that by good government we may educate our subjects into a capacity for better government; but having become instructed in European knowledge they may in some future age demand European institutions.''

This was the crux of the matter. Through the introduction of the English language a new class of natives was to be produced which to begin with would act as ''interpreters'' between the British and the millions of people governed by the British, and in the end demand the establishment of British institutions.

During the last part of the 19th century, and the first three decades of the 20th century, a number of people were selected, largely according to the judgement of British officials, for advanced studies in England. Most of them were educated in the British legal system. In the meantime, the natives were forced to learn the English language under a British system of education because without the knowledge of English they could not occupy a position of honour in any profession, or secure any employment under the government. A new elitist class was created through an alien system of education to serve as an instrument of intermediate domination (interpreters, Macaulay called them) in the service of the British crown, and it was left to this class to carry on the cultural mission of the British. I shall pause here to explain how this elitist class was used against the interest of their own people, not only in suppressing them but also in destroying their links with their historical past and their cultural traditions.

The British introduced the English language in the subcontinent on the ground that it was a language of world culture and the people of India would gain access to European and modern knowledge through this language. British teachers and Indians trained in the British educational system were then provided to run the educational institutions set up by the British to develop a new class of Western educated elite. At no stage was it envisaged that the English language should be made the language of the masses. The idea was that the elitist class should serve as the link between the rulers and the ruled and the purpose clearly was that the English language should eventually become the dominant cultural vehicle among the upper classes in the subcontinent. Before the British departed from the subcontinent they had succeeded in establishing English as the language of administration, courts, professions, and commerce. It was through the English language that the elitist class was introduced to political ideas, generally described as liberal ideas. These ideas were not all of British origin. Some of them were formulated by French philosophers and political scientists and others by American thinkers. But it is an undisputed fact that it was through the English language that the Western educated classes in India became familiar with the concepts and institutions of Western liberal democracy. These concepts included (1) the sovereignty of the people, (2) the rule of law, and (3) sanctity of human rights. While the British did not specifically preach or practise any of these concepts, they proclaimed that they intended to fulfil the obligations assumed by them under a self-created trust to civilize the people of India and to educate and prepare them for self-government. When the British Government decided to take over direct control of the territories in India from the East India Company, Queen Victoria issued a proclamation on 1st November, 1858. The proclamation said that the Queen, Defender of the Faith, had with the advice and consent of the Lords spiritual and temporal and Commons in Parliament assembled, decided ''to take upon ourselves the government of the territories in India heretofore administered in trust for us by the honourable East India Company''. The word ''trust'' in the proclamation is significant because it could only be justified in the context of a cultural mission. No one would seriously contend that the pretext of employment of surplus capital, competition for markets or space for emigration could be regarded as a trust. Imperialism adopted various intellectual formulations and theories to suppress and exploit the colonies. In Africa, the British used the theory of ''dual mandate'' which was introduced to create the right for the British to exploit the resources of the region, which placed an obligation on the British to educate and civilize the people. Here was a missionary asking for full payment for his services. In India the proclamation of the Queen said, the East India Company had been administering the territories in trust on behalf of the British Crown, but before long the British were to claim that they were holding the territories in India in trust on behalf of the people of

India – a variation of the "dual mandate" concept. Queen Victoria's proclamation called upon the people of India "to be faithful and to bear true allegiance to us". The Princes of India were given an unqualified guarantee that the British Government would scrupulously maintain any treaties and engagements made with them by the East India Company. Here the British introduced a fundamental cultural distinction between the people of India and the Princes of India. The people were required to be faithful to the British Government, the Princes of India had only to observe the terms of their treaties. They were assured that the British Government would respect "the rights, dignity and honour of native Princes as our own". No such assurance was extended to the people of India in respect of their rights, dignity and honour. The obligation which the British Government assumed in respect of the people of India was a matter of duty. The proclamation granted equal protection of the law to all classes of people without making it obligatory for the Princes to treat the people in the states according to the law. It was said that "in framing and administering the law, due regard is to be paid to the ancient rights, usages and customs of India". A general amnesty was granted to those who had indulged in rebellion as the power of the Crown had been shown "by the suppression of that rebellion in the field". Everyone was called upon to return to the "path of duty" – meaning complete submission to the Crown. It will be seen that this proclamation did not give any assurance that the educational system in India would be allowed to develop according to its own tradition. The reference to ancient rights, usages and customs of India related only to the framing and administration of the law. The proclamation accepted the same obligations toward the people of India as toward the other subjects of the British Government thus conceding in a limited sense the concept of the sovereignty of the people. I mention this to emphasize that the concept of the sovereignty of the people was never disowned by the British. It was always treated as an ideal. The royal proclamation issued by King George V, Defender of the Faith, Emperor of India, said that the Act of 1919 "points the way to full responsible government". The trust originally held by the Company was assumed by the British Government: "Ever since the welfare of India was confided to us, it has been held as a sacred trust by Our Royal House and Line." The proclamation added that the King and Parliament had always been "zealous for the moral and material advancement of India" and claimed that they had given to the people of India "the many blessings which providence has bestowed upon ourselves''. But the right of the people to self-government was restricted to domestic matters:

"The defence of India against foreign aggression is a duty of common imperial interest and pride. The control of her domestic concerns is a burden which India may legitimately aspire to take upon her own shoulders.''

It was in this context that the King expressed his understanding and sympathy for the desire of the Indian people for representative institutions.

"Starting from small beginnings this ambition has steadily strengthened its hold upon the intelligence of the country. It has pursued its course along constitutional channels with sincerity and courage. It has survived the discredit which at times and in places lawless men sought to cast upon it by acts of violence committed under the guise of patriotism.''

The proclamation then asked the representatives of the "intelligence of the country'' not to forget the interests of the masses "who cannot yet be admitted to franchise''. This was how an elitist class was being developed to act as an instrument of cultural control and domination. This class was also trained to exploit the liberal ideals and institutions. The British Government announced its commitment to liberal democratic principles but this commitment was used to undermine established cultural and political institutions. The judicial system used was an instrument of imperialism: it maintained and operated inequitable laws. Indian magistrates were not permitted to try Englishmen in India. No consideration was shown for the traditions established by the Muslims in the subcontinent for the administration of justice. In fact the whole fabric of Muslim laws and procedures was dismantled and replaced by a system which neither conformed to British practice nor reflected the liberal ideal of equality before the law. Even the basic principle that everyone should be deemed to be innocent until proved guilty was flagrantly violated by the executive and condoned by the judges who approved detention without trial of innumerable people whose opinions and activities were considered harmful to British interests.

The political institutions established by the British in India were a travesty of the Westminster model. Franchise was restricted and representation in the assemblies was distributed amongst various classes of people created by the British themselves to ensure majority support. Generous provisions were made for nominations to establish a system of patronage. What the British Government introduced in the subcontinent was not any form of liberal democracy, it introduced the game of politics, in which various sections of the population were pitched against one another to secure personal benefit or advancement. In the same way, a highly aggressive and competitive arrangement in respect of government employment was introduced. The knowledge of English was a decisive factor in this. But even in respect of appointments the Government reserved to itself the authority to "appoint to any such office any person of proved merit and ability . . . . . although the person so appointed has not been admitted to that service" in accordance with the prescribed procedure.[18] Regarding human rights, one has only to note the number of detentions without trial and the elaborate arrangements for the censorship of the press to realize that the liberal ideals were never seriously translated into practice in India.

I suggest that the institutions which the British created in the name of liberal democracy, and which were inherited as part of the Western legacy were only well designed instruments of cultural domination which created endless rivalries and confusion in the lives of the people. The greatest, and indeed the most lasting, damage was done by the introduction of the English language and the English educational system. I am using the word lasting to emphasize that the products of an alien educational system continue to occupy positions of influence and decision making in Muslim countries. They hold key offices in Government, they are dominant in the legal and educational professions and they have a natural and deep-seated personal interest in ensuring the continuance of the British cultural traditions and institutions. Any attempt to radically alter, for instance, the judicial system in countries like Pakistan and Bangladesh would immediately draw a powerful protest from the judges and the lawyers, and the students who are receiving their education and training in law at home and abroad because their social position and survival is linked with the system. The people may find this alien, tardy, incomprehensible, iniquitous and oppressive, but the elitist legal class created by the British will not allow any interference with the system – for them the death of the system would be their death. They would much rather see the masses suffer than permit themselves to be inconvenienced.

The teachers have all learnt to teach in the English language. They hold degrees from British Universities for the advancement of their career. How can they as a class be expected to do anything for the promotion and advancement of their mother-tongue or of national language. They may be no more than a small fraction of the population, and the number of students ,produced by their system of learning may add up to less than 1% of the population, but, today, they are the custodians and masters of the educational future of the people. I am not against the English language. It is a great language and it has a great literature. But people do not give up their own language because of other great languages in the world. A child must learn through the language for which he has the most intimate and deepest affection and understanding. That is the whole basis of the universally accepted notion that there is no substitute for the mother-tongue as a medium of instruction. Thinkers, writers, poets and philosophers have to think and express themselves in their own language because that is the language which they understand and which their people understand. When I suggest that our educational system can only be developed on the basis of our own language, it is not because of any dislike for the English language or for any other foreign language. It is because I believe that we will never be able to educate ourselves according to our own culture and tradition so long as we rely on any foreign language. We can go on translating all the works in English and French but we will never be able to catch up with those who think and write creatively in those languages. Translation is no compensation for creative expression. We will always be trailing behind the others. The advocates of the English language in Muslim countries should seriously re-examine their position. Two lectures have been published by the University of London, Institute of Education, by Lionel Elven, (December 1956) and the other by L. J. Lewis (February 1959). In both these lectures it is assumed that the future of education in Africa and Asia depends on the ability of the people in these areas to learn the English language. Lewis suggests that Britain should continue to provide

"special facilities for study and reflection for those men and women, whatever their previous training and experience, who find themselves as senior members of their local education services responsible for providing professional advice to their political masters and responsible for interpreting in a satisfactory professional fashion the educational aspirations of the people they serve. Such professional interpretation calls for imagination purged and judgement ripened by 'awareness of the slow, hesitant, wayward course of human life, its failures, its successes but its indomitable will to endure'. Such purging of imagination and ripening of judgement may more easily be recognised, if not come by, in this country where we are involved in educational experiment based on exceptional accumulation of experience and knowledge, and subject to a strength and wisdom such as is attainable as we are able to stand on the shoulders of those who have gone before."[19]

This is only a slightly more sophisticated version of the earlier missionary consciousness. Lewis continues to say that the British should "provide opportunity for the educational leaders of the new nations" to instruct their countrymen. Lionel Elven recalls with admiration the "very real devotion with which many an Englishman in India, the Far East and Africa had faced his responsibilities" and says that "some of the best work of the British people overseas went into teaching, into the building of schools and into the initiation of adults into modern life".[20] Margaret Read of the University of London spells out her vision of the future in even clearer terms. She is distressed by a spectacle of variety of languages in former colonies and pleads for the growth of a sense of nationhood:

"this ideal of common citizenship within each colonial territory with its extensions outwards in membership of the British Commonwealth has one of its firmest foundations in the use of English as a lingua franca. It has been one of the strongest uniting forces in this country since it is the common channel used by all citizens for political thought and cultural expression."[21]

Professor Read does not seem to notice that the language which she is recommending for adoption as a *lingua franca* is not the language of the people in the former colonies. She recognizes that the English language which has served as a common channel in England is the language used by all citizens but fails to see that this is not the case in the former colonies. English is not the language of the people in any former colony, and certainly not in any of the Muslim countries. Chamberlain, from whose pamphlet *The New Imperialism* I have quoted earlier, makes an interesting observation in his concluding paragraph. He says:

"It was easy enough for the peoples of Africa and Asia to throw off their alien conquerors in the years following the Second World War. Decolonisation proceeded at an even more breakneck pace than the original colonisation had done. But the new nations which emerged were very different from their predecessors which had been conquered. For good or ill something like a common civilisation, the main elements of which seem to derive from European political and economic ideas, has for the first time been spread over the whole globe."[22]

He hopes for the perpetuation of the post-colonial political and cultural institutions in the newly emergent countries because their main elements are derived from European ideas which are *for the first time* spread over the whole globe.

The challenge before the Muslim World has two facets: subjective and objective. The subjective facet represents a deep sense of alienation from our own culture which is the direct result of prolonged Western cultural domination. This sense of alienation expresses itself in a consciousness of inferiority, in aggression toward other people, and in our helplessness to evolve a consensus for action. The objective facet is symbolized by the Western educated elitist classes in our society which operate and control the legacy of Western cultural institutions. These classes were trained for a particular purpose and they acquired great skill in the manipulation of imperial institutions in the service of the Crown. They continue to act true to their education and training regardless of the effect on the people of their attitude and thinking. They have learnt to act naturally in opposition to the interests of the people and have drawn a curtain between the privileged few and the masses, and this curtain is the curtain of language. Western cultural imperialism has been able to influence and undermine our beliefs, values, attitudes and manners and the task before us is to reassert our identity and to reach for our destiny. I am not advocating revivalism. Societies move forward not backward. They move forward through a sustained process of cultural assimilation, cohesion and continuity. The past cannot be revived but it can be restructured and this we cannot do unless we rediscover and reinterpret the beliefs and the values enshrined in the Holy Qur'an and made available to us as a living and everlasting model in the life of the Holy Prophet, (peace be upon him).

The elitist classes in dominance today represent a major threat to our future. So long as they continue to maintain their hold on our intellectual and cultural life no change or progress will be possible. They will frustrate all our actions and isolate us not only from our past, but also from our future.

Nations have to preserve their traditions with great care and affection. I shall give but one example. When the Americans came to Pakistan they organized their own schools. The people of Pakistan could have posed no danger to them, but they would not take any risk where it was a question of preserving their cultural values. They did not want their sons and daughters to get alienated from their history or culture. They built American schools and would not send their children to any of the great English schools which are held in high esteem by the citizens of Pakistan. In contrast, we go on sending our teachers and students to foreign universities in the hope that they will come back to educate our people. All this leads not to education of the people but to the consolidation of the elitist classes.

The elitist classes draw their strength from their knowledge of a foreign language, and it is imperative that steps should be taken to restructure our social and our educational system so that our mother-tongue is adopted as the medium of instruction and our own language, our *lingua franca*. The English maintain contact with Latin and Greek because they are the languages of their culture. The Muslim world is fortunate to have one common language of faith and culture – the Arabic language in which the Holy Qur'an was revealed. Every Muslim child learns the Qur'an and the language of the Qur'an which is a part of our culture. The Muslim world could adopt this as a language of international communication and this step alone would relax the strangulating hold of the English language on our society. Once Muslim countries provide basic facilities for the learning of Arabic many of the present linguistic problems will disappear because all our languages have a natural affinity which will be expanded and strengthened by our common knowledge of Arabic.

Notes

1 *The Emergence of the Concept of Imperialism*, R. Koebner, 1957, unpublished article, Accession number JC 359 KOE, Institute of Commonwealth Studies, University of London.

2 *The New Imperialism*, M. E. Chamberlain, The Historical Association, London, 1970, p.1.

3 *Empire and After*, Rita Hinden, Essential Books Ltd. London, 1950, p. 67.

4 Ibid, pp. 67–68.

5 Ibid, p.69.

6 *Imperialism*, Edited by Philip D. Curtin, Macmillan, 1971, p.xvii.

7 *Empire and After*, Rita Hinden, p.20.

8 *British Colonisation and Coloured Tribes*, Bannister London 1938, quoted by Hinden, p.47.

9 *A True Report of the Late Discoveries*, 1583, Sir George Peckham and *Nova Britannia*, 1609, R. Johnson.

10 *Proceedings and Debates of the British Parliaments*, L. F. Stock, Washington, 1924.

11 *Outlines of Indian Constitutional History*, W. A. J. Archbold, Curzon Press, 1924, p.11.

12 Ibid, p.15.

13 Ibid, p.43.

14 *Lectures on Colonisation and Colonies*, Oxford, 1839, 1841, Vol. II, H. Merivale, p.153.

15 *Outlines of Indian Constitutional History*, p.73.

16 *Empire and After*, p.74.

17 *British Imperialism: Four Facets*. Seminar Paper, Professor D. A. Low, 1969–70.

18 Government of India Act 1919, Part 8, clause 99(1).

19 *Partnership in Overseas Education*, L. J. Lewis, 1959, pp. 11, 12.

20 *Education in the End of Empire*, Lionel Elven, December 1956, pp. 7, 8.

21 *Education and Social Change in Tropical Areas*, Margaret Read, Thomas Nelson and Sons Ltd., 1955, p.54.

22 *The New Imperialism*, pp. 42–43.

Human Rights and Duties in Islam
a Philosophic Approach
Allahbukhsh K. Brohi

It is a matter of common knowledge that in Islam man has what may be called a dual obligation to discharge: one, which is in relation to himself, styled as *Haqooqullah* or the rights of God, and the other, which is in relation to his external world, called *Haqooq-un-Nas* or *Haqooq-ul-Abad*, that is to say, the rights of society in the external world of creation. But if we were to think deeply about the religious predicament of man, this dichotomy disappears if only because the *rights of God* are ubiquitous in their range and all-embracing and *Haqooq-ul-Abad* or *Haqooq-un-nas* seem to flow from the obligation a Believer owes to God in so far as he not only acknowledges Him to be his Creator and Law-Giver but also Creator of the entire world and indeed the external world is also subject to His Law. The former category embraces duties like prayer, the need for the purification of body and mind and the latter the class of duties that regulates relationships between man and man as also between man and the state.

From the perspective which is Islamic and which in this discourse will be called a theocentric perspective, God is in the centre and man occupies a peripheral position. Man has the possibility and therefore the choice of either moving towards or away from the norm which is divinely ordained. He may be either viewed as taking a position on the radius, the line which unites God to the imaginary circumference which metaphysically considered may be called the world of the Non-Being, or as some others have done by visualizing the same conception by situating man in one of the concentric circles that enfold the divine centre and move away from the centre in a widening expansiveness beyond which lies the domain of the Non-Being. The link of the believer with God is to be conceived in the image of a traveller on his way to God along what is called *siratulmustaqim*, that is to say the straight path. He who travels farther on that road that leads to God acquires greater *qurb* (or nearness) to God.

Such is human nature that it has two co-ordinates in terms of which its essence can be specifically determined: one is the inward centre of the being of man where, so to say, man knows and feels about his real link with his Lord and in conformity with that link he means to do certain things; the second co-ordinate refers to the *way* in which this determination of man to conduct himself righteously becomes that aspect of obedience to the Divine Law by which the life of man evolves and is regulated.

It would thus appear that at all events man is in bondage to the Lord and indeed he is under an obligation to acknowledge, in word, deed and thought, this "primeval contract" that has been referred to in the Qur'an. It would be recalled: God enquired from his servants "Am I not your Lord?" and the servants replied, "Indeed thou art." (*Sura 7 verse 172*). But the progress that a human being makes on his evolutionary march is only possible if he proceeds steadily to identify this Divine Law that he is asked to obey as though it were in reality the law of his own inner being – a law, conformity with which brings relief and redemption, peace and contentment to man. To begin with, he obeys law as a matter of compulsion because, on the plane of faith, he has accepted obedience to that law as warranting his true growth. But as he proceeds further he discovers that this law is also in keeping with his deepest urge: he comes to realize that what at one time compelled obedience on his part is progressively replaced by his love and longing to do the deed in conformity with the law. That is the stage where man moves from the station of wisdom, characterized by *tussawaf*, as *Sharia* to a higher one, called *Tariqat*. This movement is not to be conceived as though the *Sharia* is abandoned but simply that the attitude of the believer towards the religious law changes. The persistent practice of obedience to law (what is called *itta'at*) has now paved the way for a new disposition where obedience to law is done out of love. There is a significant line in the Qur'an, viz. *Fitratalahillati fitrannasa alaiha, latabdeelikhalikillah zalika dinul qayyim* which explains this transformation. The whole verse in which this appears can be freely translated as follows:

"Then set your face for right religion in a right state – the nature made by Allah in which He has made man: there is no altering of Allah's creation, that is the right religion – but most people do not know." (*Sura 30 verse 30*)

The text of this verse, it would appear, sets forth the root of the matter: the Quranic position is that the religion that has been taught to man conforms to the image of nature made by God and what is more, man himself has been made in the image of the same nature. The nature of religious law itself is such that it ministers to the growth of human personality; it is designed by the Creator to enable man to flower forth into an exalted state so as to be able to reach the highest station of wisdom. Obedience to the law which is reflected in man's nature, constitutes the basis of true religion in Islam. Islam merely establishes this truth and prepares the ground for man's recognition of this law, initially on the authority of revelation, but ultimately and fundamentally from his own inward realization of the truth of this law – through right thought, through right belief and through right action. (See Author's book on *Fundamental Laws of Pakistan*, page 734. Din Muhammad Press at Karachi 1958).

From what has been said above, it must follow that, strictly speaking, all rights belong to God and all men can have are their correlates, viz. duties. Man has no rights in relation to God. And as the Qur'an describes Him as *the first* and *the last*, even as He is the *hidden* as well as the *manifest* – indeed, He is all that there is – and vastly more, of which we can form no idea!

Now if it is true that there is nothing that is outside the reach of Divine Principle or Presence, then even vestment of His Being, viz. the external world, (to which reference has been made above in relation to which man owes *Haqooq-ul-abad*) also becomes an integral part of Divine Dispensation. Included in the world of external manifestation of the Divine Principle is also the totality of mankind and the believer owes duties to it, if only because it is an implication of the overall duty he owes to God. In the Islamic conception of things, therefore, strictly speaking, there are no human rights; there are only human duties; man is in debt to God because he has acknowledged being in bondage to His law and he can redeem himself only by doing his duty – that is, fulfilling the law and discharging the debt he owes to his Master.

Having said that, in order to avoid possible misunderstanding one must take notice of the fact that from the duties that a believer owes to God and therefore to his Creator it must follow that the creatures of God or his fellow men to that extent have rights against the believer or in relation to believers. But then these rights may be described as "derivative rights" since they derive from the believer's primary duty to God. Seen from the Western Weltanschauung which may be described as an aspect of anthropocentric perspective, *man is in the centre and he is to be regarded as the measure of everything.* Here, he has rights by reason of the fact that he is the centrepiece of the universe. But from a theocratic perspective of Islam, since God is in the centre, man has only duties to God and his fellow men themselves in turn derive their rights from the believer's duty to God.

In secular societies, the concept of human rights and human freedoms has really no metaphysical foundation, and, regarded strictly from a philosophical perspective, it is difficult to comprehend their significance. And the only way to account for the notion of human rights is to see them as necessary offshoots of a political system of Governance. Such has been the history of the political struggle in the "post-protestantism" period of European History that, with the repudiation of the ecclesiastical power of the Pope at Rome, Europe got splintered into various principalities and all authority within the secular states thereafter got steadily concentrated in the persons of titular heads of those states, that is to say, the Princes became the *de facto* sovereign rulers. So much was this true that nothing belonged to anybody except under some *instrument of grant* to which the ruling sovereign was himself a party. For instance, in strict theory, all land belonged to the king; he could command services of his subject as and when he liked without paying him any compensation and for his part the king himself was above the law – his will was the source of law and nobody could take a position against it. Such was the political ethos that no one could have any rights against the titular despots if only because they were above the law.

Progressively, however, this type of relationship between the ruler and the ruled became the subject matter of controversy and was questioned, and with the growth of democratic sentiment, as it was stimulated by the writings of the deist philosophers of the eighteenth century, it came to be asserted that the king can only govern provided he had, directly or indirectly, obtained the *consent* of those he governed. In theories of politics like those that are at the base of the "social contract", of "the institution of limited government" (that is to say, government that had its powers by express grant from the people, and which amounted to a denial of any of its inherent powers) of "the sovereignty of the people", we have the enunciation of those fundamental principles of politics which came to influence the course of subsequent development of European political thought. With the march of time as a result of this approach, we have had several important landmarks in English, American and French constitutional history which tend to show how the *political* and *civil* rights of people came to be declared as inalienable, fundamental and inviolable. Governments were being distrusted everywhere and the slogan of the age was that "All power corrupts and absolute power tends to corrupt absolutely." And it was being said everywhere that the one way to deal with the evil of absolutism was to make power a check on power by bringing about democratic diffusion of power and thus ensure individual liberty. This was done on the basis of the theory of separation of powers. That theory was at first sponsored by Montesquieu, the French philosopher who wrote the famous treatise on the "Spirit of the Law" in which he suggested that if the power of the ruler was subjected to division into various organs and agents in conformity with what has subsequently been described as the theory of separation of powers the governance of the country could be carried on consistently with the claim of individual liberty.

All human rights and freedoms which are to be seen compendiously recounted in the *Universal Declaration of Human Rights*, proclaimed by United Nations on 10th December 1948, would appear to be the rights that have been wrested from the hands of a reluctant sovereign by their subjects through the Petition of Rights. All Bills of Rights were, to begin with, humbly presented for them to be acknowledged by the sovereign rulers of the time as a restraint on their despotic will. The content of civil and political rights is invariably negative; it partakes of the character of prohibitions issued to the state-power to restrain itself from doing certain things to individuals or to deny them their rights.

Thus the rights claimed in the West for the human person involve corresponding duty on the part of state-power to give effect to that right: for example, the formulation in Article 3 of Universal Declaration, viz. *every one has the right to life, liberty and security of person*, necessarily means that there is a corresponding duty on the part of the law-giver or administrator or whoever he be, who has the authority to issue the commands in the name of the state, to acknowledge a corresponding duty in favour of the subject.

Similarly, Article 4 of the same declaration says: "No one shall be held for slavery or for servitude", and Article 5 says: "No one shall be subjected to torture or cruel, inhuman or degrading treatment" – all these admonitions are virtually addressed to the state authority to restrain itself from countenancing any such action that is bound to prejudice the individual subject.

Similarly, Article 9 is couched in negative terms. It says, "No one shall be subjected to arbitrary arrest, detention or exile" and indeed several other Articles of the Universal Declaration too are cast in the negative mould – with the concomitant result that the state is being asked to respect these rights as if in the absence of these restraints, the state will trample on the rights of citizens.

The emphasis which is to be found in the Charter of the United Nations upon showing respect for human rights and securing obser-vance of human freedoms was largely due to the abuses of power of which totalitarian regimes before the second world war were guilty in that they had denied the individual any margin of worthwhile liberty and had failed to acknowledge such rights as would enable the indi-vidual to claim that he was a free person and could be trusted to secure his free development as a person.

The other classes of rights which were compendiously called economic, social and cultural rights were included in the Universal Declaration as a result of the attitude that was adopted by socialist societies at the time that the promulgation of declaration became the subject matter of discussion. These have reference to certain positive things that the state was to do in order to cater for the common needs and welfare of its people. The right to work, the right to a fair wage or leisure to which a labourer could lay claim, the right to found a fam-ily, the right to social security, etc., are couched in positive terms and require an affirmative action by the state.

Thus it was that politics and law in the last resort came to provide the organizational structure of the State and the dynamic principles by which the ideal of individual liberty can be realized and the virtually unlimited power that the modern state in a totalitarian society has acquired in our times, *pro rata* got curtailed in the name of Human Rights and Freedoms which came to be conceded to the individuals. The total deprivation of individual human rights and freedoms is a modern form of sacrifice that is demanded by totalitarian societies and indeed this undue exaltation of the state authority curiously enough postulates a sort of servitude, of slavishness on the part of man. At one time by slavery was meant total control of man over man – now that type of slavery has been legally abolished but in its place totalitarian societies impose a similar sort of control over individuals. The Charter of Liberty of the modern man is drawn up to define the limits within which state authority can operate to narrow down the sphere of individual liberty.

Enough has been said to point out that the creation of human rights and the scope of human freedoms within the framework of the Universal Declaration issued by the United Nations and also the two Covenants subsequently drawn up to accord legally binding effect to those rights and freedoms, have reference to the desire on the part of the founding fathers of the United Nations to delimit the power of the member-states, and this delimitation was somehow expected to work miracles in bringing about relief and redemption to the subjects of those member-states.

In Islam, having regard to the principles upon which the Muslim state is founded, such a phenomenon cannot possibly arise. Strictly speaking, there is no ruler within the conceptual framework of a Muslim state – this is so because here the ruler has no will of his own since he has surrendered his will at the altar of the Will of the Lord and what is more he submits to that Will and undertakes to carry out its mandates, not for the sake of his personal aggrandizement but for the sake of showing obedience to the demand of the Divine Law. A ruler who does conform to this concept is really more or less a managing director of the public affairs of citizens of the state. His power is not his own if only because the Qur'an has categorically asserted that all power belongs to God and such power as belongs to man is virtually his only because it is delegated to him on the strict condition that it would be exercised beneficially for those for whose sake it has been so delegated to him.

In other words, all power which any one has over another is a *trust* and the trustee of the power is only the owner of it in name and should the condition on which such a grant of power of ownership is made be violated, the wielder of the power becomes accountable. And it is in this sense that the ruler is accountable to the humblest subject in the realm and indeed it is this liability to account for any abuses of power, for which the victim of the abuse of such power has the absolute and unqualified right to claim redress that constitutes the most effective attribute of a just society.

Justice, as a student of Islam knows only too well, is the inviolable foundation not only of the God-made order but also of the human order which is established to reflect it. Dr Briffault, writing roughly 1350 years after the advent of Islam, makes some pertinent remarks to highlight the interplay of the dual forces of "power" and "justice" and goes on to remark, "The ethical spirit of the modern age, it must be noted, is above all characterized by the ideas of justice, fairness, fair play rather than by those of abnegation, self-sacrifice and emotional sentiments which marked the morality of religious periods.'' He then goes on to add:

"Considered abstractly and isolatedly, an individual has no rights. A right presupposes a contract; and there exists no formal or tacit contract establishing any of the claims advanced in relation to life, liberty of conduct of thought or speech, property, or any other demand made on the social organization by individuals or classes in the name of right and justice. The affirmation of the rights of man is pure unsupported fiction and dogmatic assertion.

· "Right only exists as a correlative of wrong. Apart from the circumstances that there are wrongdoers, the notion of individual right is devoid of meaning. It is because there have been men who have used their power to do violence, to oppress and exploit others, because there have been murderers, robbers, despoilers, extorters, compelling their fellow men into slavery, appropriating their labour, crushing their lives and their minds, that the notion of 'rights of man' has arisen, the rights, namely, not to be murdered, robbed, exploited, crushed. *The right of the individual is simply the right not to be wronged.* Hence all that ethical law, in its primitive form at least, is negative: 'Thou shall not . . . . .' The affirmation of human right is in truth the denial of the title to inflict wrong. It is quite true, as Nietzsche tells us, with the oppressed, it is protective, protestive. 'Thou shalt not . . . .' which means 'Thou shalt not injure me.' Manifestly it could never have originated with the oppressor himself, as a protest against his own action, as 'I shall not . . . .' It is the expression of wrongs suffered by the weak at the hands of the strong; it is the protest of the oppressed against the powerful. The oppressed weak are always morally in the right. When they protest against power, they are protesting against moral wrong; when they defend their interests, their concrete 'rights', they are defending moral Right, righteousness. Their interests and those of abstract morality necessarily coincide. From the nature of the case rebels are always right. Kings were right against pope and emperor; barons and priests were right against kings; the middle class were right against barons and priests; the proletarians are right against the middle class. The weaker are morally right.

"And the powerful are always morally wrong. Primarily power and wrong are co-extensive. All power wielded by man over man is an aggression. That power, the object of human competition, seeks the profit of the strong at the cost of the weak; all power that encroaches on equity, is unjust, oppressive. Even when expedient as an administrative function, or necessary as guidance and protection, or beneficial and blessed as leadership, power of its own nature inevitably tends and turns to abuse and oppression.

"It has long been discovered that absolute power is intrinsically bad, no matter who exercises it. The English came to perceive very definitely that to give absolute power to a saint would mean throwing open the gates of hell. Absolute power has been abolished not because rulers are bad men, but because absolute power is necessarily bad. Lord Acton well said, 'Power tends to corrupt and absolute power corrupts absolutely. Great men (meaning powerful men) are almost always bad men, even when they exercise influence and not authority, still more when you superadd the tendency or certainty of corruption by authority.' In English history there is scarcely a sovereign from William I to George I who, tried on the count of murder alone by the same standards as common delinquents, would have escaped the gallows.'' (See his *Making of Humanity*).

However, in Islam, as has been argued earlier, all power and authority belongs to God, and with man there is only delegated power which becomes a trust; everyone who becomes a recipient or a donee of such a power has to stand in awful reverence before his people towards whom and for whose sake he will be called upon to use these powers. This was acknowledged by Hazrat Khalifa Abu Bakr who said in his very first address:

"My fellow men I call God to witness, I never had any wish to hold this office; never aspired to possess it; neither in secret nor in the open, did I pray for it. I have agreed to bear this burden lest mischief raise its head. Else there is no pleasure in leadership. On the other hand, the burden placed on my shoulders is such as, I feel, I have no inherent strength to bear and so cannot fulfil my duties except with divine help. You have made me your leader although in no way am I superior to you. Co-operate with me when I am right but correct me when I commit error; obey me so long as I follow the commandments of Allah and His Prophet; but turn away from me when I deviate.''

Against such a ruler as Abu Bakr no subject could conceivably put forward a "petition of rights" and claim that his human rights be acknowledged if only because Abu Bakr himself refuses to claim any power over any one and chooses to conduct the affairs of the realm strictly in accordance with the teachings of the Book of God. For him, not his will, but God's Will is the law. Consequently the sort of constitutional battles that have been waged between the sovereign and the subjects in the west are unknown in Islamic history.

In any case, European political philosophy is not free from some paradoxes which result from the way in which its theoreticians have attempted to give us a rationale of what in a given situation is politically right and proper to do. Take, for example, the doctrine often trotted out as the greatest invention of the political genius of western mind, namely, the Doctrine of Popular Sovereignty. The doctrine is that people are somehow sovereign. But then this poses a dilemma which can be described thus: if people are the sovereign then who is the subject of the sovereign in question? People cannot be both sovereign and subject at the same time. When a question like that is raised then we are told by the apologists of the Doctrine of Popular Sovereignty that the word people here is to be written with a capital "P" and is not to be confused with the historical community which through its voters can express itself politically. "People" is a kind of corporation in which some people are continually being born and others are constantly staging an exit by dying out. It is claimed that it is a sort of juristic personality which is undying and immortal. It is this juristic personality which is the sovereign and the plurality of adult persons at any given point in history are the subjects.

One may respectfully enquire that if the *People* with a capital "P" is regarded as a corporation whose entity solely transcends time and is to be viewed as a kind of immortal stuff, then what is there to differentiate it from the doctrine of Islam which says it is *God alone Who is Sovereign*, and He alone is possessed of absolute power and He is the only true law-giver? All earthly authorities derive their powers, as though by means of delegation subject to the limitations prescribed in the law by Him to utilize those powers in *trust* for the very purposes which underlie the creation and the making of man.

In the foregoing discussion of the outline of political theory which underlies the working of social institutions in a secular society and the one that inspires the functioning of Islamic political institutions, one could see for oneself the most cardinal issue which is at stake. And it is submitted that this also constitutes the great divide between the two worlds of thought (a) of secularist thought and (b) thought anchored in religious ground which considers itself bound by what Confucius would call the *Mandate of Heaven*.

Before anyone can talk meaningfully about the theory and practice of Human Rights to which the secular societies that subscribe to the anthropocentric perspective adhere and distinguish it from the one to which monotheistic religions subscribe, one must answer several questions; e.g., what is the essential hall-mark of the human being who is supposed to have these rights? and secondly, how has the discovery been made that certain interests of a human being are to be legally protected as being relevant to his development as man?

After all every legally protected interest is a right and although from the camera point of view every biped animal appears to be a human being he may not in fact be one. Are mad people and hardened criminals to be also regarded as *persons* who are *entitled* to the enjoyment of fundamental rights? Secondly, by what yardstick have the secularist philosophers discovered the category of interests which is so important as to merit being legally protected and elevated to the status of being considered as Basic Rights of man?

To both these questions the secular philosophies are incapable of furnishing any valid answer. The sanctity that attaches to life and makes it human must have a supra-personal reference. And the dignity which we ascribe to Man must be due to the imprint of the Divine on the clay of which man is made; such a one alone reflects the truth of things in his interior consciousness; he is not a piece of the world of dead matter or mere animal existence – such a one has risen above the level of his original animal existence. Secondly, He who made us human and awarded us a high destiny of winning the reward of immortal life alone knows the basic interests which have to be protected here and now if we are to be able to grow to our full spiritual stature and reach the great goal which is our appointed destiny. The truth of man's quest can be taught only by the Prophets who claim to speak in His Holy Name, having been selected for the purpose by the divine dispensation, to *recite verses of the Lord* to the laity, to *purify* them, to teach them their *destiny* and to make them *wise*. Since man is not as yet finally made – as he is only an evolving psycho-physical organism – he cannot, left to his own slender resources, be expected to discriminate between the perennial values which he must realize in this earthly life of his, and the mere animal cravings that seem to dominate him and which he must control in order to be able to avail himself of the opportunity with which his earthly existence provides him to be able to transcend the narrower precincts of his animal self.

The content of the human duties in Islam, therefore, is such as caters for the development of those aspects of the evolving organism of man as physical-cum-spiritual life. Fulfilment of these duties is likely to help him to win the reward of higher life and be admitted to the company of elect. Here in Islam the whole approach is so radically different from the one in which human rights and freedoms are viewed in the frame of secular philosophies of Weltanschauung that there is hardly anything which is in common between the two. But enough has been said to point out at least the distinguishing features between the two to foster better understanding of the approach that Islam makes to the problem of human rights. Islam safeguards the individual by engendering in him the consciousness of his link with the Lord and guides him by the Prophetic dispensation to evolve within himself those inner resources which are to bring about fruition of all his potential.

The Western world will never be able to find a satisfactory solution to the problems that have been posed by the absence of enforcement of adequate procedures in terms of which human rights and freedoms can be respected and observed in our own time. There has been considerable discussion concerning Human Rights in the United Nations and in the related specialized agencies that deal with this aspect of the problem. There is nowadays a great deal of loose talk about human rights but it is equally true that we have not, so far, been able to see much being done in the way of improvising procedures by resort to which these rights and freedoms can be enforced on the international plane.

From the Islamic point of view, of course, the problem does not arise as these are enforced as a matter of course if only because the believer lives under the ever-seeing eye of his master – Who somehow knows what is contained even in the inner recess of his heart. And if any one manages to escape being punished for having committed the violation of the heavenly mandates here below, he will have to account for the dereliction of his duties on the last day when he will be confronted by what he did. As the Qur'an puts it, "their tongues, their hands and their feet will testify against them as to what they used to do." (Sura 24, verse 24). "Before the great judge from Whom anyhow nothing is hidden." It is this type of consciousness which brings about the inner transformation of an individual and invests him with the character of being Human.

It has been the strategy of Islam to promote this type of consciousness. This can be achieved by subjecting the child in his formative years to the influence of great teachers. It can also be brought into being as a result of the parental care which imparts to the nascent life that living impulse which lies at the back of religious tradition in which he is born. Any other institutional mode of dealing with this problem can never be effective. As the Qur'an says: "The believing person and the non-believer are not the same," – even as the seeing person is not the same as the blind person.

In conclusion let us evaluate the *Declaration of Human Rights* and such other cognate declarations for avoidance of anti-racial policies and decolonization of subject peoples made by the U.N. with a 1400-year-old Declaration of Duties which was made by the Prophet of Islam to highlight the many points of the Islamic manifesto for the Believer to follow.

The Universal Declaration of Human Rights has been held as the single greatest achievement of which the United Nations has reason to be proud, and although mere declarations of this type are not meant to be binding in international law, this Declaration was designed to represent the standard of attainment which member-states were to aspire to approximate in the pursuit of their internal and external policies to secure the dignity of the human person. The Declaration was also to embody the voice of the conscience of the international community of mankind. Human Rights and the Freedoms which had been outlined in the declaration, represented the irreducible minimum which had to be conceded in order to enable the dignity of the human person to be acknowledged and to establish norms with reference to which his claim to be considered civilized had to be assessed.

The declaration of human rights enunciates principles which have virtually to be treated as though they are inviolable. Indeed, some of the principles by now have been incorporated in many constitutions and they have invariably been invoked and applied by courts of justice in assessing the effect of a contention put forward for adjudication in respect of the claim that in a given case injustice has been perpetrated simply because these principles have been violated. The declaration is constantly appealed to and has become a sort of a touchstone by which the civilized character of a polity in our own times is to be adjudged and evaluated. Many have argued that such is the force of the Declaration of Human Rights that the United Nations cannot conceivably pass a resolution which is not in accord with the terms of the Declaration.

Enshrined in this Declaration of Human Rights there is an exhortation to the effect that the Human Rights and Freedoms contained therein are to be treated as a common standard of achievement for all peoples and for all nations. It enjoins upon every individual and every organ of the society that they, while keeping this Declaration constantly in mind shall strive by teaching and education to promote respect for these rights and freedoms and by initiating progressive measures, national and international, to secure their universal and effective recognition and observance both among the people of member-states themselves and among the people of territories under their jurisdiction.

The following Articles which refer to specific rights and freedoms which are important for our present purposes may be recalled.

Article 4: No one shall be held in slavery or servitude.

Article 21: (i) Every one has the right to take part in the Government of his country directly or through freely chosen representatives;

(ii) ....

(iii) the will of the people shall be the basis of the authority of government; and this shall be expressed in periodical genuine elections which shall be held by universal and equal suffrage and shall be held by secret vote or by equivalent free voting procedure.

The Universal Declaration of Human Rights which was proclaimed on 10th December, 1948, became the subject matter of further attention and in order to invest it with a legally binding value, two covenants were drawn up, for *political* and *economic* rights. These were drawn up along with optional protocol on civil and political rights in 1966. In both of the covenants the right of *self-determination* was made the very first Article. The declaration on the elimination of all forms of *racial discrimination* had been made earlier in 1963. In 1960 the United Nations had made the declaration of granting independence to colonial countries and peoples. Article 7 of that Declaration had said that: ''all states shall observe faithfully and strictly the provisions of the Charter of the United Nations; the Universal Declaration of Human Rights and the present Declaration.'' In the Declaration on the elimination of all forms of racial discrimination which was adopted in 1963, Article 11 had provided that:

''every State shall promote respect for an observance of human rights and fundamental freedoms in accordance with the Charter of the United Nations and shall fully and faithfully observe the provisions of the present Declaration; the Universal Declaration of Human Rights and the Declaration of the Granting of Independence to colonial countries and peoples.''

The terms of these declarations, although, not in a *strict sense* enforceable, must be carried out by member-states fully and faithfully, the argument in support thereof being that these resolutions by the General Assembly of United Nations embody the juridical conviction and consensus for the states.

In the face of these Declarations some member-states are still busy denying their subject peoples the right to be self-governed and to establish independent sovereign states, for the management of their domestic affairs. The anti-colonial revolution of our time is the most outstanding phenomenon on the contemporary international scene. Numerous countries acquired their independence after the Second World War. And indeed the contribution of the United Nations in the sphere of consummating the aspirations of the dependent peoples to obtain freedom and to establish sovereign states in the exercise of their right of self-determination is so outstandingly great that it admits of no controversy.

There are, however, still some remnants of colonialism and racial discrimination in evidence. The most outstanding of these are those that have reference to racial discrimination in the Union of South Africa. The United Nations' Human Rights covenants outlaw this nefarious practice. Human Rights Year which was celebrated in 1963 saw the practice of apartheid condemned and the General Assembly by Resolution 2142 of 27 October, 1956 recalled the mandate although the South African control has yet to be removed. Apartheid has been declared illegal and a crime against Humanity by the 1968 Tehran Conference.

At the same time, the Principle of Self-Determination is becoming a principle of codified international law and not merely a political principle or idea as was at one time upheld by the publicists who were busy crusading for the liberation of suppressed peoples of the world. Despite this in several places like Eritrea and Namibia all kind of efforts are being made to retain subject peoples in the chains and shackles of colonial rule. The rule of a white minority over preponderantly black people is a virtual denial to them of the enjoyment of the right of self-determination which, as has been commented earlier, is by now firmly recognized in the two Covenants that have been drawn up by the United Nations.

What has been said so far is only by way of a preface to the appreciation of an earlier Declaration upon the subject of dignity of man and on treating right to life, liberty and property as inviolable and even the prohibition against keeping any individual in slavery. And for that, reference must be made to the last congregational address that the Prophet of Islam made at the Farewell Pilgrimage 1400 years ago in Mecca. In this farewell address he said:

"Harken to my words, O men, for I know not whether I shall see you here another year. All customs of paganism have been abolished under my feet. The Arab is not superior to the non-Arab, the non-Arab is not superior to the Arab. You are all sons of Adam and Adam was made of earth. Verily all Muslims are brothers. Your slaves! Feed them as you feed yourselves and dress them as you dress yourselves. The blood feuds of the Time of Ignorance are prohibited. Remember Allah (in your dealings with) women. You have rights over them and they have rights over you. Verily, you should consider each other's blood, property and reputation inviolable up to the Day of Judgement. Verily, a man is responsible only for his own acts. A son is not responsible for the crimes of his father, nor is a father responsible for the crimes of his son. If a deformed Abyssinian slave holds authority over you and leads you according to the Book of Allah, obey him.''

The injunctions in mitigation of the rigours of slavery are to be understood as an exhortation to the believers to treat slaves on a par with those who claim to own them. But care should be taken to remember that this was in the context of the direct Quranic injunction which had clearly laid down the mandate that slavery was to be brought to an end.

Verse 13 of the Sura *Al Balad* is clear and imperative that the higher way the believer is asked to negotiate consists in no other virtue than that of freeing the slave and indeed, in this context numerous references can be made to the utterances of the Prophet who has admonished that one sure way of expiation is to free a slave.

It is somewhat astonishing that in spite of this clear-cut declaration contained in the Holy Book and in the utterances of the Prophet, criticism is still being voiced by the non-Muslim thinkers that Islam is all out for perpetuating slavery and that it is the Muslim peoples who are the obstacle to securing the liberation of mankind and it is they who are obstructing the onward march of mankind towards the goal of freedom. They conveniently forget that Quranic declaration against slavery had been voiced forth 1400 years ago; it had declared that the slave had to be freed. The Prophet of Islam has anticipated developments that were to take place at least 1300 years later when slavery was legally abolished. The United Nations have been proclaiming these principles only in the post-Second World War period of human history. The Prophet of Islam himself freed the slaves, so did Abu Bakr and other companions of the Prophet.

We might in this context attempt specific enumeration of the specific Human Rights in order to see them in the context of contemporary elaboration of the same as it is reflected in the Modern World.

(a) The right to life and property
The most primary right of a man is the right to live and hold such property as he possesses. These two rights were ensured by the Prophet of Islam in his address to the people on the occasion of his farewell pilgrimage when he said,

"Your blood and your property are sacrosanct until you meet your Lord, as this day and this month are holy . . . know that every Muslim is a Muslim's brother, and that the Muslims are brethren. It is only lawful to take from a brother what he gives you willingly." (*Life of Muhammad*, by Ibn Ishaq, translated by Alfred Guillaume, London, 1955, p.651).

(b) The right to freedom of opinion and expression

The right to freedom of opinion and expression was recognized very early in Islam. It was the practice of the Muslims to enquire from the Holy Prophet whether on a certain matter a divine injunction has been revealed to him. If he said that he had received no divine injunction, the Muslims freely expressed their own opinion on the matter. On the occasion of the battle of Badr the Prophet selected a particular place which he considered suitable for giving battle to the enemy. One of his companions, Hubab bin Mandhar, asked the Prophet whether he had chosen this particular place as the result of a divine revelation. The Prophet replied in the negative. At this reply, Hubab bin Mandhar suggested an alternative place for giving battle to the enemy, because he considered it to be strategically better situated. The Prophet agreed with him. (Shibli: *Sirat-al-Nabi*, Azamgadh, sixth addition, p.318)

In the *Battle of Ditch* the Holy Prophet and his companions were besieged on all sides by the Meccans and their tribal allies. Conditions were so unfavourable to the Muslims that the Prophet thought of making a separate peace with the tribe of Ghatafan which was fighting on the side of the Meccans, by agreeing to give them one third of the produce of Medina. He consulted the leaders of the Helpers, S'ad bin Ubada and S'ad bin M'adh. They said that if this was a divinely revealed injunction they could not but obey but if the matter was otherwise, they could not agree to the proposal. Therefore, the Prophet gave up the idea of making peace with Ghatafan separately. (Shibli: Ibid, p.425).

Freedom of opinion and expression have also been guaranteed in Islam by the institution of *Shura* or consultation with the people. The institution of *Shura* has been prescribed by the following verse of the Holy Qur'an:

"And whose affairs are (decided)
by Counsel among themselves."
(*Sura 42, verse 38*)

Thus every Islamic government is under an obligation to consult the people on important affairs either through a parliament or through a referendum. But *Shura* is meaningful only if there is freedom of opinion and expression. Where freedom of opinion and expression is suppressed or restricted by various means and the people are forced to think and talk in the particular way desired by their rulers, *Shura* or consultation with the people becomes meaningless.

(c) Amr bil Ma'ruf

Another human right conferred by Islam which is peculiar to Islam only, is the right of every Muslim to enjoin the good on other Muslims and forbid them from wrong-doing. The Holy Qur'an says:

"Ye are the best community that hath been raised up for mankind. You enjoin right conduct and forbid indecency and ye believe in Allah." (*Sura 3, verse 110*)

Thus every Muslim can advise another Muslim to follow the right conduct and eschew wrong-doing. This right can be exercised also in relation to the government of the day. If the government is following a policy which a Muslim considers to be not in the best interests of the country or which he thinks is opposed to the principles of Islam, he can point out the same to the government and advise it to follow another policy better suited to the interests of the country or more in accord with the principles of Islam. This is a right as well as an obligation of every Muslim and this also entails freedom of opinion and expression, for without such freedom one cannot offer any advice to the government.

(d) Right to freedom of religion and conscience

Another basic human right is the right to freedom of religion and conscience. The Holy Qur'an fully guarantees this right in the following verse:

"There is no compulsion in religion." (*Sura 2, verse 256*)

Not only are the Muslims bidden to respect freedom of religion and conscience, they are even expected to be generous to those non-Muslims who do not fight against them in the cause of religion. The Holy Qur'an says,

"Allah forbiddeth you not respecting those who warred not against you on account of religion and drove you not out of your homes that ye should show them kindness and deal justly with them. Lo! Allah loves the just dealers." (*Sura 60, verse 8*)

The Holy Prophet himself set a noble example of religious toleration when he signed a treaty with the Christians of Najran. The following are the terms of this treaty as narrated by Ibn Qayyim:

"From Muhammad, the Prophet to Abu Harth and the bishops of Najran and their priests and monks and those who live in their churches and their slaves; all of them will be under the protection of God and His Prophet; no bishop will be removed from his bishopric, no monk will be removed from his monastery and no priest will be removed from his post and there will be no change in the rights enjoyed by them so far." (Ibn Qayyim *Zad al Ma'ad* Vol. III, p.141)

As an Islamic State is an ideological State, some reservation will have to be made against non-Muslims in matters which demand complete identification with the ideology of the State. But such matters, by their very nature, are few and limited. A number of material pursuits require no particular ideology other than common morality. Non-Muslims have a very wide field in such pursuits in which no discrimination will be made against them. But if, ideologically, a non-Muslim belongs partly to foreign societies and states which may not be very friendly to Muslims, it follows that such a non-Muslim offers loyalty to the Muslim State with some mental reservations. He will be granted absolute freedom of conscience but in some vital matters of State, he cannot demand complete equality because of want of complete identification.

(e) Right to equality

Another human right is the right to equality. In the American Declaration of Independence, it was asserted as an article of faith that all men are born equal. This statement in an unqualified form is incorrect and misleading because men differ in their natural endowments and, therefore, in their achievements. It is true, however, that artificial inequalities should not be added to natural inequalities and that in certain basic needs and requirements all human beings are similar and equal. This means that there should be complete equality of opportunity.

The Holy Qur'an adumbrated its own ideal of human equality in the following verse:

"O mankind! Lo! we have created you male and female and have made you into nations and tribes so that you may know one another. Lo! the noblest of you in the sight of Allah is he who is best in conduct." (*Sura 49, verse 13*)

Thus the only superiority enjoyed by a human being over other human beings is determined by his righteous conduct. The same principle was repeated by the Prophet of Islam in his address to the Muslims on the occasion of his farewell pilgrimage when he said:

"O! people, your God is one, your father is one. No Arab has superiority over a non-Arab as no non-Arab has superiority over an Arab, neither does a man of brown colour enjoy superiority over a man of black colour, nor does a black man enjoy superiority over a man of brown colour, except by piety." (*Nail-al-Autar*, Vol. V. Cairo, 1952, p.88)

To make human equality effective in day to day life, Islam took the vital step of ensuring equality of men before the law and providing them with basic economic needs. Without these two prerequisites, human equality will remain a mere ideal untranslatable into action. As far as equality before the law is concerned, a tradition of the Prophet runs:

"From Urwah who reported from 'Ayesha who said that Usamah once recommended a woman to the Prophet. The Prophet said, some nations before you were destroyed, because they inflicted punishment on the lower class of people but did not punish the members of the higher class (when they committed a crime). By Him in whose hands is my life, if my daughter Fatimah did this, I will cut her hand." (Bukhari *Kitab-al-Hadud*)

In subsequent Islamic history, specially during the period of the first four successors of the Holy Prophet, we come across cases in which the caliphs or rulers were sued by ordinary citizens and had to appear before a judge for their trial.

As far as economic equality is concerned, Islam instituted the system of *Zakah* or poor-tax to ensure that no individual falls below a certain minimum of material well-being. The income from this tax was distributed locally to the poor and the needy section of every region or province and if some surplus was left after satisfying the needs of the common people, it was remitted to the central government. The Prophet defined *Zakah* in the following words:

"God has laid down on them a Sadaqah (tax) which is taken from the rich and returned to the poor." (Bukhari *Kitab-al-Zakat*, Vol. VI, p. 187)

Here the phrase "returned to the poor" is very significant. It indicates that the wealth taken from the rich belongs, in fact, *to the poor*.

When the Holy Prophet had consolidated his State in Medina, he took further steps towards ensuring that no orphan remained unsupported and no family whose bread-winner had died remained unhelped. He declared himself to be the patron of all those who had no patrons. If a man died leaving behind him a family which had no means of income, the Prophet, as the head of the State, himself undertook to help the bereaved family. Similarly, he financially supported all the orphans in his territory, as the head of the State, thus setting a precedent for his successors. (*Mishkat*, tr. by Dr. Robson, Lahore, 1973, Vol. II, pp. 623, 650, 651)

The institution of slavery of course was too much deeply rooted in the economic, social, political and cultural ethos of the pagan times and could not very well have been uprooted by the exhortation of a religion which had sponsored an evolutionary programme for the progressive realization of the ideal of human liberty and freedom. What else is the Qur'an, if it is not the charter of human liberty? And what else was the primary function of the Prophet, if it was not that of bringing that much measure of relief and redemption to mankind to enable it to freely worship one True God and not be overawed by the earthly authorities who used to hold sway over the lives of subject people? In Islam these earthly Rulers are made themselves subservient to the higher law, that is to say to the divine law and thus made to surrender at the altar of the will of God. In Islam, as has been observed before, the rulers became merely the *managing directors of public affairs*. The best amongst them is he who holds himself accountable for what he does in the way he conducts the affairs of his people. Power is no longer the personal property of the ruler to be used for his own purposes.

Surah Al-Balad itself, which I cannot quote in full, does not admit the redemption of a slave merely from what may be called his physical bondage but proceeds to talk of *feeding the Poor on the day of hunger* and also of *orphans, next of kin* and *some poor wretched in misery*. Thus Islam talks of the *economic* redemption of man too. It is not only redemption from hunger but also redemption from ignorance and everything else that prevents or obstructs the man from freely, independently submitting himself to the Lord of the Universe, and so obeying the one and only Ruler. He acknowledges only those as earthly rulers who in their turn accept God's law and who *rule in His name and themselves live under His law*.

The Islamic principles of private and public conduct are, therefore, designed to achieve worthwhile goals, truer ideals and abiding values, such as justice, freedom and equality. All these are mentioned in the Holy Book and illustrated in the practice of the Holy Prophet. Believers are to strive to the end that the world is made free from those soul-crushing constraints, viz. political, economic, social or cultural, which have been stifling the true growth of human personality and have posed a serious challenge to the very survival of the human race.

Islam founded its programme on a spiritual basis and invited the whole of mankind to transcend the lower level of animal life to be able to go beyond the mere ties fostered by the kinship of blood, racial superiority, linguistic arrogance, economic privilege. It invited mankind to move on to a plane of existence where, by reason of his inner excellence, man can realize the ideal of the Brotherhood of man. By becoming a self-controlled individual, a *muttaqui*, a Muslim becomes a member of the community of *Saliheens*, the righteous ones. He concerts with them to the end that the community enjoins what is right upon the rest of the world and to prohibit what is forbidden so that mankind can march forward on its way to God. Not until that attitude becomes a passion with those who claim to speak to us in the name of higher values, can the world be free from wars, from violence and from fear. The arrogance of power, of privilege is still today at war with the harmony of human life and *Fironiyat* and *Jabbariat* of petty Caesars are still in the saddle. Not until the kind of inner transformation takes place in the heart and soul of man that Islam came to foster, will there be recognition or respect for human rights or fundamental freedoms.

The claim of the West that it is the spokesman of human civilization is a spurious one. How can man be civilized if he conforms to the law merely out of the fear of the policeman – so that, when he is left to his own resources he goes on his wild ways and does what he likes? Europe has opted for the "permissive society" and has landed itself in chaos. Islam on the other hand has asked us to become members of a *disciplined society*; by disciplining ourselves we rule ourselves from within. The state enforces the law of God against those who are out to disrupt social order and pose threats to human security. Human brotherhood is possible only if we realize that, on the one hand, we are all from Adam and Adam was made of dust and on the other, to know that no power belongs to anybody except to God alone Who hath no compeer.

Universal Islamic Declaration

"In the name of God, Most Gracious, Most Merciful"

"And verily this Brotherhood of yours is a single Brotherhood, and I am your Lord, so keep your duty unto me."

During the momentous International Islamic Conference organized by the Islamic Council of Europe in London in April, 1976, a young man approached me and asked if I could explain to him very briefly the fundamental principles and salient features of the Islamic order.

Since then I found that the desire for such an explanation was not only confined to the Muslim community but was also shared by peoples of other faiths.

To satisfy this keen and widespread desire, the Islamic Council requested a number of eminent Muslim scholars and leading figures in the field of Islamic Da'wah to compile a document on the subject. The result of their efforts is this Universal Islamic Declaration. May Allah reward them for their contribution.

I earnestly hope that this document will be useful and enlightening to all people. I hope that it will not only help Muslims in realizing their cherished goal of establishing the Islamic order but would also help to dispel from the minds of many people the confusion and misapprehensions caused by the spread of false and misleading notions about Islam.

Let us all hope and pray that the dawn of the 15th century of the Hijra will herald an era of peace and prosperity, righteousness and justice throughout the world. Allah has placed a great responsibility on the Muslim *Ummah* to strive for such an era, as Allah says in *Al Qur'an*.

"You are the best qualified community that hath been raised by mankind.
Ye enjoin right conduct and forbid wrong doing,
and ye believe in Allah." (*Al Imran* 3–110)

> Salem Azzam, Secretary General
> London 26th Jumad Al-Ula
> 12th April 1980

"O mankind! Now hath a proof from your Lord come unto you, and We have
sent down unto you a clear Light;

As for those who believe in Allah, and hold fast unto Him, them He will cause
to enter into His mercy and grace, and will guide them unto Him by a straight
path."

(*Al Qur'an Al-Nisa: 174, 175*)

1 Preamble

WHEREAS mankind's convenant with Allah – may He be praised and
glorified (*Al Qur'an Al-A'raf* 7:172) – binds us all in an unbreakable
relationship of complete and abiding submission to His will and His
commands, and whereas this commitment was reaffirmed in *Al Qur'an*
when Allah made His Covenant with the prophets saying:

"Behold that which I have given you of the Scripture and knowledge. And
afterward there will come unto you a messenger, confirming that which ye
posses. Ye shall believe in him and ye shall help", and asking: "Do you
agree, and will ye take up My burden (which I lay upon you), in this matter?"

"They answered: 'We agree'. He said: 'Then bear witness.
I will be a witness with you'".
(*Al Qur'an, Al-Imran* 3:81);

WHEREAS this covenant makes the believers the bearers and trustees
of the Divine Message, enjoins them to establish that which is good
and to forbid that which is evil, builds human personality and society
on justice and establishes religion (*din*) in its completeness. (*Al
Qur'an, Al Shura* 42:13);

WHEREAS Islam is a complete code of life suitable for all people and
all times, and Allah's mandate is eternal and universal and applies to
every sphere of human conduct and life, without any distinction between the spiritual and the temporal;

WHEREAS Islam enjoins the Muslim *Ummah* to establish a just and humane world order, providing every opportunity for the all-round development of man and society in an environment free from all forms of exploitation and inequity;

WHEREAS Islam is a dynamic faith, making the believers conscious of their destiny and providing them with guidance for the maximum development of their talents and potentialities;

WHEREAS the Islamic law (*Shariah*) not only confers generous rights and privileges upon the believers but also places upon them certain obligations and responsibilities;

WHEREAS the Muslim *Ummah* is duty-bound to fulfil its covenant with Allah by establishing the Islamic order and translating into practice the ideals and principles of Islam in its own life, thus presenting the message and model of Islam to others.

II Islam's approach to life

In the light of the above and sharing the widespread longing among Muslim people for the establishment of a truly Islamic order, we, Muslims, as humble servants of Allah and as members of the universal brotherhood of Islam, at the beginning of the fifteenth century of the Islamic era,

DO HEREBY BEAR WITNESS TO AND IN FULL CONSCIOUS-NESS OF OUR FAILINGS AND LIMITATIONS SOLEMNLY AFFIRM THAT:

Islam approaches life and its problems in their totality. Being a complete and perfect code of life, it holds no brief for partial reforms or compromise solutions. It starts by making man conscious of his unique position in the universe, not as a self-sufficient being but as a part, a very important part, of Allah's creation. It is only by becoming conscious of their true relationship with Allah and His creation that men and women can function successfully in this world.

Islam brings man close to Allah and enables him to gain a true perception of reality and builds, on that basis, his relationship in harmony with the entire creation. Islam emphasizes that man has been created as Allah's vicegerent (*Khalifa*) (*Al Qur'an 2:30*), and all that exists is there for him to harness. Allah has endowed him with great potentialities and has provided all that he needs in the world around him. However, to make the best use of Allah's bounties, man needs Divine guidance. Allah has provided this guidance in its final form in *Al Qur'an* and the traditions of the Prophet Muhammad (*Sunnah*). This guidance is an unfailing recipe for success in this world and in the hereafter. Islam is a faith, a way of life, and a movement for the establishment of the Islamic order in the world. It is in this context that the believers must study and resolve all issues in every age and place.

Oneness of Allah (*Tawhid*) is the foundation of Islam. It affirms that Allah and Allah alone is our Creator, Sustainer, Guide and Lord; that He has no partners; that His will and authority is supreme and encompasses the entire universe; that He is the Law Giver, and to Him we must submit and surrender.

Tawhid has its corollary in the unity of His creation. It demolishes all distinctions based on race, colour, caste, lineage, wealth and power. It leads to the establishment of relationships between human beings on the basis of equality. It integrates man and nature, which complement each other in Allah's scheme of creation.

Oneness of Allah also means the unity of life which leads to the elimination of all distinctions between the spiritual and the physical, the religious and the secular. Under this concept the whole fabric of life is governed by one law and the goal of the believers becomes the realization of the Divine will.

Ever since the beginning of creation, Allah has sent prophets who conveyed His message to mankind. Thus we have a chain of prophets beginning with Adam and ending with Muhammad (Peace be upon them). He also revealed Books of Guidance to the Prophets Moses, David, Jesus and Muhammad (Peace be upon them). *Al Qur'an*, the Book revealed to the Prophet Muhammad (Peace be upon him), is the last and final Book of Guidance, and the Prophet Muhammad (Peace be upon him), is the last and final Prophet, after whom there will be none other.

Al Qur'an is the word of Allah. In it is preserved the Divine revelation unalloyed by human interpolation of any kind. It is the essence of all the messages previously sent to mankind by Allah. In it is embodied a framework for the conduct of human affairs. It contains explicit criteria for judging between right and wrong and principles for the individual and collective conduct of men and women. In it are warnings for mankind as well as a promise of guidance and support for those who seek Allah's help. *Al Qur'an* presents a path – the Straight Path (*Sirat al mustaqim*) – which, when followed, revolutionizes life and leads to the establishment of an order based on truth, justice, virtue and goodness.

Man, as Allah's *Khalifa*, has a pivotal role to play in this world. Islam prepares him well for this role and provides him with guidance for the development of his character and for the establishment of a just society. For purification of the self, he is required to offer prayers (*Salat*) five times a day. Prayers strengthen man's commitment to Allah, refresh his loyalty to truth and invigorate him to work for the realization of his ideals.

Prayer is supplemented by fasting (*Sawm*) in the month of Ramadan to discipline and control his life. Alms (*Zakah*) commit man's worldly possessions to the achievement of the Divine purposes in the socio-economic field.

The above are the methods by which man's body, his soul and his possessions are harnessed in the service of virtue, truth and justice. It is also obligatory on Muslims who are able to do so, to perform pilgrimage (*Hajj*) once in their lifetime. This obligation, among other things, is an index of unity of the Muslim *Ummah* – a community of faith and a symbol of the unity of mankind.

A universal order can be created only on the basis of a universal faith and not by serving the gods of race, colour, territory or wealth. The ideal of man's brotherhood seeks and finds its realization in Islam.

Establishment of justice on earth is one of the basic objectives for which Allah sent His prophets and His guidance (*Al Qur'an, Al Hadid* 57:25). All human beings have rights upon all that Allah has provided, and as such Allah's bounties are to be shared equitably. The poor and the needy have the right to share in the wealth of the rich (*Al Qur'an, Adh Dhariyat*, 51:19). It is the religious duty of Muslims to harness these resources to serve the ends of justice, to promote goodness and virtue, and to eliminate evil and vice (*Al Qur'an, Al Imran* 3:110). Allah's resources must not be allowed to become instruments of oppression and exploitation by any individual or section of society or state.

It is only the mandate of Allah which confers legitimacy on governments, rulers and institutions, and legitimate power and authority can be derived only in accordance with the mandate laid down in *Al Qur'an* and *As Sunnah* of the Prophet Muhammad (Peace be upon him).

Islam urges the believers actively to pursue, acquire and advance knowledge and fully approves the intuitive, rational and empirical methods of so doing. It confers on all human beings the right to an honourable life, freedom of worship, expression, movement and thought and the guaranteed right to retain legitimately acquired wealth.

Any system of government is Islamic as long as it upholds the mandatory principles laid down by *Al Qur'an* and *As Sunnah*. Apart from this mandatory requirement there is considerable flexibility in the form which an Islamic government may adopt. It is through this flexibility that Islam caters to the requirements of every age and place.

The objective of the Islamic movement is not simply to come to power by any means, but to see that the institutions of state and society are mobilized to serve mankind by pursuing policies which further the distinctive objectives of Islam. It is, therefore, imperative that Islam's policy guidelines are spelt out and translated into practice.

The primary duties of state are to establish justice in all spheres of life and to nurture and strengthen the unity of the *Ummah*. These objectives can only be achieved when the just expectations of people are fulfilled; and when differences in rank, power, wealth and family ties are not permitted to undermine the socio-political process of Islam.

There are no intermediaries between Allah and man. Allah's guidance is available to all in the form of His Book, *Al Qur'an* and in the life example of His Prophet, the *Sunnah*. They clearly state the ideals, values and principles that man needs in order to build his individual and collective life on truth and justice. There exists in this guidance a built-in mechanism to meet the demands of changing times and evolution is possible within this framework.

Islam aims at creating a model society. Its strategy is to mould the individual in accordance with the tenets of Islam, to organize and mobilize him within a social movement for progress and development and to establish an Islamic Order by building society and state, their institutions and policies, at national and international levels.

Islam's primary focus is on the individual. By inspiring the individual with a new consciousness (*Iman*), social development is achieved. By making the individual righteous, trustworthy and duty-conscious (*Muttaqi*), he is enabled to change the world for the better.

Islam has emphasized the importance of institutions but has made it clear that institutions cannot yield the best results unless the men who manage them have a firm commitment to Islam and are capable of bearing the trust that has been placed in them.

Individuals inspired by this idealism and fortified by moral training become the prime movers in the establishment of an Islamic World Order. The *Ummah* is not expected to be a passive spectator of human exploitation, nor of the perpetration of tryanny and injustice. It is called upon to organize itself in the form of a movement for social change and reconstruction, and to come forward to help the oppressed and the persecuted of the world. Islam exhorts the believers to strive incessantly to establish Allah's will on earth. It makes it obligatory on all Muslims to struggle against every obstacle that stands in the way of achieving this goal. This effort is known as *Jihad*.

III The crisis of contemporary civilization

It is a matter of deep concern that the contemporary world is passing through a period of grave crisis threatening human civilization. It is not that man lacks the resources that are needed to maintain high levels of culture and honourable living. The threat to civilization comes from the fact that man today is unable to utilize fully and righteously the vast resources he has come to acquire. With the help of science, technology, and economic power, he has made impressive material progress, but has not been able to achieve fraternity, equity, and piety. Man's historic experiments with secular systems, such as capitalism and communism, have failed to realize that just and humane society for which he has yearned and sacrificed so much.

The capitalist system inevitably leads to exploitation of the poor and the establishment of hegemony of the rich and the privileged. It has been the root cause of various forms of imperialism.

The communist system, a secular alternative to capitalism, views society's problems in materialistic terms and sacrifices all freedoms in order to implement its policies. It leads to regimentation and authoritarianism, and state monopoly of the means of production leads to the creation of a bureaucratic control of thought and initiative, and a new oligarchy.

Both capitalism and communism have failed to create that balanced society wherein the demands of freedom, justice, respect for the individual and socio-economic efficiency, are achieved in harmony. The imperialisms, of both the capitalist and the communist type, seek to control the world by relentless economic and political exploitation, often under attractive slogans and labels.

IV Framework for an Islamic Order

1 State policy

Muslims are committed to the sincere and effective pursuit of the guiding principles of state policy as ordained by Allah and His Prophet, which include the following:

(a) The *Sharia* is the supreme law of the Muslim community and must be enforced in its entirety in all aspects of life. Each and every Muslim country must explicitly make *Sharia* the criterion by which to judge the public and private conduct of all, rulers and ruled alike, and the chief source of all legislation in the country.

(b) Political power must be exercised within the framework of *Sharia*. It is neither valid nor exercisable except by and on behalf of the community through the process of mutual consultation (*Shura*). No one is authorized to arrogate to himself the right to rule by personal discretion.

(c) It is the obligation and right of every person to participate in the political process, and political authority is to be entrusted to those who are worthy of it according to the Islamic criterion of knowledge, trustworthiness and capability.

(d) All political power, whether legislative, executive or judicial, is exercisable within the limits set out by Allah and His Prophet for the promotion and enforcement of the values prescribed by Islam.

(e) Obedience to the legitimately constituted authority is obligatory on people so long as it is in conformity with the *Sharia*.

(f) All persons in authority are bound by the rules of the *Sharia*, both in regard to their personal as well as public conduct.

(g) All citizens are equal before the law.

(h) People have the right to question the decisions of their rulers and to seek and obtain remedies for wrongs committed by them.

(i) The rights of people to life, liberty, honour and property as guaranteed by Allah and His Prophet can in no circumstances be abrogated or suspended.

(j) The civil and religious rights of minorities shall be upheld and protected.

2 Economic policy

The Islamic economic system is based on social justice, equity, moderation and balanced relationships. It is a universal system embodying eternal values which safeguard man's rights while constantly reminding him of his obligations to himself and to society. It forbids all forms of exploitation and honours labour, encourages man to earn his living by honest means, and to spend his earnings in a rational way. Its salient features are:

(a) All natural resources are a trust (*Amanah*) from Allah and man is individually and collectively custodian (*Mustakhlif*) of these resources. Man's economic effort and its reward are determined within the context of this framework of trust.

(b) Wealth must be acquired through effort and by lawful means. It should be saved, retained and used only in ways approved by Allah and His Prophet.

(c) Wealth should be justly distributed. When personal wealth has satisfied the legitimate needs of its owner, the surplus is required to satisfy the needs of others.

(d) All resources available to man in general and to the *Ummah* in particular, must always be put to optimum use; no one has the right to hoard them or to keep them idle, or to squander them or to use them for wanton display, be it the individual, the community or the state.

(e) Development is an essential requirement, and participation in economic activity is obligatory on every Muslim. He must labour hard, and always seek to produce more than is necessary for his personal needs, because then alone would he be able to participate in the process of *Zakah* and to contribute to the well-being of others.

(f) Every worker is entitled to a fair recompense for his or her work. There must be no discrimination based on race, colour, religion or sex.

(g) The procurement of wealth and the production of goods must be lawful in terms of the *Sharia*. Usury (*Riba*), gambling, hoarding, etc. are forbidden sources of income.

(h) The principles of equality and brotherhood require the just sharing of resources in prosperity as well as in adversity, *Zakah, Sadaqat, Al'Afw* and inheritance are some of the means for the equitable distribution of wealth and resources in society.

(i) Persons incapable of looking after their own needs, owing to permanent or temporary incapacity, have a just call upon the wealth of society. They are the responsibility of society which must ensure supply of basic necessities of food, clothing, shelter, education and health care, to all of them irrespective of their age, sex, colour or religion.

(j) The economic power of the *Ummah* shall be structured in such a way that there is co-operation and sharing within the *Ummah* and maximum self-reliance therein.

3 Educational policy

Education is an important corner-stone of the Islamic system. Pursuit of knowledge is obligatory for all Muslims, including knowledge of skills, crafts and vocations. Some of the basic principles of Islamic educational policy are:

(a) There shall be universal basic education for all men and women in society, and adequate national resources shall be made available for this purpose.

(b) The purpose of education shall be to produce people who are imbued with Islamic learning and character and are capable of meeting all the economic, social, political, technological, physical, intellectual and aesthetic needs of society.

(c) The two parallel streams of secular and religious education prevailing today in the Muslim World should be fused together so as to provide an Islamic vision for those engaged in education, and to enable them to reconstruct human thought, in all its forms, on the foundations of Islam.

4 Social policy

The social institutions of mosque, family, local community, social consultative bodies, socio-economic co-operatives, etc., are an integral part of the Islamic system, and should be established and strengthened on the Islamic principles of brotherhood (*Ukhuwwah*) and mutual help (*Takaful*). The fundamental objectives of Islamic social policy are:

(a) Affirmation, restoration and consolidation of the dignity, integrity and honour of the individual.

(b) Protection and strengthening of the family as the basic unit of society, with particular emphasis on kindness and respect to parents.

(c) Ensuring that women enjoy full rights – legal, social, cultural, economic, educational and political – which Islam has guaranteed to them.

(d) Self-reliance, mutual consultation, social cohesion and co-operation in all aspects of national life.

5 Defence policy

Defence of Islam and Muslim lands is the sacred duty of all Muslims. While Islam stands for peace, it also enjoins Muslims to be ever ready to deter and repulse aggression. To fulfil this duty, the Muslim countries should:

(a) Develop their defence potentials to the maximum.

(b) Strive for the earliest achievement of self-sufficiency in defence production.

(c) Establish the closest possible co-operation in every field of defence activity.

(d) Consider aggression against any Muslim country as aggression against the entire Muslim world.

V Co-operation among the Muslim states

Further co-operation among Muslim states requires that:

(a) The Muslim world should establish an Islamic Fund for Mutual Assistance (*Baitul Mal*), through which assistance to Muslim countries should be administered.

(b) The Muslim world should set up a monetary reserve of its own and take expeditious steps to establish a common currency system.

(c) A common market among Muslim countries should be established.

(d) The Muslim world should establish its own institutions to control and operate the "service sector", viz. banking, insurance, travel, shipping, packaging, transport, advertizing, and marketing, etc.

(e) The Muslim world should co-ordinate production policies and agreed programmes for improving and developing the techniques and quality of agricultural and industrial production in different countries. The primary aim in this regard should be:

(i) To create sufficient agricultural capacity and food reserves.

(ii) To produce raw materials for consumption in the industrial sector

(iii) To rationalize the development of industry, particularly heavy and basic industries, in order to make the Muslim world self-sufficient in essential supplies of capital goods and defence equipment.

(f) The Muslim world should formulate a joint approach to secure fair and stable prices for its raw material and natural resources. It must enjoy and exercise complete sovereignty with regard to their production, pricing, marketing and usage. The Muslim states may also establish a common fund in order to acquire effective capability for market intervention and price support.

(g) The Muslim world should seek a fundamental restructuring of the present international monetary and economic system so as to make its operation fair and equitable for the developing countries and to give them their due share in decision-making.

(h) The Muslim states should establish a Muslim World Court to resolve and/or adjudicate on all inter-state disputes.

(i) The Muslim states should establish a Permanent Commission to formulate information and educational policies for the Muslim world as a whole, and should develop the full range of expertise, techniques and production facilities in mass media.

(j) The Muslim world should take an active interest in the welfare of Muslim minorities in non-Muslim countries. It is incumbent upon it to see that they are not denied human rights, and enjoy full freedom to practise their Islamic way of life.

(k) Arabic, the language of *Al Qur'an*, should be developed as the *lingua franca* of the Muslim *Ummah* and every effort should be made to achieve this objective.

VI Liberation of Muslim lands

The subjugation of Muslim people and the occupation of their lands in certain parts of the world is a matter of grave concern to us. The most painful of these is the usurpation and occupation of the holy city of Jerusalem (Al Qudus). It is the sacred duty of the *Ummah* to mobilize itself fully and strive relentlessly to liberate Jerusalem and all other Muslim lands.

VII Unity of the Ummah

The people of the Muslim world should prevail upon their governments to adopt this framework as a principle of state policy, to be followed by statutory treaty arrangements leading to greater unity of the *Ummah* as envisaged by Islam.

DECLARATION AND RESOLVE

The affairs of the *Ummah*, divided into nation-states, are presently in disarray because:

(a) In spite of public declarations of commitment to Islam, Islamic principles have not been implemented in the life of its people and institutions.

(b) Real power is, by and large, in the hands of people whose hearts are not imbued with the teachings of Islam and the spirit of Muslim solidarity, and who tend to put their own interests above those of the Muslim *Ummah*.

(c) The vast resources of the *Ummah* are being grossly wasted. In many cases they are being used for purposes held to be illegal and immoral by *Al Qur'an*. Instead of being utilized for the removal of economic imbalance and social injustice in the *Ummah*, wealth is used in a manner that benefits forces that are inimical to Islam and the Muslim *Ummah*.

We therefore, declare that the objectives of the Islamic Order can be achieved only *IF:*

(a) The Muslim *Ummah* dedicates itself to practising the principles of Islam at the individual and collective levels, and abolishes all forms of domination, exploitation, all distinctions, discriminations and all un-Islamic systems, laws and customs that have permeated Muslim society.

(b) A truly Islamic leadership emerges in the Muslim *Ummah* in all fields; capable of leading the people through the strength of its moral calibre and not through force, coercion or manipulation; which trusts its people and is trusted by them; which regards itself as accountable to the *Ummah* and above all to Allah.

It is under such an inspiring leadership and with a clear commitment to Islamic principles that Muslims all over the world would be integrated into one organic community, and would be able to transform the mandate of Allah into reality.

O people of the Muslim Ummah, in every Muslim country where the prevailing order does not fully conform to the teachings of Islam, it is your sacred duty to struggle for change.
O people of the Muslim Ummah, stand firm and do your utmost to fulfil your obligation to build a truly Islamic society.

So help us Allah, You are the best Protector and the best Helper.

Reference index

Subject index